Information Manipulation and Its Impact Across All Industries

Maryam Ebrahimi
Independent Researcher, Germany

A volume in the Advances in Social Networking and Online Communities (ASNOC) Book Series

IGI Global
PUBLISHER of TIMELY KNOWLEDGE

Published in the United States of America by
IGI Global
Information Science Reference (an imprint of IGI Global)
701 E. Chocolate Avenue
Hershey PA, USA 17033
Tel: 717-533-8845
Fax: 717-533-8661
E-mail: cust@igi-global.com
Web site: http://www.igi-global.com

Library of Congress Cataloging-in-Publication Data

Names: Ebrahimi, Maryam, 1980- editor.
Title: Information manipulation and its impact across all industries / Maryam Ebrahimi, editor.
Description: Hershey, PA : Information Science Reference, [2022] | Includes bibliographical references and index. | Summary: "This book is a collective resource with comprehensive knowledge in the areas of misinformation and disinformation, not only about misinformation/ disinformation in social media and politics, but also discusses misinformation and disinformation in other fields particularly organization, health, and the economy"-- Provided by publisher.
Identifiers: LCCN 2021031970 (print) | LCCN 2021031971 (ebook) | ISBN 9781799882350 (hardcover) | ISBN 9781799882367 (paperback) | ISBN 9781799882374 (ebook)
Subjects: LCSH: Information society--Political aspects. | Disinformation--Political aspects. | Social media--Political aspects. | Truthfulness and falsehood--Political aspects.
Classification: LCC HM851 .I5317 2022 (print) | LCC HM851 (ebook) | DDC 303.48/33--dc23
LC record available at https://lccn.loc.gov/2021031970
LC ebook record available at https://lccn.loc.gov/2021031971

This book is published in the IGI Global book series Advances in Social Networking and Online Communities (ASNOC) (ISSN: 2328-1405; eISSN: 2328-1413)

British Cataloguing in Publication Data
A Cataloguing in Publication record for this book is available from the British Library.

Advances in Social Networking and Online Communities (ASNOC) Book Series

ISSN:2328-1405
EISSN:2328-1413

Editor-in-Chief: Hakikur Rahman, Ansted University Sustainability Research Institute, Malaysia

MISSION

The advancements of internet technologies and the creation of various social networks provide a new channel of knowledge development processes that's dependent on social networking and online communities. This emerging concept of social innovation is comprised of ideas and strategies designed to improve society.

The **Advances in Social Networking and Online Communities** book series serves as a forum for scholars and practitioners to present comprehensive research on the social, cultural, organizational, and human issues related to the use of virtual communities and social networking. This series will provide an analytical approach to the holistic and newly emerging concepts of online knowledge communities and social networks.

COVERAGE

- Knowledge Management System Architectures, Infrastructure, and Middleware
- Information and Data Management
- Communication and Management of Knowledge in R&D Networks
- Leveraging Knowledge Communication in Social Networks
- Technology Orientation and Capitalization of Knowledge
- Knowledge as Capacity for Action
- Performance Evaluation and Benchmarking of Deployed Systems
- Current State and Future Development of the Institutional Knowledge Management
- Broadband Infrastructure and the New Wireless Network Solutions
- Knowledge Chains

The Advances in Social Networking and Online Communities (ASNOC) Book Series (ISSN 2328-1405) is published by IGI Global, 701 E. Chocolate Avenue, Hershey, PA 17033-1240, USA, www.igi-global.com. This series is composed of titles available for purchase individually; each title is edited to be contextually exclusive from any other title within the series. For pricing and ordering information please visit http://www.igi-global.com/book-series/advances-social-networking-online-communities/37168. Postmaster: Send all address changes to above address.

Titles in this Series

For a list of additional titles in this series, please visit:
http://www.igi-global.com/book-series/advances-social-networking-online-communities/37168

E-Collaboration Technologies and Strategies for Competitive Advantage Amid Challenging Times
Jingyuan Zhao (University of Toronto, Canada) and Joseph Richards (California State University, Sacrameto, USA)
Information Science Reference • © 2021 • 346pp • H/C (ISBN: 9781799877646) • US $195.00

Analyzing Global Social Media Cnsumption
Patrick Kanyi Wamuyu (United States International University – Africa, Kenya)
Information Science Reference • © 2021 • 358pp • H/C (ISBN: 9781799847182) • US $195.00

Global Perspectives on Social Media Communications, Trade Unionism, and Transnational Advocacy
Floribert Patrick C. Endong (University of Calabar, Nigeria)
Information Science Reference • © 2020 • 300pp • H/C (ISBN: 9781799831389) • US $195.00

Electronic Hive Minds on Social Media Emerging Research and Opportunities
Shalin Hai-Jew (Kansas State University, USA)
Information Science Reference • © 2019 • 358pp • H/C (ISBN: 9781522593690) • US $205.00

Hidden Link Prediction in Stochastic Social Networks
Babita Pandey (Lovely Professional University, India) and Aditya Khamparia (Lovely Professional University, India)
Information Science Reference • © 2019 • 281pp • H/C (ISBN: 9781522590965) • US $195.00

For an entire list of titles in this series, please visit:
http://www.igi-global.com/book-series/advances-social-networking-online-communities/37168

IGI Global
PUBLISHER of TIMELY KNOWLEDGE

701 East Chocolate Avenue, Hershey, PA 17033, USA
Tel: 717-533-8845 x100 • Fax: 717-533-8661
E-Mail: cust@igi-global.com • www.igi-global.com

Table of Contents

Detailed Table of Contents

Information has various definitions and combinations, which have to be regarded for proper information management. The purpose of this study is to clarify the concepts of information, misinformation, and disinformation for having a better understanding of their dimensions as well as to explain the patterns and motives of diffusion of misinformation and disinformation. The present study examines studies of a social diffusion model of information, misinformation, and disinformation as well as a prevention framework of misinformation. Knowing these concepts and their dimensions provides the basis for more accurate and comprehensive analysis in this area. Skills of critical thinking and information evaluation in the forms of information literacy and web literacy can prevent users from publishing, retrieving, and using misinformation and disinformation.

Infodemic refers to the influx of inaccurate or deceptive information on social media during a pandemic. The sharing of unverified COVID-19 information on social media is pervasive in Malaysia, which leads to adverse consequences stemming from misinformation, disinformation, and mal-information. Drawing upon the cognitive load theory (CLT) and self-determination theory (SDT), this research examined the antecedents driving unverified COVID-19 information sharing on social media in Malaysia. Based on 309 validated online survey responses, the PLS-SEM analysis revealed that except for trust towards online information; the proposed factors, self-disclosure, information overload, entertainment, and fear of missing out (FoMo), were found to predict the intention to share unverified COVID-19 information sharing on social media in Malaysia. Theoretical implications are discussed through CLT and SDT, and practical recommendations for government agencies, social media administrators, and public members to curb unverified COVID-19 information sharing on social media in Malaysia are offered.

With the advent and widespread use of information and communication technologies, the need for information has become part of the daily work of individuals. Recently, social networks are one of the most important topics in cyberspace. This study seeks to identify and rank the opportunities and threats of social media for the society. Three hundred seventy students active in social networks are selected by clustering sampling method. A conceptual model is developed based on the review of theoretical literature and five opportunities of social network including electronic learning, filling leisure time, organizing social groups, getting to know about diverse cultures, possibility of conversation, as well as five threats include sharing anti values, abusing, dissemination of misinformation, internet addiction, and malacious communication have significant effect on the students.

The highest degree of impact is observed nowadays from the bodies that finance the media. The information community of journalists and television companies are the tools for influencing society. As a result, the picture shown to the audience does not coincide with reality, so the people don't trust the media. Thus, there is a need to find alternatives to what viewers see on the screen of official television channels. This demand also creates a supply, which, having convincing facts and evidence of its innocence, forms an audience. The purpose of the chapter is to consider a practical attempt to counteract the process of manipulation of public consciousness. To achieve this goal, the author of this chapter set the following research tasks: to study the available scientific sources on the topic of manipulative influence on people, to compare the facts provided by the official media, and the means of the YouTube network, and to find a logical explanation for the emergence of the internet party in Ukraine.

The use of internet and new media technologies provide new ways of communicating and online searching for health information. False health-related information as a result of the lack of reliable scientific sources is intentionally or unintentionally created and disseminated and can have negative effects on people's health. The purpose of this study is to identify strategies for counteracting online health misinformation from the perspective of health professionals using content analysis approach. From the analysis, strategies for dealing with the effects of misinformation include training of health staff at all levels, improving public awareness, and filtering or fact-checking. It is revealed that the most important way to cope with health misinformation in cyberspace is to enhance public awareness, which can reduce its detrimental impact to a great extent.

Data has become the new trading currency in today's competitive environment. The human factor is still seen as a significant threat through social engineering channels, despite the advanced technological controls implemented by organizations. Companies can implement appropriate technical solutions, but they are still unable to control the human factor. The aim of the chapter is to better understand the role of human factors in information security. For this purpose, it provides a model that focuses on human-security elements including management commitment, skills, experiences, self-efficacy of human resources, and security culture and training as the vulnerable factors in information security issues. Quantitative methodology and statistical technique are used for analysis. Thus, the main contribution of this research is to present a model of human resource factors in information security that can be applied in several case studies, and the results can be compared.

Facing diverse unverified and verified sources of information, users have to be considerably notified of the best accessible information sources to make informed decisions. The main purpose of this study is to determine the relationship between information literacy and the ability to detect fake news based on structural equation model using data from 300 samples selected through cluster sampling. It is indicated that there is a relationship between information literacy and the ability to spot fake news. Therefore, users should have prerequisite skills to distinguish between fake news and factual content by way of improving the quality of literacy programs of education institutions and promoting a culture of reading and critical thinking.

Misleading statements and outright lies by governmental figures might reduce economic growth rates and would result in a substantially lower level of economic well-being. The lie is the induction of false belief with the aim of misleading the audience in any way possible. Although a liar knows lying has its costs, he lies in the hope of gaining short-term benefits. Lies accumulated reduce trust, increase transaction costs in the business environment, create dysfunctional balances, all of which are factors in the decline of well-being. The aim of this study is to analyze the economics literature on lies in terms of lying's effects on harming social capital, destroying the expected functions of institutions, increasing transaction costs, and creating asymmetric information.

Profit manipulation refers to bringing reported profits closer to the intended level, which is classified into categories of earnings management, falsification, and creative accounting practices. It is extremely difficult to detect manipulated financial statements using standard business audit procedures because there is a lack of knowledge about extensions and features of management fraud. Auditors have a shortage of the experience to detect falsified financial statements, and managers deliberately attempt to deceive auditors using new methods. The goal of this study is to review mathematical techniques to detect profit management practices and to compare the average profit management and ability to predict earnings management of the accrual and revenue models. The motivation behind this chapter is to provide a basis to compare techniques on detecting financial manipulation.

Preface

OVERVIEW

Persistent misconceptions that can carry risks for public can be the result of both misinformation and disinformation. Despite the history of information manipulation from the past, the advent of modern technology has led to rapid and widespread dissemination of misinformation. Recognizing the impact of misinformation on society is especially important when it has a greater potential scope and attracts a larger population.

Information manipulation generally focuses on areas such as economics and finance, society, health, etc. Accordingly, the present book examines the effects of misinformation and disinformation on organizations, human resources, governments and citizens. In this book, we also describe the models and approaches of detecting misinformation and disinformation, and also anti-misinformation measures, laws and policies. This book can be considered a dynamic resource for managers, engineers, researchers, teachers, advanced students, professors, academics and professional institutions that cover topics such as cybersecurity, online health misinformation and social capital.

DESCRIPTION

It has become clear to almost everyone that the information contained on websites and other digital media is not necessarily accurate and credible, and may even be misleading. For countries, economies and individuals, controlling and dealing with misinformation and disinformation has become a challenge. Misinformation means that inaccurate information is spread unintentionally and accidentally. This confuses the audience because the information is not interpreted correctly and the information is wrong and out of date, which of course is not necessarily intentional. Disinformation means that misleading information is deliberately spread. For example, websites do not have a specific author and contact address, and there is no correct citation for the information.

As deliberately spread misinformation in the form of news, fake news is not a new phenomenon, but it put completely on the international agenda in the 2016 US presidential election. Real progress in understanding or controlling this phenomenon should occur in humans, not machines, because the actions and behaviors that are often associated with this concept, including manipulation, misinformation, lies, rumors, conspiracy theories, have existed since humans have been in contact with each other. However, Kalsens (2018) believes that new ways of producing, distributing and consuming fake news have been provided by new communication technologies, which makes it more difficult to distinguish trusted information. The definition given of fake news also includes intentionally spread misinformation in the format of news. Prior to verification, information can be defined as unverified information, and information that has been verified to be incorrect is misinformation that can lead to fear, hatred, and wonder. Unverified information that can be true is called a rumor or a real rumor (Wu et al., 2019).

The emergence of a "post-fact" world was one of the most dramatic developments of 2016, in terms of Fukuyama (2017), which challenged almost all credible sources of information with contradictory facts of doubtful quality and origin. One cannot be sure that good information triumphs over bad information in a world without a gatekeeper.

According to estimates provided in Freitas et al. (2013), approximately 34% of the world's population, or 2.4 billion people, have access to the Internet, and this access and use of the Internet is very widespread, especially in industrial areas, such as Europe with 518 million users. People seem to believe everything they read on the Internet. Because there is no intermediary between the producer and the consumer of information to validate the news that was published in the past. Information constitutes a form of power, and to the extent that information has been becoming cheaper and more accessible. Russia, China, and other countries have now taken an active role in undermining the credibility of information, which is a new form of warfare. By employing large numbers of trolls and bots to overwhelm social media with disinformation like Russia, or by using tens of thousands of censorship forces like China, the old authoritarian forces often tried to respond dialectically and control the Internet. However, the use of the weapon of dissemination of disinformation by authoritarian powers is also very undesirable in itself. At the same time, people are willing to believe everything and do not care about its accuracy. On the other hand, it can be said that institutions have always been under the control of the elites, and these institutions and the control of the elites over them are weakened by the presence of the Internet (Fukuyama, 2017).

As a main political communication channel, for example, Twitter played a prominent role in the 2012 election, and its role remains strong. As a threat to democracy that has recently become the center of public debate, political misinformation published on social media was noticed during 2012. Old rumors are repackaged in the form of new news by party websites and shared by influential Twitter users. Usually in the form of exaggeration, the rebirth of rumors is often accompanied by content change, however, at the end of the selection period, this process stops. Hence according to Shin et al., (2018) the inconsistency of content dissemination and the mechanism of message change over time should be observed by digital media researchers.

The volume of available online health information, as well as the search for such information, has increased with the increasing use of the Internet. Europe, for example, saw a 10 percent increase in health-related searches from 2005 to 2007. As a powerful medium for information and marketing, the Internet can also be used for misinformation and mismarketing purposes. Misleading information along with inaccuracies, imbalances, non-compliance with accepted scientific standards may lead to adverse consequences for patients, including increased health care costs (e.g., the purchase of new drugs through cheaper options and be persuaded to use non-pharmacological treatments) and injury or death (e.g., persuading patients to buy drugs that are not fully approved and there are more credible alternatives to them) (Freitas et al., 2013).

Although misinformation may sometimes be spread by social media, these platforms are often also a place to correct misinformation. Social media often offers a combination of scientific, medical, and government information as well as quasi-scientific research, some of which is used to correct misinformation. As a social network, Facebook is likely to facilitate communicating scientific content. Due to the inclusion of weakly connected networks, Facebook allows for a diversification of the information flow and therefore, according to Bode and Vraga (2017) has lower levels of homogeneity compared to other platforms (such as face-to-face networks), resulting in a greater chance of accidental exposure or exposure without intention to search for news and other content.

In today's world, vaccination can lead to profound emotional reactions and controversial debates (Hausman, 2020). These debates are generally about forced or recommended vaccine injection systems, which have led to disputes between relatives and friends and sparked legal debates. Also, because the misinformation framework is based on the idea that science is the only realm of truth, the prevalence of conspiracy theories and blatantly false ideas presented as the truth leads to a weakening of social functions and public health, and even the disintegration of even completely pluralistic communities.

The epidemic of coronavirus (Covid-19) since December 2019 has caused a heavy burden and a growing number of hospitalizations. Traditional platforms and social media were disseminating information with considerable speed and without barriers as public health and health care officials sought to identify and restrain the virus spread. Medical disinformation, due to the impact of the disease and the lack of information related to it, quickly spread on various social networks. Because such a phenomenon is somewhat worrying at the individual and public health levels, and similar trends are also reported in other cases, including Ebola and Zika outbreaks, governing institutions are aware of its impact and are working to control it (Kouzy, et al., 2020).

As a relatively new dimension of misinformation, we can refer to fake news produced for financial gain. Among economics theorists, few agree that information does not need to be presented equally to different groups of subjects. Because investors do not weigh information properly, rely on poor samples, and do not recognize what the market already knows, getting more and more information is of little benefit to them. Because of the fact that predictions of current events are always somewhat uncertain and make it difficult to distinguish between true and false information, stock market data is particularly susceptible to all kinds of misinformation (Polak, 2012).

In order to reduce the misstatement and thus declared profit fluctuation, companies are required to publish their domestic and global output. As profits in US are usually overstated, and this does not cause serious harm, however, the risks of being under-appreciated in credit markets and markets overpriced can be caused by the periods of excessive overstatement. Also, high hurdle rates, which reduces investment can be made from overstated Return on Equities (ROEs). Satisfaction with debt and asset prices is more common today than it was before the financial crisis, in which it played a major role. But when there is bad information about the value of assets and credit risks, it becomes more difficult to limit the price of debt and assets. Profit misstatement also lead to asset bubbles and thus increase economy cyclical fluctuations (Smithers, 2019).

Focusing on information security, this book also addresses information security issues as a major challenge for most organizations. Some technological solutions have been developed in this regards and more solutions are being implemented, but the mentioned issue is still a concern. Also, technological solutions need to be considered from a broader human and managerial perspective since they are relied on information security policies and organizational strategies. Management is primarily responsible for business affairs and, therefore, has a significant impact on each business activity. Primarily as a managerial and business issue, senior managers should be aware of the importance of developing and implementing information security policy and pay more attention to the effective implementation of security controls. Organizational factors including the type of industry, size and structure of the organization have a great impact on the implementation of information security management. According to studies, negligent employees or contractors, hackers or criminals, system failures are accounts for 39%, 37%, 24% of all accidents, respectively. Therefore, it can be said that perhaps the weakest loop in information security is the human factor (Soomro et al., 2016).

Since cybersecurity has become a global issue, more than 50 countries have formally issued a strategy document specifying their official position on cyberspace, cybercrime, and/or cybersecurity. Huge amounts of potential revenue from the sharing of illegal movies, music, and other forms of digital media are lost each year. Although the confidentiality, integrity or availability of shared media is not necessarily affected by this illegal sharing, this directly affects the financial status of the legal rights owner of a given media. Also, the country's vital infrastructure can be threatened by Cyber terrorists or enemy specialists through cyberspace. This can be done by affecting access to intelligence services by using denial-of-service attacks indirectly, or by directly attacking the critical infrastructures such as national electricity system that attacks to them include not only the loss of integrity or access to information resources, but also the availability of such critical services. In this case, the well-being of the whole society is threatened, neither the information itself nor the user of individual information (Solms and Niekerk, 2013).

TARGET AUDIENCE

By providing comprehensive knowledge on information manipulation and its impact on all industries, this book seeks to provide a comprehensive resource that targets managers, engineers, researchers, teachers, advanced students, professors, academics, and professional institutions.

ORGANIZATION OF THE BOOK

The 10 chapters of this book are summarized below:

Chapter 1, '*Information, Misinformation, and Disinformation: Social Diffusion and Misinformation Prevention*', written by Mahshid Ebrahimi: The model for disseminating social information, misinformation and disinformation as well as the framework for preventing misinformation is examined in this book. Research show that information literacy including critical thinking and information evaluation skills, and web literacy can prevent the dissemination, retrieval and use of misinformation busers.

Chapter 2, '*Antecedents Driving the Intention to Share Unverified COVID-19 Information on Social Media*', written by Thong Bing Tai, Tze Wei Liew, Su-Mae Tan, and Mohammad Tariqul Islam Khan: Theoretical implications are discussed through cognitive load theory (CLT) and self-determination theory (SDT), and practical recommendations for government agencies, social media administrators, and public members to curb unverified COVID-19 information sharing on social media in Malaysia are offered. The anticidnets of unconfirmed COVID-19 information sharing on social media in Malaysia, based on CLT and SDT, has been investigated and theoretical concepts are discussed through the CLT and SDT in this study. Also, in order to prevent unverified COVID-19 information from being shared on social media in Malaysia, some practical advice is provided to government agencies, social media managers and members of the public.

Chapter 3, '*Opportunities and Threats Analysis Caused by Social Media*', written by Elina Ahmadi: Aiming to identify and rank social media opportunities and threats to society, a conceptual model based on a review of theoretical literature is presented in this study, which includes five social networking opportunities including e-learning, leisure time filling, organizing social groups, familiarity with different cultures, possibility of conversation, as well as five threats to students including sharing counter-values, abuse, and publishing misinformation, internet addiction, and bad communication.

Chapter 4, '*The Phenomenon of Counteracting for the Information Manipulation: Ukrainian Aspect*', written by Nadezhda Lebedeva: The research tasks covered in this chapter include studying the available scientific sources on the influence of the people, comparing the facts presented by the official media and YouTube, and finding a reasonable explanation for the emergence of the internet party in Ukraine.

Chapter 5, '*Counteracting Online Health Misinformation*', written by Mahshid Ebrahimi: The present chapter aimed to identify strategies to deal with online health misinformation from the health professionals perspective using a content analysis approach. Based on the analysis of this study, strategies to deal with the effects of misinformation include training health workers at all levels, improving public awareness, and filtering or investigating the facts.

Chapter 6, '*A Model of Human Factors in Cyber Security*', written by Maryam Ebrahimi: In order to achieve the purpose of this chapter, which is to better understand the role of human factors in information security, a model is presented that focuses on human security elements including management commitment, and human resources experiences, skills and self-efficacy, security culture, and education as vulnerable factors in information security issues.

Chapter 7, '*Information Literacy and Its Effects on Spotting Misinformation*', written by John Ryan: Determining the relationship between information literacy and the ability to detect fake news based on the structural equation is the aim of this chapter, which ultimately concludes that by improving the quality of educational institutions' literacy programs and promoting a culture of reading and critical thinking, users should acquire the necessary skills to distinguish between fake news and real content.

Chapter 8, '*Lies and Deceit vs. Social Capital*', written by John Ryan: The present chapter seeks to analyze the economic literature in terms of the impact of lies on harm to social capital, destroying the institutions expected performance, creating asymmetric information and increasing transaction costs.

Chapter 9, '*The Detection of Profit Manipulation: Assessing the Ability of the Accrual and Revenue Models*', written by Maryam Ebrahimi: This chapter reviews mathematical techniques for identifying earnings management practices and comparing average earnings management and the ability to predict earnings management of accrual and revenue models.

Chapter 10, '*Misinformation in the Global Crisis of Coronavirus*', written by Elina Ahmadi: This chapter focuses on studies to trace misinformation on popular social media because the dissemination of such information can cause risks to public health. In addition, the impact of social media on social phobia and lifestyle with regard to the corona virus is examined.

To assist and advise the European Commission on how to understand and combat the fake news and misinformation phenomenon, 38 experts in a new expert group on fake news and online misinformation were appointed by the Commission in January 2018, according to a by Kalsnes (2018). Due to the multifaceted and evolving issue of misinformation, this group is strongly opposed to simplistic solutions such as censorship of freedom of expression and their report suggested to act based on the following five pillars: (1) increasing the digital information ecosystem transparency (2) promoting literacy in the field of media and information to combat misinformation and help users to direct the digital media environment; (3) providing tools to empower users and journalists against misinformation and strengthen positive partnerships with rapidly evolving information technologies; (4) maintaining the diversity and sustainability of the European news media ecosystem; (5) Continuous review of the impact of misinformation in Europe to evaluate the actions taken by various actors and continuously adjust the necessary responses. By enacting new legal measures, some countries have tried to make ban in the release of fake news. Other measures can be also done by users, readers, viewers and listeners of information to counterfeit fake news. Children and students with media literacy and education can distinguish between trusted and less trusted sources, and for this reason, government programs have been developed in some countries. New fact-finding services are also being developed with the increasing spread of fake news.

REFERENCES

Bode, L., & Vraga, E. K. (2017). See something, say something: Correction of global health misinformation on social media. *Health Communication*, 1–11. doi:10.1080/10410236.2017.1331312 PMID:28622038

Freitas, J. D., Falls, B. A., Haque, O. S., & Bursztajn, H. J. (2013). Vulnerabilities to misinformation in online pharmaceutical marketing. *Journal of the Royal Society of Medicine*, *106*(5), 184–189. doi:10.1177/0141076813476679 PMID:23761527

Fukuyama, F. (2017). *The emergence of a post-fact world*. Retrieved from https://www.project-syndicate.org/onpoint/the-emergence-of-a-post-fact-world-by-francis-fukuyama-2017-01

Hausman, B. L. (2020). Against misinformation. *Journal for Research and Debate*, *3*(8), 1–4. PMID:33017160

Kalsnes, B. (2018). *Fake news*. *Oxford Research Encyclopedia of Communication*. doi:10.1093/acrefore/9780190228613.013.809

Kouzy, R., Jaoude, J. A., Kraitem, A., Alam, M. B. E., Karam, B., Adib, E., Zarka, J., Traboulsi, C., Akl, E. W., & Baddour, K. (2020). Coronavirus goes viral: Quantifying the COVID-19 misinformation epidemic on Twitter. *Cureus*, *12*(3), e7255. doi:10.7759/cureus.7255 PMID:32292669

Polak, M. (2012). The misinformation effect in financial markets-an emergence issue in behavioral finance, e-finance. *Financial Internet Quarterly*, *8*(3), 55–61.

Shin, J., Jian, L., Driscoll, K., & Bar, F. (2018). The diffusion of misinformation on social media: Temporal pattern, message, and source. *Computers in Human Behavior*, *83*, 278–287. Advance online publication. doi:10.1016/j.chb.2018.02.008

Smithers, A. (2019). *Productivity and the bonus culture*. Oxford University Press. doi:10.1093/oso/9780198836117.001.0001

Solms, R. V., & Niekerk, J. V. (2013). From information security to cyber security. *Computers & Security*, *38*, 9–102.

Soomro, Z. H., Hussain Shah, M., & Ahmed, J. (2016). Information security management needs more holistic approach: A literature review. *International Journal of Information Management*, *36*(2), 215–225. doi:10.1016/j.ijinfomgt.2015.11.009

Wu, L., Morstatter, F., Carley, K. M., & Liu, H. (2019). Misinformation in social media: Definition, manipulation, and detection. *SIGKDD Explorations*, *21*(2), 80–90. doi:10.1145/3373464.3373475

Chapter 1
Information, Misinformation, and Disinformation:
Social Diffusion and Misinformation Prevention

Mahshid Ebrahimi
Independent Researcher, Germany

ABSTRACT

Information has various definitions and combinations, which have to be regarded for proper information management. The purpose of this study is to clarify the concepts of information, misinformation, and disinformation for having a better understanding of their dimensions as well as to explain the patterns and motives of diffusion of misinformation and disinformation. The present study examines studies of a social diffusion model of information, misinformation, and disinformation as well as a prevention framework of misinformation. Knowing these concepts and their dimensions provides the basis for more accurate and comprehensive analysis in this area. Skills of critical thinking and information evaluation in the forms of information literacy and web literacy can prevent users from publishing, retrieving, and using misinformation and disinformation.

INTRODUCTION

The emergence of the information society, changing the information environment and the importance of information as a vital element of various economic, occupational, educational, research and recreational activities of different segments of society

DOI: 10.4018/978-1-7998-8235-0.ch001

has led to increasing attention to the issue of human-information interaction. The pervasiveness and widespread use of information by academic disciplines and the general public has led to a variety of definitions of information. More than 600 years after the advent of the word information, its meaning has not yet been established and a consensus has not been formed about it.

After an in-depth examination of the word information, Brock & Dhillon (2001) stated that it is almost anything and everything, and attributed it to the Aether also called quintessence (fifth element), the substance that permeated everything; But its exact meaning was unknown. A creative way to explore the concept of information is to analyze its compound. One of the neglected dimensions of information combinations is the negative components of information such as information bombardment, information pollution also called info pollution, information explosion, information overload, misinformation, and disinformation.

Social networks, as the latest form of information and communication technologies of the present age, have provided a platform for the presentation of ideas and opinions, and have greatly increased the speed of information penetration. Today, most social decisions are made based on information that is collected through personal and social networks as important channels of knowledge (Qiu et al., 2013). The ease of disseminating information on social media is like a double-edged sword that, while useful, has devastating effects on human-information interactions and poses fundamental challenges. One of the challenges is the uncontrolled increase in creation, manipulation, sharing, and consumption of information without spatial and temporal limitations through social networks and the spread of misinformation and disinformation, so that it has become difficult to distinguish true information from false and misleading information.

The purpose of this study is to clarify the concepts of information, misinformation, and disinformation, provide a better understanding of their commonalities, differences, and relationships, and explain the patterns and motives for the diffusion of information, misinformation, and disinformation. Additionally, this chapter reviews the social diffusion model of information, misinformation, and disinformation proposed by Karlova and Fisher (2013) and the misinformation prevention framework developed by Koohang and Weiss (2003).

INFORMATION

One of the assumptions of information is the assumption that information is true. The criterion of truth makes it possible to distinguish between the concepts of information, misinformation, and disinformation. Despite the relatively long history of debating fact and lie, no universally accepted theory or definition of fact has been presented. In addition, Tabatabai (1990) argued that fact is the same as truth or right and is called a mental proposition that corresponds to reality; but an illusion, a lie, or a falsehood implies that mental proposition that does not correspond to reality. Truth means perception in accordance with reality. Any proposition that corresponds to reality is the truth. However, many thinkers do not consider truth to mean that perception corresponds to reality and offer other definitions of truth. Positivists, for example, believe that truth is the agreement of all minds at once on a proposition.

Truth is a feature of a statement. A statement or proposition can be true or false. When submitting a statement, asking if it is correct or incorrect will have the usual answer. It is correct if the statement describes the state of the world as it is or if it conforms to one of the universal methods. A strong assumption about information is that the information is correct. If this assumption is not true, the meanings associated with that information can be misleading, and incorrect information cannot inform perception or action.

The two main different frameworks in the criteria used to make decisions about reality are the correspondence theory of truth and the coherence theory of truth. In fact, these are not testable theories themselves, but they can be used to extract substantive theories. They use completely different criteria to judge the truth of a particular theory and the hypotheses, propositions, or claims that emerge from that theory. In other words, the two theories are not comparable (Custers, 2019).

Theories within the framework of correspondence use empirical accuracy as the ultimate standard for judging truth. In other words, signs in the environment that say something about this world are used to make valid judgments about the natural world. It is assumed that the natural world provides tangible indicators of the intangible aspects of the phenomenon. Most importantly, in correspondence theory, there is no need to explain how the signs of the phenomenon relate to specific judgments. The only thing that matters is that it is empirically accurate or not, given a certain standard by which this accuracy can be assessed (Custers, 2019).

As the ultimate standard for judging truth, theories within the framework of coherence use rationality or logical stability. Because this criterion is relatively weak, in practice it often extends to coherence, a stronger criterion. Complete incompatibilities cannot be resolved this way. If two claims are inconsistent, they are contradictory and therefore at least one must be false (Custers, 2019).

The interdisciplinary nature of the concept of information on the one hand and the interest of experts in various fields on this concept on the other hand has led to the multiplicity and diversity of definitions, and this has made it difficult to have a comprehensive definition. English dictionaries provide a range of definitions such as news, data, knowledge, informing, knowledge gained from learning, ideas expressed, records recorded, awareness and learning for information. Information is the name for the content that is exchanged with the outside world. As a result, the feeling is added to it and it adapts to the environment. This definition places more emphasis on the effective processes of information sharing than the information itself.

Some researchers (Davenport and Prusak, 1998; Walsham, 2001; Ulrich, 2001) have defined data as one of the ways to reach the meaning of information. Data is the raw fact of the world. When data finds meaning and connection in context, it becomes information. This relationship between data, information and meaning is often agreed upon. However, De George (2003) clearly distinguishes between data and information; because the data make no claims about the truth; while the information does this.

Figure 1. Information map adopted from Floridi (2011)

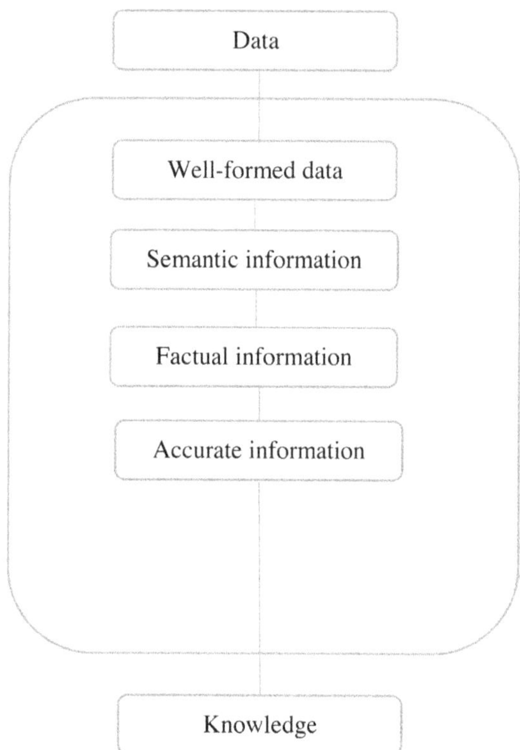

By analyzing multiple definitions of information, Floridi (2011) has defined data equivalent to data along with meaning. The information map by Floridi in Figure 1 shows how information is placed in a hierarchical structure between data and knowledge. In fact, in order to form information, the data must be well-formed, meaningful and honest. The first condition is that the data set be correctly placed in one or more datasets according to the rules. The second condition is that the data match the selected meanings. The third condition allows the individual to accurately distinguish between information, misinformation and disinformation. New knowledge can be created based on available information and existing knowledge and through various cognitive processes such as learning, communication, and reasoning. Some scholars have criticized the concept of continuity and hierarchical data, information and knowledge, and believe that although there is coherence between them; but this coherence is not hierarchical.

Table 1. Information quality specifications

Information quality specifications	Description
Available	The available information should be easily accessible by authorized users so that they can obtain it in the appropriate format and at the right time to meet their needs.
Accurate	Accurate information is free of errors. In some cases, incorrect information is generated; this is because incorrect data enters the conversion process, which is usually called garbage in, garbage out.
Complete	Complete information contains all the important facts that are necessary for a decision.
Economic	Information production should be relatively cost-effective. Decision makers must always balance the value of information with its total cost.
Flexible	Flexible information can be used for a variety of purposes.
Relevant	Relevant information is information that is available for a situation or problem and can help solve a problem. Relevant information is important for decision makers.
Reliable	Reliable information can be trusted by users. In many cases, the reliability of the information depends on the reliability of the data collection method.
Secure	Information must be protected from unauthorized users.
Simple	Information should be simple, not complex. Excessive information can overflow information. In this way, the decision maker has a lot of information and cannot determine what is really important. Timely information means that information is delivered whenever needed.
Timely	Timely information means that information is delivered whenever needed.
Verifiable	The information must be verifiable. This means that they can be checked to make sure they are correct. It may be possible to prove the accuracy of the information by examining many sources for the same information.

(Stair and Reynolds, 2017)

In this regard, Bhatt (2001) believes that whenever the data are related and the necessary context and interpretation is considered for them, information emerges that can be used to make decisions. In contrast to this definition, data that has a special meaning for a person, it may not make sense to another person. Therefore, it can be said that information is processed data, understandable and usable for a specific need that makes sense for a person or individuals in a particular context. However, true information regardless of its context, as shown in Table 1, has characteristics such as availability, accuracy, completeness, cost-effectiveness, flexibility, relevance, reliability, security, simplicity, timeliness, and verifiability (Stair and Reynolds, 2017).

MISINFORMATION

There are almost very few references to the negative forms of information, or in other words, misinformation is considered equivalent to false information. Stahl (2006) cited the same definition without providing further analysis or discussion, and another group has argued. Fox (1983) clearly described the relationship between information and misinformation. He believed that information does not have to be true, in the sense that there is no reason why information should be true. The information may be incorrect. Misinformation is a form of information, and misinformation, although wrong, is still information and can still be informative. Lewis et al. (2016) disagreed with Fox's view on raising awareness of misinformation. They believe that misinformation is misleading, incomplete, or incorrect.

To define misinformation, Watson (1990) focused on the purpose of creating misinformation, and misinformation is information that is intended to mislead, deceive, and undermine the confidence of individuals, organizations, or governments. This misinformation can take many forms, including incomplete, outdated, biased, deceptive, inconsistent, incorrectly translated data, software incompatibilities, unauthorized corrections, actual errors, and scientific misconduct. Misinformation may be false, vague, probable, or unreliable. According to Lewandowsky et al. (2012), misinformation seems more comprehensive. They believed that misinformation that occurs during a dynamic event or during a knowledge update is inevitable and unintentional. However, there are other sources of incorrect information that are probably less reliable. They pointed out certain sources of misinformation, which include:

Rumors and legends: Communities have struggled for centuries with misinformation about the spread of rumors. Even fiction can lead to misconceptions about facts.

Governments and politicians: Governments and politicians can be powerful sources of misinformation, either inadvertently or intentionally.

Non-governmental organizations with personal interests: Trade guilds interests have a long history. They try to influence the public discourse by announcing misinformation. As recently, regular campaigns against corporate interests have been led by interested nonprofits.

Media: Although the media literally seeks to inform the public but they are exposed to the spread of misinformation.

To evaluate the accuracy of any information, four factors are considered. These factors are identified by asking four questions, which are:

Message compatibility: It refers to the consistency of information with other beliefs of an individual.

Message integrity: The information have any internal integration without any contradictions to form a credible narrative.

Source credit: The information is from a valid source.

Public acceptance: It refers to checking whether others believe this information.

In general, according to the definitions and explanations provided for misinformation, this type of information can be considered synonymous with wrong, incorrect, inaccurate, incomplete information are published unintentionally.

DISINFORMATION

The origins of disinformation go back to the 1950s, when it was defined as misinformation that was intentionally misleading. Given the political and cultural climate of the Soviet Union at the time, Karlova and Fisher (2013) stated disinformation is as a result of Stalinist intelligence control policies. Although there are policymakers, academics and the media who believe that disinformation is obsolete after the Cold War; however, by the end of 1986, the term disinformation was not listed in the British Encyclopedia and was mistakenly believed to be a synonym for misinformation. But in fact, disinformation is very different from misinformation. In other words, misinformation, when published intentionally and deliberately in order to deceive, will lead to the creation of disinformation. Disinformation arises when the information process is incomplete. When semantic content is incorrect, it is a case of misinformation, and if the source of the information is aware of its erroneous nature, then it is disinformation. In other words, disinformation is incorrect information that the source is aware of being wrong. When a person jokes or speaks sarcastically, even though the person is aware that the talk is wrong, because there is no intention of deception, so it is not disinformation.

Fallis (2009) analyzed disinformation to prove the difference between disinformation and misinformation. He pointed to a set of conditions that may lead to disinformation. While misinformation is generally incorrect, but disinformation is not always false, it is just misleading. Therefore, disinformation is not a subset of misinformation. Although disinformation may have something in common with misinformation, but disinformation is intentionally misleading. The motive behind such deception is unknown, but it includes personal motivation, social motivation such as benevolent reasons such as lying about a particular group and joining cultural values, and conflicting reasons such as manipulating a competitor's stock price and damaging one's reputation. As simple examples of disinformation include deceptive advertisements in business and government, fake documents, tampered images, fake maps, Internet fraud, and fake websites. Providing disinformation has been around for centuries. What distinguishes disinformation from misinformation is the unintentional spread of incorrect information. The difference between the two is in their goals.

Fetzer (2004) stated that disinformation is more or less tantamount to lying. In other words, it is a lie that the narrator believes to be false and is intended to mislead. Disinformation includes incomplete, inaccurate and misleading information that is disseminated with the aim of deceiving others about the truth. This is how Fetzer described the main features of disinformation:

- Disinformation is often the product of a technically advanced and well-designed misleading process.
- Disinformation may not come directly from the source who intends to defraud.
- Disinformation often includes items such as verbal or written communications, including manipulated images, fake videos, and more.
- Disinformation can be widely or purposefully distributed among specific individuals or organizations.
- Goals of disinformation are often intended to deceive a person or group of people.
- Terms such as lie, counterintelligence, seductive information, and misleading information are synonymous with disinformation.

In general, with regard to the definitions given for disinformation, it must be acknowledged that in all these definitions there is agreement on two key aspects of disinformation, which include false information and intent to mislead.

DIFFUSION MODEL

Information, misinformation and disinformation have been less the subject of theoretical research in information science. Recently, the Internet and websites not only provide reliable and up-to-date information, they also store and present information containing deceptions and mistakes. In addition, the pervasiveness of the Internet and the abundance of information it provides have expanded the meaning and concept of information. As a result of changes in Internet communication interactions, especially the number of participants in such interactions, information integration is disrupted. These interferences on the Internet can be defined as social, technical, or semantic errors that lead to the formation of information, misinformation, or disinformation. Therefore, it is necessary to restore criteria to distinguish information from misinformation, and disinformation, especially in today's society, despite the speed of information transfer through the Internet.

It is difficult to distinguish between information, misinformation, and disinformation, and this difficulty becomes more complicated when misinformation and disinformation are considered as a subset of information or a type of misinformation. However, misinformation is unintentional dissemination of misleading and wrong information. In general, the truth or falsity of information can be proven by referring to sufficient evidence. This issue has become important with the analysis of social media. Although making a lie at a remarkable time is a challenging operation, but usually the accuracy of the information can be identified. It is much more difficult to discern the intention to mislead, because it requires an understanding of people's mental processes.

By referring to three key criteria called ABC – (Accuracy, Balance, and Credibility), the intent to mislead by disinformation can be demonstrated, which are (Nimmo, 2016):

The accuracy of verbal statements: Those who speak in the position of officials are obliged to ensure the honesty and correctness of any statement that arises from their position and executive duty.

Balance in the report: Their reports ensure a proper balance in the use of commentators.

Validity of selected resources: It is necessary to ensure the authenticity of the sources cited.

Criteria for distinguishing websites presenting information, misinformation, and disinformation have been proposed by Tarcza & Buker (2001), which include:

Information: Informational websites provide real information. They identify the author, source, and owners of the information, and the information provided by them is credible. This information is accurate and error free and is updated regularly.

Misinformation: This information causes confusion, because they are presented in contrast to previous information or in order to correct the incorrect communication process. Misinformation includes mistakes and subject matter information are old.

Disinformation: Information that is intentionally misleading and deceptive. The true author of such information is unknown. There is no contact address or reference to the source, date of insertion or update of information and even a brief description of the author.

Tudjman & Mikelic (2003) introduced five criteria for evaluating information: authority, accuracy, objectivity, currency and coverage. Karlova and Fisher (2013) relying on the five characteristics of truth, completeness, being up-to-date, having useful information, and being deceptive, compared information, misinformation and disinformation.

Table 2. A summary of features of information, misinformation, and disinformation

	Information	Misinformation	Disinformation
True	Yes	Could be Yes and No, depending on context and time	Could be Yes and No, depending on context and time
Complete	Could be Yes and No, depending on context and time	Could be Yes and No, depending on context and time	Could be Yes and No, depending on context and time
Current	Yes	Could be Yes and No, depending on context and time	Could be Yes and No, depending on context and time
Informative	Yes	Yes	Yes
Deceptive	No	No	Yes

Karlova and Fisher, 2013)

The diffusion model of information, misinformation, and disinformation is presented in Figure 2 by Karlova and Fisher (2013). Features of this model include:

Figure 2. The social diffusion model of information, misinformation, and disinformation
Source: Karlova and Fisher, 2013

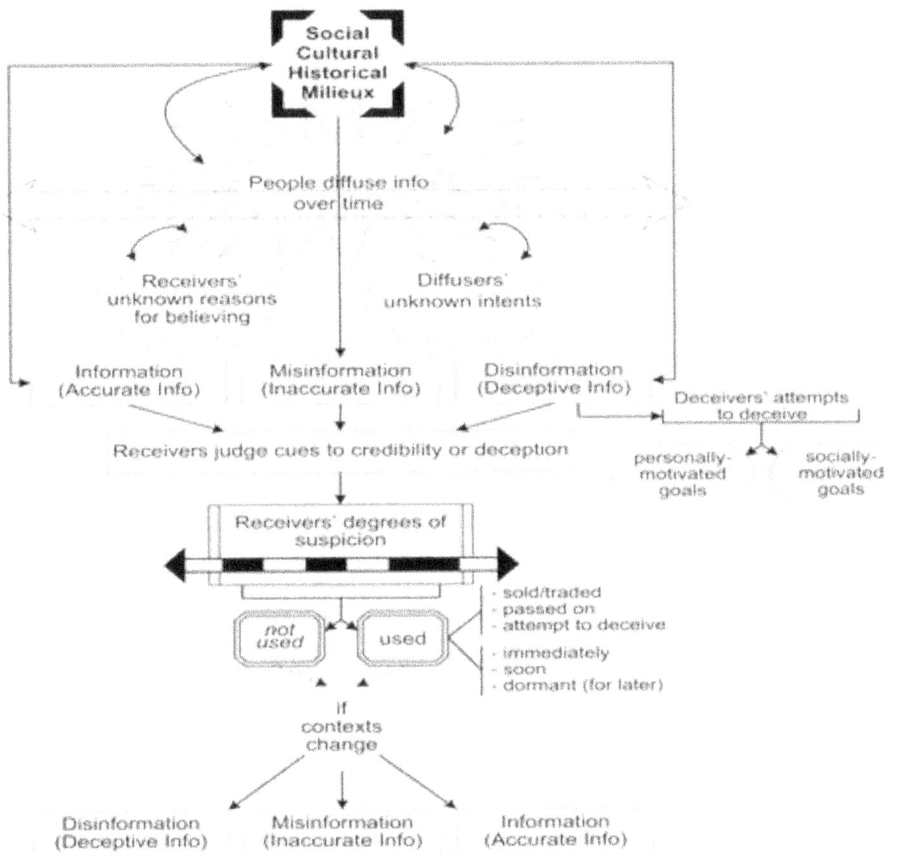

Milieux

Information is not generally formed in a vacuum. This model seeks to learn and be aware of the context. Environmental factors such as social, cultural and historical aspects can affect the perception and use of information, misinformation, and disinformation. In this model, information, misinformation, and disinformation are mediated through social, cultural and historical.

Diffusion

Social networks are used to spread information, misinformation and disinformation over time. People share information even if they do not believe it. Naturally, with the diffusion of information, signs of inaccuracy or deception may change, disappear or appear. Diffusion of information may be fast or time consuming. Some social media technologies, such as Twitter and Facebook, are faster at the diffusion of information, misinformation, and disinformation.

Unknowns

The purposes behind the diffusion of information, misinformation, and disinformation to people, governments and businesses are unknown. Determining the exact human intention of an action at any given moment is a difficult task. People may be reluctant to express their true intentions, unable to remember their original intentions, or unable to articulate them. There may be benevolent or contradictory motives behind the diffusion misinformation, and disinformation, but the nature or extent of the intention alone cannot determine. Information, misinformation and disinformation may be diffused without the belief of the speaker. Even in the case of expressing a statement of belief, the intents behind the phrase are not clear.

Deception

In producing misinformation, deceivers try to deceive people. Given any motive, deception does not guarantee the achievement of their goals. Deception allows for the achievement of malicious (such as embezzlement of a colleague) and benevolent (such as lying about a surprise party for a friend) goals. Such goals indicate the complexity of deception. It is better to consider the signs of deception as context-dependent or relationship-related.

Judgement

Recipients judge their credibility using information quality assessment criteria and signs of deception. Deceivers use credentials to deceive. Despite the efforts of the deceivers, none of the efforts may succeed, which largely depends on the extent to which the recipients are suspicious of misinformation or disinformation. Recipients use their information literacy skills to judge information, misinformation, and disinformation

Use

Information is used by people, governments and businesses to make decisions and take action. Correcting misinformation can provide opportunities for meaningful participation, public awareness and education, and the provision of business services.

Individuals can use misinformation to influence or control others, as governments do. Misinformation and disinformation, if detected, can be sold or traded. The world is changing day by day and it is possible to turn information into misinformation or vice versa.

Social media is increasingly used to generate and exchange information. However, there are insufficient control mechanisms in this medium and it has raised concerns about the validity of the information circulating. This has attracted the attention of researchers, but little is known about the factors that allow people to identify misinformation and disinformation (Dabbous et al., 2021).

THE MISINFORMATION PREVENTION FRAMEWORK

Figure 3. Misinformation prevention framework
Source: Koohang and Weiss, 2003

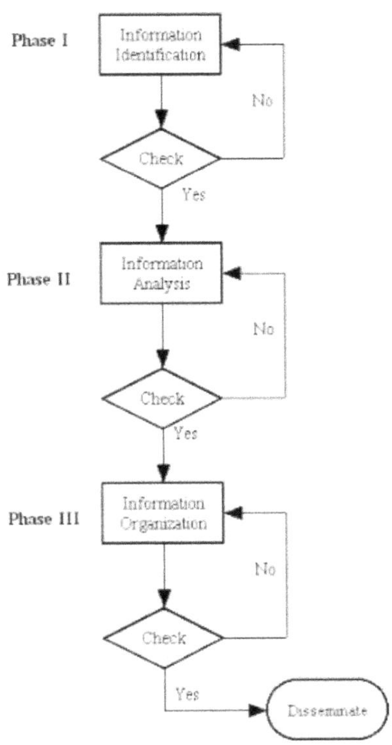

Diffusion of real information has become a challenge for the organizations and individuals responsible for it. The framework (Figure 3) can be used as a guide to prevent the diffusion of misinformation. This framework consists of three stages (Koohang and Weiss 2003):

1. Information identification,
2. Information analysis, and
3. Information organization.

Under this framework, only the information architect will be responsible for all stages of the misinformation prevention framework and will strive to minimize or eliminate misinformation before publishing information. After completing each step, a checkpoint is critical to make sure all steps in each step are followed correctly.

Phase 1- Information Identification

This step is to identify the information that needs to be defined and described. The nature of the information must be specified; in other words, what the information is intended to accomplish should be defined. Assessing information needs is one of the main tasks of this step. To do this, techniques including direct observation, interviews and surveys are used. This step deals specifically with:

- Define and describe information.
- Identify the nature of information.
- Understand and define what the information is intended to do.
- Understand information needs.

Phase 2- Information Analysis

Information analysis is the most important step that requires high accuracy. Information analysis can include a map that outlines the overall functionality of information, information source, information architecture, and content. The analysis phase determines the value of the information that is ultimately used to make the right decisions. This step determines the accuracy, completeness and relevance of the information. This step specifies internal and external controls to ensure the reliability of the information. It also validates information and can refer to information sources for this purpose. The validity and legality of the information is checked at this stage. In general, the analysis phase examines the relationship between information, information context, and users who have access to the information.

Information for having quality must have characteristics that include usefulness, uniqueness and accuracy of information. Information should not be derivative, repetitive or dubious. Information must meet the purpose. It must be real. It should not be biased. Facts and opinions should be separated from the information collected. Facts are events that actually happened. They are accurate, verifiable, clear and accurate. Opinions are thoughts, views, judgments, and feelings that are not supported by facts. Incompatibility between information obtained from different sources must be confirmed. The frequency of information updates must also be verified. The information of the sponsors must be verified. In most cases, the motivations and goals of the sponsoring organization must be considered. This may help to clarify and intelligently analyze possible bias. Information must be credible and sourced from reputable sources. Attention should be paid to credible and credible sources that may be more useful for gathering facts. Verifying the credibility and affiliation of the person or persons who compiled this information is a critical task. This step deals specifically with:

- Identify internal and external controls that ensure information is reliable.
- Verification and validation of information.
- Confirmation of valid information and legality of information.
- Includes a map that outlines the overall functionality of information, information source, information architecture, and content.
- Identify the scope of information.
- Separation of facts and opinions from each other.
- Confirmation of information sponsors.
- Check for information inconsistencies.
- Confirmation of credentials and affiliation of the author of the information.

Phase 3- Information Organization

This step is about organizing the information for the diffusion. At this stage, information must be customized for a specific environment and must be organized so that it can be easily found and understood. Information should be presented in a clearly and logically organized format for the use of the target audience. Information must be labeled clearly and appropriately. An information map is beneficial for information organization. Information should not be cluttered. The information must be legible and accurate. Key points should be highlighted. It must be structured to include headings, bold words, tables, and figures. This step deals specifically with:

- Customization for a specific context.
- Find and understand information easily.
- Convenient and clear labeling.
- Transparent and logical formatting.
- Includes information map.

- Identify clear navigation elements.
- Identify key points.
- Determine and include visual clarity.

DISCUSSION

Structural and content features must be evaluated to assess the validity of web information. Online contexts have speed, link structure, multimedia and interaction. On the other hand, they have lack of referencing and organizational contracts. These differentiate the evaluation of web information from the evaluation of traditional information sources. In addition, evaluating the credibility of information resources in areas such as health, e-commerce, and political decision-making is important because of its impact on individuals and social lives. In addition, assessment skills vary among different users according to their needs, context and abilities. Lack of assessment skills is a consequence of variables such as experience, age, tasks and etc. (Keshavarz, 2014).

CONCLUSION

This study tried to clarify the concepts of information, misinformation, and disinformation. It reviewed a diffusion model of information, misinformation, and disinformation as well as a misinformation prevention framework. The chapter provides a basis for the concepts explored and a list of criteria by which credibility of information could be assessed. Websites around the world play important roles simultaneously as a source, message and media. In addition, with the prevalence of web resources in research and education, traditional information evaluation skills are not sufficient to validate. To deal with the day-to-day problems of the digital environment and the information that comes with it, new information skills need to be created for users of websites and these information resources. Users need to think critically to distinguish reality from false information.

REFERENCES

Bhatt, G. (2001). Knowledge management in organization. *Journal of Knowledge Management*, *5*(1), 68–75. doi:10.1108/13673270110384419

Brock, F. J., & Dhillon, G. S. (2001). Managerial information: The basics. *Journal of International Information Management*, *10*(2), 45–59.

Custers, E. J. F. M. (2019). Theories of truth and teaching clinical reasoning and problem solving. *Advances in Health Sciences Education: Theory and Practice*, *24*(4), 839–848. doi:10.100710459-018-09871-4 PMID:30671703

Dabbous, A., Barakat, K. A., & Navarro, B. Q. (2021). *Fake news detection and social media trust: a cross-cultural perspective.* Behavior and Information Technology. Retrieved from https://www.tandfonline.com/doi/full/10.1080/01449 29X.2021.1963475

Davenport, T. H., & Prusak, L. (1998). *Working knowledge: How organizations manage what they know*. Harvard Business School Press.

De George, R. T. (2003). *The ethics of information technology and business.* Blackwell. doi:10.1002/9780470774144

Fallis, D. (2009). *A conceptual analysis of disinformation.* Paper presented at the iConference.

Fisher, K. E., Erdelez, S., & McKechnie, L. E. F. (2005). *Theories of information behavior*. Information Today, Inc.

Floridi, L. (2011). *The philosophy of information.* Oxford University Press. doi:10.1093/acprof:oso/9780199232383.001.0001

Fox, C. J. (1983). *Information and misinformation: An investigation of the notions of information, misinformation, informing, and misinforming*. Greenwood.

Karlova, N. A., & Fisher, K. E. (2013). *A social diffusion model of misinformation and disinformation for understanding human information behaviour.* Retrieved from http://www.informationr.net/ir/18-1/paper573.html

Keshavarz, H. (2014). How credible is information on the web: Reflections on misinformation and disinformation. *Infopreneurship Journal*, *1*(2), 1–17.

Koohang, A., & Weiss, E. (2003). Misinformation: Toward Creating a Prevention Framework. *Information Science*. Retrieved from https://proceedings.informingscience.org/IS2003Proceedings/docs/025Kooha.pdf

Lewandowsky, S. U., Ecker, K. H., Seifert, C. M., Schwarz, N., & Cook, J. (2012). Misinformation and its correction. *Psychological Science in the Public Interest*, *13*(3), 106–131. doi:10.1177/1529100612451018 PMID:26173286

Lewis, A., Lord, A. S., Czeisler, B. M., & Caplan, A. (2016). Public education and misinformation on brain death in mainstream media. *Clinical Transplantation*, *9*(30), 1082–1089. doi:10.1111/ctr.12791 PMID:27314625

Nimmo, B. (2016). *Identifying disinformation: An ABC approach*. Institute for European Studies. Policy Brief. Retrieved from http://www.ies. be/node/3612

Qiu, L., Rui, H., & Whinston, A. (2013). Information Exchange in Prediction Markets: Do Social Net-works Promote Forecast Efficiency? *System Sciences (HICSS), 46th Hawaii International Conference on System Sciences*, 3982-3991. 10.1109/HICSS.2013.269

Stahl, B. (2006). On the difference or equality of information, misinformation, and disinformation: A critical research perspective. *Informing Science Journal*, *9*, 83–96. doi:10.28945/473

Stair, R., & Reynolds, G. (2017). *Principles of information systems*. Course Technology.

Tabatabai, M. H. (1990). *The principles of philosophy and the method of realism*. Sadra Publishing.

Tudjman, M., & Mikelic, N. (2003). Information science: Science about information, misinformation and disinformation. *Informing Science*, *4*, 1513–1527.

Ulrich, W. (2001). A philosophical staircase for information systems definition, design, and development. *Journal of Information Technology Theory and Application*, *3*(3), 55–84.

Walsham, G. (2001). *Making a world of difference - IT in a global context*. Wiley.

Watson, B. W. (1990). *United States intelligence: An encyclopedia*. Garland Publishing, Inc.

Chapter 2
Antecedents Driving the Intention to Share Unverified COVID-19 Information on Social Media

Thong Bing Tai
Multimedia University, Malaysia

Su-Mae Tan
Multimedia University, Malaysia

Tze Wei Liew
Multimedia University, Malaysia

Mohammad Tariqul Islam Khan
Multimedia University, Malaysia

ABSTRACT

Infodemic refers to the influx of inaccurate or deceptive information on social media during a pandemic. The sharing of unverified COVID-19 information on social media is pervasive in Malaysia, which leads to adverse consequences stemming from misinformation, disinformation, and mal-information. Drawing upon the cognitive load theory (CLT) and self-determination theory (SDT), this research examined the antecedents driving unverified COVID-19 information sharing on social media in Malaysia. Based on 309 validated online survey responses, the PLS-SEM analysis revealed that except for trust towards online information; the proposed factors, self-disclosure, information overload, entertainment, and fear of missing out (FoMo), were found to predict the intention to share unverified COVID-19 information sharing on social media in Malaysia. Theoretical implications are discussed through CLT and SDT, and practical recommendations for government agencies, social media administrators, and public members to curb unverified COVID-19 information sharing on social media in Malaysia are offered.

DOI: 10.4018/978-1-7998-8235-0.ch002

INTRODUCTION

In response to the COVID-19 pandemic, Dr. Tedros Adhanom Ghebreyesus, the director of the World Health Organization (WHO), noted that "We're not just fighting an epidemic; we're fighting an infodemic. Fake news spreads faster and more easily than this virus, and is just as dangerous." (Twitter, 2020). The statement characterizes *infodemic,* which concerns the influx of inaccurate or deceptive information during a disease outbreak. In the age of information abundance, social media has become a popular choice for people to exchange news and information. Unfortunately, social media has also become a tool for perpetuating unverified health information regarding COVID-19.

Notably, the three categories concerning unverified health information are misinformation, disinformation, and mal-information. Misinformation refers to false information that is inadvertently or unintentionally forwarded. For instance, during March 2020, a notion that drinking warm water can inhibit and even kill the invading virus with stomach acid emerged. The baseless information was regrettably disseminated widely and rapidly through social media (Ambrose, 2020). Disinformation refers to the fabrication and sharing of fake news with malicious intentions. During the early Ebola outbreak, certain parties have intentionally fabricated and disseminated the rumors that healthcare workers were harvesting patients' organs (Dzieza, 2014) and that the Ebola virus was a government's hoax to receive fundings and donations (Cheung, 2015). Mal-information refers to the deliberate distortion of the original information misused and repurposed with malicious intentions. For instance, certain parties manufactured the Covid-Vegan memes by stitching together a picture depicting a large amount of vegan food on a supermarket shelf with the caption claiming that people were avoiding vegan products amid the pandemic (Chiorando, 2020).

According to Lewandowsky et al. (2012), people rarely retract or correct unverified information that they have shared, even when they have realized later the need to perform the retractions. Unverified information related to daily affairs tends to be repeatedly diffused through the sharing on social media for a long time (Wen & Zhang., 2018). This is worrying as unverified COVID-19 information can cause adverse public reactions such as over-reacting and under-reacting as well as self-isolation behaviors (Zarocostas, 2020; Pennycook et al., 2020). Furthermore, misleading information can cause citizens to hold and exhibit unproductive views and actions that inhibit strategies aimed at improving the pandemic situation (Kanekar & Thombre, 2019).

From a theoretical perspective, research on the behavioral and psychological factors that drive the intention to share unverified COVID-19 information on social media is scant. While studies on unverified information sharing have been conducted in Singapore, United States, Italy, and Nigeria (Chen, 2015; Pennycooka & David, 2019; Rovetta & Bhagavathula, 2020; Apuke & Omar, 2020); similar investigation has yet to be conducted in Malaysia. Thus, understanding to what extent these factors affect the intention to share unverified COVID-19 information on social media can provide unique insights into theory and practice. Formally, the research question of this study was formulated as:

RQ: What are the antecedents that drive the intention to share unverified COVID-19 information on social media in Malaysia?

This study enriches the literature on unverified health information by providing theoretical contributions. Although prior studies have examined the spread of misinformation on social media (Chen et al., 2015; Wen & Zhang, 2018; Talwar et al., 2019; Talwar et al., 2020), research regarding misinformation in the context of the COVID-19 pandemic is scarce. As an extension to the scant research on health-related misinformation (Apuke & Omar, 2020; Islam et al., 2020; Laato et al., 2020), this study is the first to investigate the antecedents of unverified COVID-19 information sharing on social media in Malaysia. Further, the findings of this study can help mitigate the propagation of panic and misinformation concerning COVID-19 on social media (Ahmad & Murad, 2020). Against this backdrop, this study attempts to understand why people tend to share unverified COVID-19 information on social media and discover the current trend of what social media platforms that people most utilized to spread unverified COVID-19 information.

The inclusion of both cognitive load theory (CLT) and self-determination theory (SDT) provides unique insights into the research. Given the recent prevalence of social media infodemic (Talwar et al., 2019; Islam et al., 2020; Laato et al., 2020; Cinelli et al., 2020), the findings of this study clarify the relationship between unverified COVID-19 information sharing on social media and the factors that are predominantly related to users' personal characteristics such as self-disclosure, trust towards online information, information overload, entertainment, and fear of missing out (FoMo). To mitigate the negative impacts of unverified health information mediated by social media during the prolonged pandemic, this study offers several practical recommendations which enable the users to collect, use, share and re-share the correct knowledge and information on COVID-19 through social media; as well as guiding users to check the credibility of information actively.

The following section presents the background regarding disseminating unverified COVID-19 information on social media in Malaysia. The subsequent section then discusses the literature review on two theories mentioned previously that excavate the predictor factors to form the conceptual framework and hypotheses of this study. The methodology section discusses the methods of data collection and statistical analysis applied in this study. The final sections present the discussion, implications, and future work concerning misinformation and unverified information sharing behaviors.

BACKGROUND

The Dissemination of Unverified COVID-19 Information on Social Media in Malaysia

About 81% of Malaysians are active on social media platforms, and Malaysia's social media penetration rate is considered among the highest in the world (Department of Statistics Malaysia, 2020). Issues surrounding COVID-19 have become the most discussed topics in social media (Ahmed et al., 2020), and Malaysians are highly dependent on social media to acquire news, instructions, or updates related to the pandemic. Like many countries worldwide, the sharing of unverified COVID-19 information on social media is notably evident in Malaysia. In response, the Malaysian government has effectuated awareness campaigns to discourage unverified COVID-19 information sharing. The Malaysian Communications and Multimedia Commission (MCMC) has also established a fact-checking portal, i.e., "sebenarnya. my," for citizens and public members to validate acquired information. Moreover, the national government has also imposed legal measures leading to fines and possible imprisonment of culprits involved in sharing unverified COVID-19 information. Specifically, the act of intentionally spreading fake news triggering public panic and fear, is punishable by law through a maximum fine of RM100,000 (~USD24,300) or a maximum imprisonment term of three years, or both (Terry, 2021).

Despite these measures, the sharing of unverified COVID-19 information on social media remains pervasive in Malaysia (ISIS Malaysia, 2020). People must have digital media literacy, which requires skills and intents to verify and interpret information to mitigate the sharing of unverified COVID-19 news on social media (Guess et al., 2020). The present study aimed to examine the antecedents that drive Malaysians to share unverified COVID-19 information on social media. In particular, this study draws upon cognitive load theory as well as self-determination theory to form the research framework with the following variables: self-disclosure, trust towards online information, information overload, entertainment, and fear of missing out (FoMo). The incorporation of cognitive load theory and self-determination theory in the research framework hinges on the *personal characteristics* of social media users. For instance, the need for autonomy of social media users can be fulfilled through the sharing of unverified COVID-19 information in the forms of images, infographics, statements, videos, and memes. During a prolonged pandemic, social media users may start to respond "numbly" to acquired information (Richard & Thomas, 2021), which leads to their disinterest in validating COVID-19 information. Social media users with different psychological needs may react differently to COVID-19 information, fueled by their trust toward online information, self-disclosure tendency, and the degree to which they find entertainment when sharing COVID-19 information on social media. For instance, there is a subtrend in which young TikTokers aged between 18 and 30 years old are adopting and perpetuating COVID-19 anti-vaccination and conspiracy theories; and this is attributed to their low media literacy and lack of ability to assess online information critically.

LITERATURE REVIEW

Two theories — cognitive load theory and self-determination theory, form the present study's research framework. The cognitive load theory (CLT) incorporates the role of information overload and trust toward online information; whereas, the self-determination theory (SDT) proposes the following factors — self-disclosure, fear of missing out, and entertainment, as antecedents that drive the intention to share unverified COVID-19 information on social media in Malaysia.

Cognitive Load Theory

The cognitive load theory (CLT) is primarily related to the learning process. Sweller (1988) proposed the CLT to describe the limited amount of information "chunks" that can be held and processed in a person's working memory at a given period. The CLT has been applied to investigate human behavior in the online environment (Yen et al., 2015; Quinn, 2018; Chan, 2020), such as sharing unverified information on social media (Laato et al., 2020; Islam, 2020). The cognitive load can be distinguished into three different types:

1. Germane load relates to the effectiveness of selecting, organizing, and integrating the information (words and images) into mental frames for intrinsic load processing.
2. Intrinsic load relates to how easily a person holds information (verbal and visual) in working memory based on their characteristics such as expertise level and age.
3. Extraneous load is associated with direct external factors such as the media or interface design that shape how the information is presented (novelty and complexity).

Both extraneous and intrinsic cognitive load contributes to *information overload*, where the amount of information to be processed exceeds mental capacity (Jackson & Farzaneh., 2012). Framed within the context of social media engagement, the bombardment of diverse news or information in the forms of rich multimedia that converges images, animations, videos, spoken voice, sound, or music can maximize cognitive processing within the limits of working memory — by imposing a load on both the visual (used for processing on-screen text/images/animations/videos) and verbal (used for processing spoken voice, sound, music) sensory channels of individuals. Relatedly, social media platforms can convey multimedia information from multiple sources simultaneously, which can cause a split-attention effect among users, thereby reducing cognitive ability to critically assess the online information (Yang and Lim, 2011; Laato et al., 2020; Islam, 2020).

Information overload is evident in an infodemic with an influx of new information regarding pandemics on social media. Accordingly, studies have focused on the role of information overload in health crises, such as the recent COVID-19 pandemic (Ahmed, 2020) and the SARS outbreak in 2003 (Kaigo, 2003). Information overload occurs in novel situations when people need guidance on how to manage the situations (e.g., How to prevent COVID-19 disease? Am I safe for this type of vaccine?). In line with the CLT, the influx of novel COVID-19 information can overload people's cognitive capacity, which in return diminish their ability or motivation to verify the COVID-19 information's authenticity (Laato et al., 2020; Islam,2020). Relatedly, such a phenomenon stems from people's inherent nature to avoid information that is hard to conceptualize (Sweller, 2011). It has been reported that information overload can cause psychological discomfort, such as the sense of ill-being or fatigue (Swar et al., 2017; Whelan, Islam, & Brooks., 2020). Thus, people are less devoted to verifying information sources that are especially novel and large in numbers (Maier et al., 2014; Whelan et al., 2020). Thus, it was proposed that:

H_1: Information overload is positively related to the intention to share unverified COVID-19 information on social media.

Intrinsic load, which associates with users' experience, familiarity, or expertise levels with certain subjects or internet experiences, can impact trust towards online information. In particular, the lack of expertise or experience can lead to decreased critical thinking about the authenticity regarding the information and the sources — and this, in turn, can prompt social media users to trust the information online easily (Khan & Idris., 2019; Talwar et al., 2019; Laato et al., 2020). Social media users who hold more trust in online information will be more likely to share unverified information rather than appraise the information's authenticity. As such, this study predicted that:

H_2: Trust toward online information is positively related to the intention to share unverified COVID-19 information on social media.

Theory of Self-determination

The self-determination theory (SDT) is formulated to study people's goal-driven behaviors concerning their motivation and personality (Ryan & Deci, 2017). In recent years, SDT has been used frequently to examine the relationship between human's psychological needs and social media behaviors (Chen & Jang., 2010; Ferguson et al., 2015; Karahanna et al., 2018; Kozan et al., 2019; Adjei et al., 2020; Fang et al., 2020), as well as the sharing of unverified COVID-19 information on social media (Talwar et al., 2019).

As noted by Gagné & Deci (2005), human motivation can be divided into three types:

1. *Amotivation*, which is related to people who have a lack of intention to behave,
2. *Intrinsic motivation* is related to wholly autonomous people from their inherent interests and is not mediated by extrinsic motives,
3. *Extrinsic motivation* is where people's initial reactions depend on their perception of contingency to achieve the desired outcome.

The present study focused on extrinsic motivation as the COVID-19 pandemic can be judged as an external regulation (social context and external contingency factor) that stimulates a person's initiative and active engagement toward certain activities (Ryan & Deci, 2017; Talwar et al., 2019). For instance, the sharing of unverified COVID-19 information on social media could be motivated by the sense of duty stemming from external support (the convenience of disseminating information on social media) and external pressure (worrying about the COVID-19 pandemic). The internalization of extrinsic motivation is a process that turns external causes into endorsed values (nutrition or intrinsic rewards), which motivates people to react more self-determinedly. However, this does not mean people will be entirely internally driven and act autonomously, as they are still subjected to external pressure such as stemming from the COVID-19 crisis. Accordingly, social media users acquire intrinsic rewards based on three psychological needs: relatedness, competence, and autonomy (Ryan & Deci., 2000) — and these have behavioral implications on unverified COVID-19 information sharing on social media (Laato et al., 2020; Talwar et al., 2019).

Self-disclosure is a communication form that reveals personal information, intimate feelings such as aspirations and fears, as well as personal thoughts with others (Jourard, & Friedman, 1970; Gibbs et al., 2006). As per the SDT, the need for relatedness is the desire to care for others and stay close and connected with others; this social need is particularly amplified during the COVID-19 crisis. The tendency to disclose personal details on social media is related to increasing mutual understanding and strengthening relationships to meet their needs for relatedness (Ryan & Deci., 2000; Talwar et al., 2019). Nonetheless, people may also disclose more personal information on social media for narcissistic intentions by dispensing self-promotional content with socio-emotional details to gain more popularity (Winter et al., 2014; Christofides, Muise, & Desmarais., 2009); and this may contribute to the sharing of unverified COVID-19 information on social media. Collectively, people who tend to self-disclose on social media are more likely to share COVID-19 information, including unverified ones on social media — not due to purely malicious intentions; rather, due to their desires to provide social support and keeping the community informed as to fulfill their relatedness needs (Talwar et al., 2020). Therefore, it was predicted that:

H_3: Self-disclosure is positively related to the intention to share unverified COVID-19 information on social media.

Competence refers to the ability to experience and master a particular task based on skills and abilities. The need for competence and relatedness as per the SDT theory is associated with the *fear of missing out (FoMo)* phenomenon (Deci & Ryan., 1985; Przybylski et al., 2013). In particular, FoMo reflects the pervasive anxiety of social media users about others having rewarding experiences compared to them. Specifically, FoMo may stem from the fear of social exclusion (Blackwell et al., 2017), which may be triggered by the perceived lack of competence and relatedness; and the need to feel popular and belong socially (Beyens et al., 2016). FoMo may cause people to behave more recklessly online, make critical comments, and engage in online gossip (Nottingham Trent University, 2016). By the same token, sharing information online can satisfy people's psychological deficit of competence and relatedness needs that contribute to the formation of FoMo. Compounded by the sense of loneliness and boredom during lockdowns (Banerjee & Rai., 2020); the recklessness and vulnerability of social media users afflicted by FoMo can prompt them to engage in unverified COVID-19 information sharing on social media (Yu et al., 2020; Talwar et al., 2019). As such, this study proposed that:

H_4: Fear of missing out (FoMo) is positively related to the intention to share unverified COVID-19 information on social media.

Entertainment refers to the engagement of social media to fulfill the need for pleasure as well as to moderate negative emotions such as anxiety; mainly through social media features surrounding "likes", comments, and exchange of novel information (Ma, Lee, & Goh., 2011; Thompson et al., 2020). The need for entertainment relates to people's tendency to consume news (Diddi, & LaRose., 2006), utilize social media tools (won Kim., 2014), share Facebook links with entertainment content (Baek et al., 2011), express personal views through clicks (e.g., Facebook Like), as well as to search and share useful information to garner joy and relaxation via online social relationships (Lin & Lu, 2011; won Kim, 2014).

The distinguishment between internal and external motives for sharing health information for entertainment purposes remains unclear, in particular during the COVID-19 pandemic. It has been asserted that entertainment may relate to extrinsic motivation because the pandemic poses health, financial, and lifestyle implications to people's life (Apuke, & Omar, 2021). Nonetheless, it has also been argued that entertainment relates to intrinsic motivation (Deci et al., 1994). For instance, learning new information while experiencing entertainment is related to self-regulation activities in seeking knowledge, accomplishment, or stimulating experience to meet the needs for autonomy (Deci & Ryan, 2000; Ha, Yoon, & Zhang, 2013). However, the need to experience entertainment through learning and exchanging new information as well as amassing likes and comments may prompt social media users to share COVID-19 information indiscriminately, including unverified ones, on social media. It was thus was predicted that:

H_5: Entertainment is positively related to the intention to share unverified COVID-19 information on social media.

METHODOLOGY

Data Collection

The present study targeted social media users in Malaysia as potential survey respondents. The study authors disseminated the invitation to participate in the online survey on Facebook, Instagram, WhatsApp, WeChat, Linked In, and Google Classroom. Data was collected between 3rd March 2021 and 1st June 2021. The formation of the survey questions was gauged in closed-ended questions, and a 5-points Likert scale ranging between strongly disagree (1) and strongly agree (5). The survey items were adapted from well-established questionnaires used in prior studies (see Table 1).

G*Power analysis was conducted to calculate the minimum sample size for PLS-SEM analysis. For five predictors, a medium effect size $f^2 = 0.15$, with $\alpha = .05$ and $1 - \beta = .95$, the required sample size was 138. In addition, both Kirchherr & Charles (2018) suggested a higher sample size to reduce bias selection and increase sampling diversity for the online survey. Hence, a total of 309 targeted respondents was collected. There was no missing data because of the "required" button afforded by the Google Form, and thus, all items were filled out. Therefore, the researcher fully utilized the 309 results from the online survey.

Table 1. Measurement of variables

Variables	Sources	No	Original items	Modified items
Self-disclosure	Krasnova et al. (2009)	SD1	I have a comprehensive profile on Facebook.	I have a comprehensive profile on social media.
	Krasnova et al. (2009)	SD2	I have a detailed profile on Facebook.	I have a detailed profile on social media.
	Krasnova et al. (2009)	SD3	My profile tells a lot about me.	My social media profile tells a lot about me.
	Krasnova et al. (2009)	SD4	From my Facebook profile it would be easy to find out my preferences in music, movies or books.	From my social media profile it would be easy to find out my preferences in music, movies or books.
Trust towards online information	Laato et al. (2020)	TOI1	I trust the information that is shared on social media.	I trust the Coronavirus (COVID-19) information that is shared on social media.
	Laato et al. (2020)	TOI2	I trust the news that is shared on social media.	I trust the Coronavirus (COVID-19) news that is shared on social media.
Information overload	Laato et al. (2020)	IO1	I am often distracted by the excessive amount of information on social media about Coronavirus (COVID-19).	I am often distracted by the excessive amount of Coronavirus (COVID-19) information on social media.
	Laato et al. (2020)	IO2	I find that I am overwhelmed by the amount of information that I process on a daily basis from social media about Coronavirus (COVID-19).	I find that I am overwhelmed by the amount of Coronavirus (COVID-19) information that I process on a daily basis from social media.
	Laato et al. (2020)	IO3	I receive too much information regarding the Coronavirus (COVID-19) pandemic to form a coherent picture of what's happening.	I receive too much Coronavirus (COVID-19) information to form a coherent picture of what's happening.
	Bock et al. (2010)	IO4	I cannot assimilate all the information that I read.	I cannot absorb all the Coronavirus (COVID-19) information that I read.
Entertainment	Chen et al. (2015)	ENT1	I feel enjoyment while sharing.	I feel enjoyable while sharing information during the COVID-19 pandemic.
	Chen et al. (2015)	ENT2	Sharing is a good way to relax.	Sharing information is a good way to relax during the COVID-19 pandemic.
	Chen et al. (2015)	ENT3	Sharing is a good way of killing time.	Sharing information is a good way of killing time during the COVID-19 pandemic.
	Chen et al. (2015)	ENT4	Sharing is good for keeping boredom away.	Sharing information is good for keeping boredom away during the COVID-19 pandemic.

Continued on following page

Table 1. Continued

Variables	Sources	No	Original items	Modified items
Fear of missing out	Hoetjes. (2013)	FoMO1	I get nervous that I might be missing out on something important.	I get nervous that I might be missing out on something important during the COVID-19 pandemic.
	Przybylski et al. (2013)	FoMO2	I fear others have more rewarding experiences than me.	I fear others have more rewarding experiences than me during the COVID-19 pandemic.
	Przybylski et al. (2013)	FoMO3	I get worried when I find out my friends are having fun without me.	I get worried when I find out my friends are having fun without me during the COVID-19 pandemic.
	Przybylski et al. (2013)	FoMO4	When I miss out on a planned get-together it bothers me.	During the COVID-19 pandemic, when I miss out on a planned get-together it bothers me.
Unverified COVID-19 information sharing on social media	Laato et al. (2020)	UIS1	I often share information or news on COVID-19 without checking its authenticity.	I often share Coronavirus (COVID-19) related information or news without checking its authenticity.
	Laato et al. (2020)	UIS2	I share information or news on COVID-19 without checking facts through trusted sources.	I share Coronavirus (COVID-19) related information or news without checking facts through trusted sources.
	Laato et al. (2020)	UIS3	I share information or news on COVID-19 without verifying it.	I share Coronavirus (COVID-19) related information or news without verifying it.
	Laato et al. (2020)	UIS4	I share information or news on COVID-19 even if sometimes I feel the information may not be correct.	I share Coronavirus (COVID-19) related information or news even if sometimes I feel the information may not be correct.
	Anderson, & Rainie. (2017)	UIS5	Most users just read the headline, comment and share without digesting the entire article or thinking critically about its content.	I share Coronavirus (COVID-19) related information or news depending on the headline but not the entire article.

Statistical Analysis

To proceed with the statistical analyses, the study screens normality of the data at the initial stage. The normality test shows that the data is assumed to have normal distribution as the items for all the constructs range within ± 1.96 (George and Mallery, 2010). Even though the data shows a normal distribution, the study proceeds with the variance-based PLS-SEM estimation to test the proposed framework. The justification lies in the exploratory nature of the variables, distribution-free analysis, bootstrapping method of path coefficients, and the study's sample size (Hair, Hult, Ringle, and Sarstedt, 2014). PLS-SEM involves both measurement and structural models, where the measurement model assesses the reliability (i.e., composite reliability and Cronbach's alpha) and validity (i.e., convergent and discriminant validity) of the constructs, and then, the structural model estimates the relationships. The significance of path coefficients is achieved via the bootstrapping method, which reduces the standard error of the model (Hair et al., 2014). The predictability of the model is assessed by the coefficient of determination (R^2).

RESULTS

Respondent's Profile

The demographic profile of the survey respondents showed the mix between female and male were equal (female = 51.5%). The majority of the respondents were aged between 21 and 30 years old. Over 80% of respondents were Chinese, followed by Malay and Indian ethnic groups. Most of the respondents lived in Malaysia's southern regions — Melaka, Johor, and Negeri Sembilan. A large majority of the respondents (89.3%) reported living with family members or children. Respondents indicated Facebook (29.8%), Instagram (25.6%), and WhatsApp (20.1%) as their most utilized social media platforms. Accordingly, the respondent reported that they preferred Facebook (39.8%), Instagram (32.4%), and WhatsApp (18.1%) as social media platforms for sharing information.

Composite Reliability and Convergent Validity

As shown in Table 2, the results described the composite reliability and convergent validity for all the six constructs. The outer loadings of all the items are higher than 0.7 ensuring a high level of internal consistency (Hair et al. 2014). With the high level of loadings, the values of Cronbach's alpha meet the threshold value, which is above 0.7. Consistently, the composite reliability of all constructs achieved the minimum required value of 0.7 to ensure acceptable composite reliability. The average variance extracted (AVE) is evaluated to establish the convergent validity of items in the construct. The AVE values of all constructs are above 0.5, ensuring achievement of convergent validity and indicates the degree of correlation of all items of a certain construct.

Table 2. Composite reliability and convergent validity

Variables	Items	Loadings	Cronbach's α	CR	AVE
Self-disclosure (SD)	SD1	0.842	0.829	0.886	0.662
	SD2	0.784			
	SD3	0.846			
	SD4	0.779			
Trust towards online information (TOI)	TOI1	0.888	0.766	0.895	0.810
	TOI2	0.911			
Information overload (IO)	IO1	0.793	0.842	0.893	0.677
	IO2	0.873			
	IO3	0.845			
	IO4	0.777			
Entertainment (ENT)	ENT1	0.844	0.879	0.917	0.734
	ENT2	0.860			
	ENT3	0.881			
	ENT4	0.841			
Fear of missing out (FoMO)	FoMO1	0.769	0.828	0.884	0.657
	FoMO2	0.808			
	FoMO3	0.819			
	FoMO4	0.845			
Unverified COVID-19 information sharing (UIS)	UIS1	0.841	0.9030	0.928	0.720
	UIS2	0.857			
	UIS3	0.871			
	UIS4	0.839			
	UIS5	0.833			

Note: The sample size is 309.

Discriminant Validity

To ensure that the variables in the model are distinct from each other, discriminant validity is estimated via the Fornell-Larcker criterion and Heterotrait-monotrait (HTMT) Measurement Model. Discriminant validity is achieved using the Fornell-Larcker criterion, where the square root of AVE is higher than the largest correlated values of any other variables within the respective rows and columns in the table. Table 3 shows the results of the Fornell-Larcker criterion. Discriminant validity is better gauged by the Heterotrait-monotrait (HTMT) Measurement Model. As shown in Table 4, the result reveals that the HTMT values of all constructs are less than 0.90 achieving the acceptable values to establish discriminant validity (Henseler et al. 2015).

Table 3. Discriminant Validity (Fornell-Larcker's criterion)

	[1]	[2]	[3]	[4]	[5]	[6]
[1] SD	**0.813**					
[2] TOI	0.356	**0.900**				
[3] IO	0.273	0.238	**0.822**			
[4] ENT	0.394	0.314	0.293	**0.856**		
[5] FoMO	0.380	0.267	0.254	0.355	**0.810**	
[6] UIS	0.443	0.342	0.355	0.394	0.382	**0.848**

Note: SD= Self-disclosure; TOI= Trust towards online information; IO= Information overload; ENT= Entertainment; FoMO= Fear of missing out; UIS= Unverified COVID-19 information sharing. The highlighted diagonal shows the square root of the AVE.

Table 4. Discriminant validity (HTMT)

	[1]	[2]	[3]	[4]	[5]	[6]
[1] SD						
[2] TOI	0.411					
[3] IO	0.262	0.310				
[4] ENT	0.391	0.362	0.298			
[5] FoMO	0.379	0.363	0.244	0.355		
[6] UIS	0.467	0.408	0.344	0.388	0.370	

Note: SD= Self-disclosure; TOI= Trust towards online information; IO= Information overload; ENT= Entertainment; FoMO= Fear of missing out; UIS= Unverified COVID-19 information sharing

Hypotheses Testing

To test the relationship between independent and dependent variables, the significant values of the path coefficient were evaluated. The results are reported in Table 5. It is observed that self-disclosure is positive and significantly related to the unverified COVID-19 information sharing. Similarly, information overload significantly predicts sharing of unverified COVID-19 information. It is likely that too much information might cause unverified information sharing related to COVID-19. The significant path coefficients are documented for entertainment and fear of missing out as well, but at a lower significance level. Entertainment has a positive and statistically significant impact on unverified COVID-19 information sharing if there is an issue of entertainment. This means that individuals tend to share unverified COVID-19 information. Fear of missing out also contributes to unverified COVID-19 information sharing. Fear of missing out is positive and statistically significant in predicting unverified COVID-19 information sharing. Therefore, hypotheses H1, H3, H4, and H5 are supported by the data, where hypothesis H2 is not supported. Figure 1 shows the PLS-SEM diagram of the empirical model.

Table 5. Results of hypothesis testing

Hypotheses	Paths	Path coefficients	P-values	T-values	Remarks
H1	SD→UIS	0.227**	0.022	2.005	Supported
H2	TOI→UIS	0.127	0.114	1.206	Not Supported
H3	IO→UIS	0.176**	0.026	1.942	Supported
H4	ENT→UIS	0.156*	0.077	1.424	Supported
H5	FoMO→UIS	0.162*	0.084	1.379	Supported

Note: SD= Self-disclosure; TOI= Trust towards online information; IO= Information overload; ENT= Entertainment; FoMO= Fear of missing out; UIS= Unverified COVID-19 information sharing

Figure 1. PLS-SEM diagram of the model

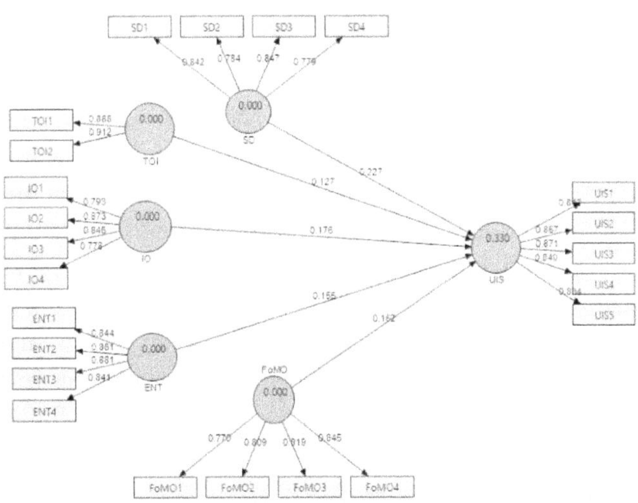

Predictive Accuracy and Predictive Relevance

The coefficient of determination (R2) indicates the model's predictive accuracy. The significant variables — self-disclosure, information overload, entertainment, and fear of missing out, can predict a 33.0% variation in the unverified COVID-19 information sharing (see Table 6). This reveals a weak to moderate level of predictive accuracy. The predictive relevance (Q2) of this model is 0.237 indicating a medium level of predictive relevance.

Table 6. Predictive accuracy and predictive relevance

Endogenous construct	R square	Q square
UIS	0.330	0.237

Note: UIS= Unverified COVID-19 information sharing

DISCUSSION

This research revealed that the intention to share unverified COVID-19 information in Malaysia was predicted by self-disclosure, information overload, entertainment, and fear of missing out (FoMo). Self-disclosure was the strongest predictor of unverified COVID-19 information sharing on social media during the pandemic outbreak in Malaysia. Social media users with a higher tendency to disclose personal details, including self-promotional contents and socio-emotional information, also share unverified COVID-19 related information on social media to meet their need for relatedness or competence; which conforms with prior findings with WhatsApp users (Talwar et al., 2019).

Information overload was found to have a significant and positive impact on sharing unverified COVID-19 information on social media in Malaysia. Coherent with the CLT, people are less devoted to verifying information sources that are especially novel and large in numbers, as information overload can impose people's cognitive capacity, ability and, after that, cause psychological discomfort as well as less motivation toward certain activities. This finding aligns with the prior observation with Bangladeshi social media users — specifically, it was shown that information overload was the main antecedent that influenced intention to share unverified information on social media (Laato et al., 2010). Furthermore, this finding parallels a study demonstrating that information overload can lead to social media fatigue; and this factor was found to be the strongest predictor of misinformation sharing behavior on social media (Islam et al., 2020).

Entertainment has a positive relationship with unverified COVID-19 information sharing on social media, albeit showing a weaker effect comparatively. This demonstrates that social media users in Malaysia who seek pleasure or moderate negative emotions by learning and exchanging new information on social media platforms are more likely to share COVID-19 information indiscriminately. This finding contrasts with Apuke & Omar (2021), which demonstrated that entertainment was not associated with COVID-19 fake news sharing. Apuke & Omar (2021) argued that the social media users might have viewed the pandemic as a serious issue and hence did not assign entertainment values to the sharing of the news content. On the other hand, the finding of this research implies that social media users in Malaysia find enjoyment in sharing COVID-19 information on social media platforms, which consequently drives intention to share unverified COVID-19 information on social media.

Fear of missing out (FoMo) has a positive relationship with unverified COVID-19 information sharing on social media in Malaysia, albeit indicating a weaker effect comparatively. This implies that social media users in Malaysia who have the anxiety that others have rewarding experiences compared to them are more likely to engage in unverified COVID-19 information sharing on social media. This observation is in line with the SDT insofar as FoMo stems from people's need for competence and relatedness to feel popular and belonged socially — and these unfulfilled needs can prompt social media users to behave recklessly online, including unverified information sharing on social media platforms.

Interestingly, trust towards online information did not predict intention to share unverified COVID-19 information on social media in Malaysia. This finding stands in stark contrast with Laato et al (2020), which reported online information trust as the strongest predictor of unverified health information sharing behaviors. In a similar vein, this finding diverges from recent studies — for instance, Talwar et al. (2019) indicated that there was a significant positive relationship between online trust and fake news sharing; and Khan & Idris (2019) reported that trust in online information might cause the sharing of unverified information on social media. Hence, this result suggests that social media users in Malaysia who engage in unverified COVID-19 information on social media are not driven by their tendency to trust the information online.

IMPLICATIONS

Theoretical Implications

This research contributes to the literature on misinformation, particularly in unverified COVID-19 information sharing behavior on social media. The findings of this study endorsed the roles of self-disclosure and information overload as the two primary antecedents that drive the intention to share unverified COVID-19 information sharing on social media, which reinforces recent findings on misinformation sharing intentions during the pandemic (Talwar et al., 2019; Islam, 2020). Furthermore, the results from this research supported recent findings demonstrating the positive association between FoMo and fake news sharing (Talwar et al., 2019). Beyond these, when contrasted with current research, some novel findings are derived from this study: 1) social media user's trust toward online information did not predict the intention to share unverified COVID-19 information on social media in Malaysia, and 2) enjoyment predicted the intention to share unverified COVID-19 information on social media in Malaysia. As this study is the first to examine the antecedents of unverified COVID-19 information sharing on social media in Malaysia, these findings provide significant insights unique to the context of social media users in Malaysia.

Lastly, this study extends the misinformation or unverified COVID-19 information sharing on social media construct (Talwar et al., 2019; Islam et al., 2020; Laato et al., 2020) by incorporating a new sub-component, "UIS5: I share Coronavirus (COVID-19) related information or news depending on the headline but not the entire article". This hinges on people's tendency to share social media information upon reading the headlines rather than the full-text contents — a view which was supported by Anderson & Rainie (2017). The inclusion of this new sub-component thus reflects the sharing misbehaviors in social media platforms that offer an influx of media-rich information, where users tend to heuristically rely on surface cues such as headlines while filtering out other contents when evaluating online information..

Practical Implications

The findings of this research have some implications for the Malaysian government agencies, social media platform administrators, and public members. To counter information load due to COVID-19 information influx on social media, social media administrators can sort or sift through health-related information to assess information authenticity. Subsequently, social media administrators can affix trusted news with endorsement labels/logos that display the verification status of the information for users to observe, such that users may not need to decide on the credibility of the information by themselves. Further, social media administrators can include reminders in social media platforms to discourage social media users from sharing unverified information about COVID-19. Interestingly, social media platforms administrators have started utilizing AI (e.g., machine learning) to assist human reviewers in sifting through fake or misleading news on social media to mitigate the influx of unverified information during the pandemic.

The government agencies can also create fact-checking portals for citizens or public members to easily and rapidly verify acquired unverified COVID-19 information in Malaysia. Furthermore, the government can generate awareness campaigns through social media platforms, radios, SMS, and TVs to remind the public members in Malaysia not to engage in unverified COVID-19 information sharing on social media. Because the intention to share unverified COVID-19 information on social media in Malaysia is driven by psychological needs, the government agencies can implore the public to have positive mindsets and attitudes during the pandemic by promoting the importance of healthy social and familial support and relationships. This may contribute to reduced anxiety, boredom, frustration, or FoMo — which are psychological that drive intention to share unverified COVID-19 information on social media in Malaysia.

LIMITATIONS AND RECOMMENDATIONS FOR FUTURE RESEARCH

This research has some limitations. Firstly, the respondents of this study were mainly from the southern region of Malaysia. Hence, similar studies can be conducted with respondents from other Malaysian areas to obtain more representative and generalizable findings concerning the antecedents of unverified COVID-19 information sharing on social media in Malaysia. Secondly, the level of predictive accuracy was considered weak to moderate. The five predictor variables — self-disclosure, information overload, entertainment, trust towards information, and fear of missing out, can predict 33.0% of the variation in the unverified COVID-19 information sharing, leaving 67% unexplained. This implies other variables influencing unverified COVID-19 information sharing behavior on social media in Malaysia, thereby warranting further studies to discover or examine other possible factors.

CONCLUSION

This study examined the antecedents that drive the intention to share unverified COVID-19 information on social media in Malaysia, predicated on the cognitive load theory (CLT) and self-determination theory (SDT). Based on the results of variance-based PLS-SEM analysis, it is clear that the psychological factors of self-disclosure contributed the most to the unverified COVID-19 information sharing in Malaysia. Information overload, entertainment, and fear of missing out (FoMo) also drive the intention of unverified COVID-19 information sharing on social media in Malaysia. This study is the first empirical investigation on unverified COVID-19 information on social media in Malaysia and hence offers significant insights unique to the context of social media users in Malaysia. It is interesting to note that trust towards online information did not predict the intention of sharing unverified COVID-19 information in Malaysia. This study provides practical recommendations to curb the unverified COVID-19 information sharing on social media in Malaysia.

REFERENCES

Adjei, J. K., Adams, S., Mensah, I. K., Tobbin, P. E., & Odei-Appiah, S. (2020). Digital Identity Management on Social Media: Exploring the Factors That Influence Personal Information Disclosure on Social Media. *Sustainability*, *12*(23), 9994. doi:10.3390u12239994

Ahmad, A. R., & Murad, H. R. (2020). The impact of social media on panic during the COVID-19 pandemic in Iraqi Kurdistan: Online questionnaire study. *Journal of Medical Internet Research*, *22*(5), e19556. doi:10.2196/19556 PMID:32369026

Ahmed, M. E., Rabin, M. R. I., & Chowdhury, F. N. (2020). *COVID-19: Social media sentiment analysis on reopening*. arXiv preprint arXiv:2006.00804.

Ambrose, S. (2020). *M'sia Health Minister Drew Flak for Suggesting That Drinking Hot Water Would Prevent COVID-19*. Retrieved from https://goodyfeed.com/msia-health-minister-covid19/

Anderson, J., & Rainie, L. (2017). The future of truth and misinformation online. Pew Research Center.

Apuke, O. D., & Omar, B. (2021). Fake news and COVID-19: Modelling the predictors of fake news sharing among social media users. *Telematics and Informatics*, *56*, 101475. doi:10.1016/j.tele.2020.101475

Baek, K., Holton, A., Harp, D., & Yaschur, C. (2011). The links that bind: Uncovering novel motivations for linking on Facebook. *Computers in Human Behavior*, *27*(6), 2243–2248. doi:10.1016/j.chb.2011.07.003

Banerjee, D., & Rai, M. (2020). *Social isolation in COVID-19: The impact of loneliness*. Academic Press.

Baumeister, R. F., DeWall, C. N., Ciarocco, N. J., & Twenge, J. M. (2005). Social exclusion impairs self-regulation. *Journal of Personality and Social Psychology, 88*(4), 589–604. doi:10.1037/0022-3514.88.4.589 PMID:15796662

Beyens, I., Frison, E., & Eggermont, S. (2016). "I don't want to miss a thing": Adolescents' fear of missing out and its relationship to adolescents' social needs, Facebook use, and Facebook related stress. *Computers in Human Behavior, 64*, 1–8. doi:10.1016/j.chb.2016.05.083

Blackwell, D., Leaman, C., Tramposch, R., Osborne, C., & Liss, M. (2017). Extraversion, neuroticism, attachment style and fear of missing out as predictors of social media use and addiction. *Personality and Individual Differences, 116*, 69–72. doi:10.1016/j.paid.2017.04.039

Bock, G. W., Mahmood, M., Sharma, S., & Kang, Y. J. (2010). The impact of information overload and contribution overload on continued usage of electronic knowledge repositories. *Journal of Organizational Computing and Electronic Commerce, 20*(3), 257–278. doi:10.1080/10919392.2010.494530

Chan, A. K., Nickson, C. P., Rudolph, J. W., Lee, A., & Joynt, G. M. (2020). *Social media for rapid knowledge dissemination: early experience from the COVID-19 pandemic*. Academic Press.

Chen, K. C., & Jang, S. J. (2010). Motivation in online learning: Testing a model of self-determination theory. *Computers in Human Behavior, 26*(4), 741–752. doi:10.1016/j.chb.2010.01.011

Chen, X., Sin, S. C. J., Theng, Y. L., & Lee, C. S. (2015). Why students share misinformation on social media: Motivation, gender, and study-level differences. *Journal of Academic Librarianship, 41*(5), 583–592. doi:10.1016/j.acalib.2015.07.003

Cheung, E. (2015). An outbreak of fear, rumours and stigma: Psychosocial support for the Ebola virus disease outbreak in West Africa. *Intervention (Amstelveen, Netherlands), 13*(1), 70–76. doi:10.1097/WTF.0000000000000079

Chiorando, M. (2020). *Snopes Debunks Meme Claiming No One Is Buying Vegan Food During Coronavirus Stockpiling*. Retrieved from https://plantbasednews.org/news/snopes-debunks-meme-no-one-buying-vegan-food-coronavirus/

Christofides, E., Muise, A., & Desmarais, S. (2009). Information disclosure and control on Facebook: Are they two sides of the same coin or two different processes? *Cyberpsychology & Behavior, 12*(3), 341–345. doi:10.1089/cpb.2008.0226 PMID:19250020

Cinelli, M., Quattrociocchi, W., Galeazzi, A., Valensise, C. M., Brugnoli, E., Schmidt, A. L., Zola, P., Zollo, F., & Scala, A. (2020). The COVID-19 social media infodemic. *Scientific Reports*, *10*(1), 1–10. doi:10.103841598-020-73510-5 PMID:33024152

Deci, E. L., Eghrari, H., Patrick, B. C., & Leone, D. R. (1994). Facilitating internalization: The self-determination theory perspective. *Journal of Personality*, *62*(1), 119–142. doi:10.1111/j.1467-6494.1994.tb00797.x PMID:8169757

Deci, E. L., & Ryan, R. M. (1985). The general causality orientations scale: Self-determination in personality. *Journal of Research in Personality*, *19*(2), 109–134. doi:10.1016/0092-6566(85)90023-6

Diddi, A., & LaRose, R. (2006). Getting hooked on news: Uses and gratifications and the formation of news habits among college students in an Internet environment. *Journal of Broadcasting & Electronic Media*, *50*(2), 193–210. doi:10.120715506878jobem5002_2

Dzieza, J. (2014). *Fake news sites are using Facebook to spread Ebola panic*. Retrieved from https://www.theverge.com/2014/10/22/7028983/fake-news-sites-are-using-facebook-to-spread-ebola-panic

Fang, J., Wang, X., Wen, Z., & Zhou, J. (2020). Fear of missing out and problematic social media use as mediators between emotional support from social media and phubbing behavior. *Addictive Behaviors*, *107*, 106430. doi:10.1016/j.addbeh.2020.106430 PMID:32289745

Ferguson, R., Gutberg, J., Schattke, K., Paulin, M., & Jost, N. (2015). Self-determination theory, social media and charitable causes: An in-depth analysis of autonomous motivation. *European Journal of Social Psychology*, *45*(3), 298–307. doi:10.1002/ejsp.2038

Gagné, M., & Deci, E. L. (2005). Self-determination theory and work motivation. *Journal of Organizational Behavior*, *26*(4), 331–362. doi:10.1002/job.322

Gibbs, J. L., Ellison, N. B., & Heino, R. D. (2006). Self-Presentation in Online Personals: The Role of Anticipated Future Interaction, Self-Disclosure, and Perceived Sucess in Internet Dating. *Communication Research*, *33*(2), 152–177. doi:10.1177/0093650205285368

Guess, A. M., Lerner, M., Lyons, B., Montgomery, J. M., Nyhan, B., Reifler, J., & Sircar, N. (2020). A digital media literacy intervention increases discernment between mainstream and false news in the United States and India. *Proceedings of the National Academy of Sciences of the United States of America*, *117*(27), 15536–15545. doi:10.1073/pnas.1920498117 PMID:32571950

Ha, L., Yoon, K., & Zhang, X. (2013). Consumption and dependency of social network sites as a news medium: A comparison between college students and general population. *Journal of Communication and Media Research, 5*(1), 1.

Hair, J. F., Hult, G. T. M., Ringle, C., & Sarstedt, M. (2014). *A primer on partial least squares structural equation modeling*. Sage.

Henseler, J., Ringle, C. M., & Sarstedt, M. (2015). A new criterion for assessing discriminant validity in variance-based structural equation modeling. *Journal of the Academy of Marketing Science, 43*(1), 115–135. doi:10.100711747-014-0403-8

Hoetjes, M. (2013). *(Compulsive) Mobile Phone Checking Behavior Out of a Fear of Missing Out: Development, Psychometric Properties and Test-Retest Reliability of a C-FoMO-Scale Beata Hato ANR: 610304*. Academic Press.

Islam, A. N., Laato, S., Talukder, S., & Sutinen, E. (2020). Misinformation sharing and social media fatigue during COVID-19: An affordance and cognitive load perspective. *Technological Forecasting and Social Change, 159*, 120201. doi:10.1016/j.techfore.2020.120201 PMID:32834137

Jackson, T. W., & Farzaneh, P. (2012). Theory-based model of factors affecting information overload. *International Journal of Information Management, 32*(6), 523–532. doi:10.1016/j.ijinfomgt.2012.04.006

Jia-lin, W., & Zeng-yi, Z. (2018). The Generation, Dissemination, Identification and Control of Misinformation—A Review of Existing Studies. *Science and Society, 8*(3), 108–122.

Jourard, S. M., & Friedman, R. (1970). Experimenter-subject" distance" and self-disclosure. *Journal of Personality and Social Psychology, 15*(3), 278–282. doi:10.1037/h0029388 PMID:5485418

Kaigo, M. (2003). Initial Findings in the Perceptions and Behavioural Change by News on SARS in Japan. *Media Asia, 30*(4), 216–219. doi:10.1080/01296612.2003.11726728

Kanekar, A. S., & Thombre, A. (2019). Fake medical news: Avoiding pitfalls and perils. *Family Medicine and Community Health, 7*(4), e000142. doi:10.1136/fmch-2019-000142 PMID:32148726

Karahanna, E., Xu, S. X., Xu, Y., & Zhang, N. A. (2018). The needs–affordances–features perspective for the use of social media. *Management Information Systems Quarterly, 42*(3), 737–756. doi:10.25300/MISQ/2018/11492

Khan, M. L., & Idris, I. K. (2019). Recognise misinformation and verify before sharing: A reasoned action and information literacy perspective. *Behaviour & Information Technology, 38*(12), 1194–1212. doi:10.1080/0144929X.2019.1578828

Kirchherr, J., & Charles, K. (2018). Enhancing the sample diversity of snowball samples: Recommendations from a research project on anti-dam movements in Southeast Asia. *PLoS One, 13*(8), e0201710. doi:10.1371/journal.pone.0201710 PMID:30133457

Kozan, H., Baloğlu, M., Kesici, Ş., & Arpaci, İ. (2019). *The role of personality and psychological needs on the problematic internet use and problematic social media use*. Academic Press.

Krasnova, H., Kolesnikova, E., & Guenther, O. (2009). *"It won't happen to me!" Self-disclosure in online social networks*. Academic Press.

Laato, S., Islam, A. N., Islam, M. N., & Whelan, E. (2020). What drives unverified information sharing and cyberchondria during the COVID-19 pandemic? *European Journal of Information Systems, 29*(3), 288–305. doi:10.1080/0960085X.2020.1770632

Lewandowsky, S., Ecker, U. K., Seifert, C. M., Schwarz, N., & Cook, J. (2012). Misinformation and its correction: Continued influence and successful debiasing. *Psychological Science in the Public Interest, 13*(3), 106–131. doi:10.1177/1529100612451018 PMID:26173286

Ma, L., Lee, C. S., & Goh, D. H. L. (2011, June). That's news to me: The influence of perceived gratifications and personal experience on news sharing in social media. In *Proceedings of the 11th annual international ACM/IEEE joint conference on Digital libraries* (pp. 141-144). 10.1145/1998076.1998103

Maier, J., & Richter, T. (2014). Fostering multiple text comprehension: How metacognitive strategies and motivation moderate the text-belief consistency effect. Ryan. *Metacognition and Learning, 9*(1), 51–74. doi:10.100711409-013-9111-x

Napoleoncat. (2020). *Social media users in Malaysia*. Retrieved from https://napoleoncat.com/stats/social-media-users-in-malaysia/2020/03

Nottingham Trent University. (2016). *FOMO, a vicious circle for social media users*. Retrieved from: https://www.ntu.ac.uk/about-us/news/news-articles/2016/10/fomo-a-vicious-circle-for-social-media-users

Pennycook, G., McPhetres, J., Zhang, Y., Lu, J. G., & Rand, D. G. (2020). Fighting COVID-19 misinformation on social media: Experimental evidence for a scalable accuracy-nudge intervention. *Psychological Science, 31*(7), 770–780. doi:10.1177/0956797620939054 PMID:32603243

Pennycook, G., & Rand, D. G. (2019). Fighting misinformation on social media using crowdsourced judgments of news source quality. *Proceedings of the National Academy of Sciences of the United States of America, 116*(7), 2521–2526. doi:10.1073/pnas.1806781116 PMID:30692252

Przybylski, A. K., Murayama, K., DeHaan, C. R., & Gladwell, V. (2013). Motivational, emotional, and behavioral correlates of fear of missing out. *Computers in Human Behavior, 29*(4), 1841–1848. doi:10.1016/j.chb.2013.02.014

Quinn, K. (2018). Cognitive effects of social media use: A case of older adults. *Social Media + Society, 4*(3), 2056305118787203. doi:10.1177/2056305118787203

Richard, F. M., & Hübl, T. (2021). *Harvard Health Blog. Numb from the news? Understanding why and what to do may help.* Retrieved from https://www.health.harvard.edu/blog/numb-from-the-news-understanding-why-and-what-to-do-may-help-2021031822176

Rovetta, A., & Bhagavathula, A. S. (2020). COVID-19-related web search behaviors and infodemic attitudes in Italy: Infodemiological study. *JMIR Public Health and Surveillance, 6*(2), e19374. doi:10.2196/19374 PMID:32338613

Ryan, R. M., & Deci, E. L. (2000). Self-determination theory and the facilitation of intrinsic motivation, social development, and well-being. *The American Psychologist, 55*(1), 68–78. doi:10.1037/0003-066X.55.1.68 PMID:11392867

Ryan, R. M., & Deci, E. L. (2017). *Self-determination theory: Basic psychological needs in motivation, development, and wellness*. Guilford Publications. doi:10.1521/978.14625/28806

Swar, B., Hameed, T., & Reychav, I. (2017). Information overload, psychological ill-being, and behavioral intention to continue online healthcare information search. *Computers in Human Behavior, 70*, 416–425. doi:10.1016/j.chb.2016.12.068

Sweller, J. (2011). Cognitive load theory. *Psychology of Learning and Motivation, 55*, 37–76. doi:10.1016/B978-0-12-387691-1.00002-8

Talwar, S., Dhir, A., Kaur, P., Zafar, N., & Alrasheedy, M. (2019). Why do people share fake news? Associations between the dark side of social media use and fake news sharing behavior. *Journal of Retailing and Consumer Services*, *51*, 72–82. doi:10.1016/j.jretconser.2019.05.026

Talwar, S., Dhir, A., Singh, D., Virk, G. S., & Salo, J. (2020). Sharing of fake news on social media: Application of the honeycomb framework and the third-person effect hypothesis. *Journal of Retailing and Consumer Services*, *57*, 102197. doi:10.1016/j.jretconser.2020.102197

Terry, A. (2021). *Jurist. Legal News and Commentary. Malaysia government uses emergency powers to enforce anti fake-news law*. Retrieved from https://www.jurist.org/news/2021/03/malaysia-government-uses-emergency-powers-to-enforce-anti-fake-news-law/

Thompson, N., Wang, X., & Daya, P. (2020). Determinants of news sharing behavior on social media. *Journal of Computer Information Systems*, *60*(6), 593–601. doi:10.1080/08874417.2019.1566803

Twitter. (2020). *World Health Organization (WHO) Live with @DrTedros on health security from the @MunSecConf. #MSC2020*. https://twitter.com/WHO/status/1228680399733194756

Whelan, E., Islam, A. N., & Brooks, S. (2020). Applying the SOBC paradigm to explain how social media overload affects academic performance. *Computers & Education*, *143*, 103692. doi:10.1016/j.compedu.2019.103692

Whelan, E., Islam, A. N., & Brooks, S. (2020). Is boredom proneness related to social media overload and fatigue? A stress–strain–outcome approach. *Internet Research*, *30*(3), 869–887. doi:10.1108/INTR-03-2019-0112

Winter, S., Neubaum, G., Eimler, S. C., Gordon, V., Theil, J., Herrmann, J., Meinert, J., & Krämer, N. C. (2014). Another brick in the Facebook wall–How personality traits relate to the content of status updates. *Computers in Human Behavior*, *34*, 194–202. doi:10.1016/j.chb.2014.01.048

won Kim, J. (2014). Scan and click: The uses and gratifications of social recommendation systems. *Computers in Human Behavior, 33*, 184-191.

Yang, Y., & Lim, H. (2011). A cognitive ability measuring system with cognitive loading task. In *Future Information Technology* (pp. 325–328). Springer.

Yen, C. H., Chen, I. C., Lai, S. C., & Chuang, Y. R. (2015). An analytics-based approach to managing cognitive load by using log data of learning management systems and footprints of social media. *Journal of Educational Technology & Society*, *18*(4), 141–158.

Yu, S. C., Chen, H. R., Liu, A. C., & Lee, H. Y. (2020, December). Toward COVID-19 Information: Infodemic or Fear of Missing Out? []. Multidisciplinary Digital Publishing Institute.]. *Health Care*, *8*(4), 550.

Zarocostas, J. (2020). How to fight an infodemic. *Lancet*, *395*(10225), 676.

KEY TERMS AND DEFINITIONS

Cognitive Load Theory: A theory that describes how many "chunks" of information that humans can be held and processed in their working memory at a given period.

Entertainment: Engaging social media to fulfill the need for pleasure and moderate negative emotions such as anxiety, mainly through features surrounding likes, comments, and exchange of novel information.

Fear of Missing Out (FoMo): The pervasive anxiety of social media users about others having rewarding experiences compared to them.

Infodemic: An influx of inaccurate or deceptive information on social media during a pandemic.

Information Overload: Occurs when too much information and messages on media far exceed one's information demand and processing capability.

Self-Determination Theory: A theory that explains how human personality and motivation promote specific tasks and behavior by three essentially psychological needs: autonomy, relatedness, and competence. Autonomy implies freedom of personal choice, relatedness signifies a person's relationship with others, while competence refers to people's skills and abilities to master a specific task.

Self-Disclosure: Describes social media user's communication form through descriptive disclosure that reveals personal information, while evaluative disclosure expresses personal feelings such as aspirations and fears, as well as personal thoughts with others.

Social Media: An internet-based communication platform that facilitates users to share and exchange information, including unverified ones.

Trust Toward Online Information: The belief that one's online information is valuable mediates by the expertise level and critical thinking skills.

Unverified Information: The source of the message that is uncertain or not authentic, forming misinformation, disinformation, and mal-information.

Chapter 3
Opportunities and Threats Analysis Caused by Social Media

Elina Ahmadi
Independent Researcher, Australia

ABSTRACT

With the advent and widespread use of information and communication technologies, the need for information has become part of the daily work of individuals. Recently, social networks are one of the most important topics in cyberspace. This study seeks to identify and rank the opportunities and threats of social media for the society. Three hundred seventy students active in social networks are selected by clustering sampling method. A conceptual model is developed based on the review of theoretical literature and five opportunities of social network including electronic learning, filling leisure time, organizing social groups, getting to know about diverse cultures, possibility of conversation, as well as five threats include sharing anti values, abusing, dissemination of misinformation, internet addiction, and malacious communication have significant effect on the students.

INTRODUCTION

Technological evolution in communication channels has led to the creation of a new system that speaks a universal language. Humans communicate with others by generating and distributing digital codes and tokens in the space of interconnected computer networks, or the Internet. This communication, which is formed in

DOI: 10.4018/978-1-7998-8235-0.ch003

the moment, is called "virtual communication" due to the lack of face to face communication. The virtual world includes the Internet and the World Wide Web.

According to Toffler (1980), human societies have gone through two periods of revolution: agriculture and industry, and are now in the late post-industrial or information age, based on electronics and computers. An age in which power, wealth and security are created on the basis of knowledge and speed is its characteristic and information is its most valuable commodity. This latest world, which is expanding rapidly and has affected all aspects of life on Earth, is based on modern information technology and communication media and continues to grow and flourish in a non-physical space, which is called cyberspace.

The advent of information and communication technology has opened a new window on the world and its influence in various aspects of human life has caused great changes in society, which is called the information revolution. People try to use it in various ways by increasing their knowledge in this field. With the increasing development of information technology and its use, a new era in the life of societies has begun to be called the information society, and entering this course requires the necessary arrangements and facilities.

At the recent past, information and communication technology is an integral part of human life and the emergence of new forms of communication and large information and communication networks has paved the way for new social spaces as boundless spaces that affect the relationships, dimensions and social skills of individuals. The age of transition from an industry-based society to an information-based society, in other words, the transition from the physical world into the virtual world requires recognizing the characteristics of the virtual world. The information and communication revolution has rapidly transformed the world economy, culture and politics and turned the world into a global village. .

In the information age, changes are taking place in a geometric progression, with speed, knowledge, and creative and dynamic management at the forefront. Therefore, it is necessary to know the new technologies and consequently how to use them correctly, quickly and optimally. Cyberspace is a platform that generates numerous threats and opportunities for human beings and societies. Harms and crimes in cyberspace have capacities and characteristics, including globalization, decentralization, digitalization, and networking, as well as access based on time and virtual work. In this regard, having a system of legislation, policy-making and cybercrime are plays a great role to diminish crimes. Students are the most widely users of cyberspace; therefore, the important issue and challenge in this field is what opportunities and threats cyberspace creates for students.

SOCIAL MEDIA

Social media is a medium that is designed to interact and publish content on the Internet through social interaction, has a very high availability and use scalable publishing techniques in it. Social Media is an Internet-centric application that allows people to create and share concepts (Kaplan, 2010) Social media comes in a variety of forms, such as social networks, Internet forums, blogs, social blogs, microblogs, wikis, podcasts, images, videos. There were just very limited number of social network sites in the late 1990's and users could only create personal profiles and connect with "friends" (Boyd & Ellison, 2007). Their technologies were Web 1.0, consisted as static web pages and file management. Around 2001, professional social network sites began to emerge and users could interact and collaborate with each other for business and professional purposes. Then, technologies of Web 2.0 created an online environment for sharing electronic media and content.

Table 1. Social media categories

Category	Functionality
Social networks such as Facebook	Create a profile Connect with people with similar interests and backgrounds
Bookmarking sites such as Tagging	Save, bookmark, and share links Users can "tag" links to others for easy searching and sharing
Social News such as Digg	Post and share news and stories Users can vote for new items. The item that gets the most votes wins and is displayed as the most important news
Media Sharing such as YouTube, Instagram, and SlideShare	Upload and share media items (such as images and video) Some offer other features such as personal profile, commenting and voting
Blog Comments and Forums such as WordPress and Blogger	Post stories, comments or extensive comments At the end of each "post", members can send messages and make conversations
Micro Blogging such as Twitter	Send and receive short updates that are sent to anyone who subscribes
Passion-Centric sites such as TheSamba	Communicating with users who have common interests or hobbies
Community sites such as BlackPlanet	Relationships with users with shared values, beliefs or other identities
Opportunistic sites such as LinkedIn, Academia, and ResearchGate	Support for professional and business communications and collaboration

(Sahoo and Krotov, 2018)

In addition to engaging in social media conversations, organizations need to start activities that help explain why consumers buy or do not buy their products or services. Conversations on social media provide knowledge to organizations that can have a positive impact on product branding and customer relationships. These conversations are done at all stages of the purchasing process. Social media allows individuals to quickly transfer information through self-replication. Social networks have an internal capability for this repetition, and businesses find that using social networks in this way can achieve a wider range of customers (Brooks et al., 2014).

Figure 1. Number of active users in millions
Source: Sahoo and Krotov, 2018

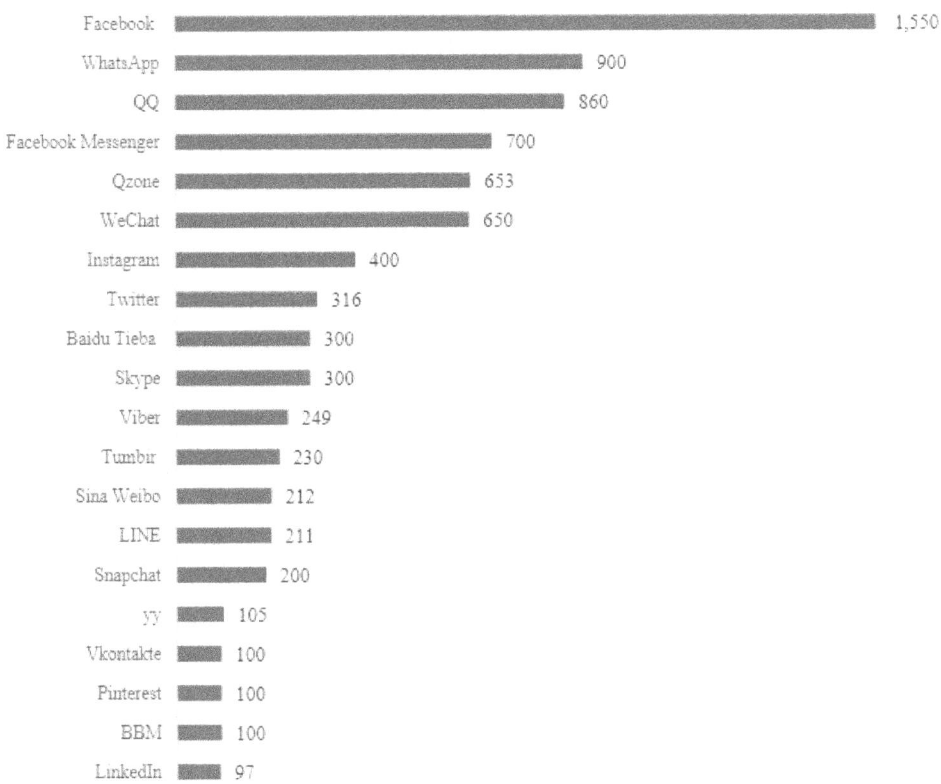

A social network is a social structure made up of nodes (usually individual or organizational) that have one or more specific types of dependencies, such as ideas and financial exchanges, friends, relatives, web links, disease transmission (epidemiology). Mathematically, a social network is a graph in which each participant in the network is read as an actor. Problems and their solutions play a role in how organizations are run and to what extent individuals achieve their goals. Hu and Racherla (2008) argue that the social network is a group of collaborative entities that work together.

METHODOLOGY

The present article is applied and developmental based on the type of purpose, because it seeks to develop a conceptual model to examine the views of students of a university about the opportunities and threats of social network and its applications for students of the university. Also, the present research method is a combined method including quantitative methods (descriptive, survey) and qualitative (focus group and content analysis). The research steps are as follows:

In the first step, by studying the literature, the set of opportunities and threats of social networks are reviewed and identified from the perspective of university students, and their components and effects are explained based on scientific documents.

In the second step, using the method of field studies and semi-structured interviews with professors and experts at the university and also qualitative analysis of the findings of the previous step, the set of factors in the form of opportunities and threats of various social networks for students is determined. In this step, finally, the research model, which includes a set of factors and how they work, is explained based on the theoretical scientific literature and related background.

In the third step, a questionnaire is designed for students based on the identified factors and valid scientific theories. The validity of the questionnaire is assessed based on the content validity method. In this way, the questionnaire has been approved and finalized by applying the necessary changes and corrections based on the opinions of professors and experts. Cronbach's alpha method is used to assess the reliability of the questionnaire. Then the questionnaire is distributed and collected in statistical samples, 370 students from different faculties who which use social networks by clustering method.

In the fourth step, the information obtained from the questionnaires were analyzed using SPSS statistical analysis software in two sections: descriptive and inferential statistics. In the descriptive statistics section, the demographic data of the selected sample is reviewed and analyzed. In the inferential statistics section, research hypotheses are tested and decisions are made to confirm or reject them. In this section, Kolmogorov-Smirnov test is used to check the normality of data distribution, and one-sample t-test and sign test are used to test research hypotheses.

In the fifth step, by ranking analysis and Friedman test, the ranking of the factors identified in the previous step is determined, and based on the results of students' views on the opportunities and threats of social networks for students, executive suggestions are provided.

In the sixth step, after summarizing and concluding the research process, emphasizing the applicability of the research for the university, practical solutions to reduce social network threats and use social networking opportunities for students are presented.

CONCEPTUAL MODEL

Based on the review of theoretical literature and research background, as well as the formation of a focus group and expert meeting with the presence of nine experts (including seven professors, dimensions of the conceptual model of the present study are designed as follows and the semi-structured questionnaire of field studies is based on this conceptual model.

Figure 2. The conceptual research model

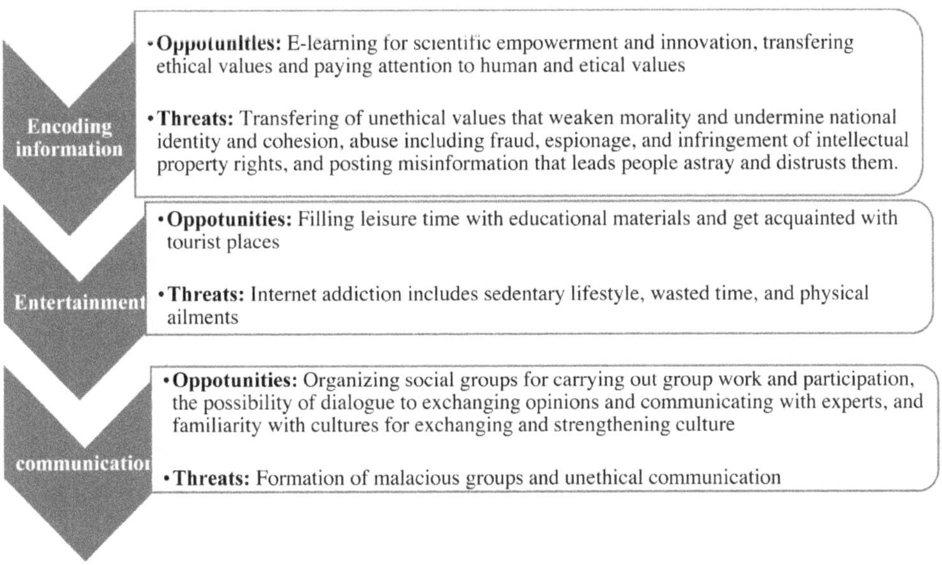

STATISTICAL ANALYSIS

Poplulation and Sample

The statistical population of this research is students of a university who are members and do activities in social networks. Besides, the Cochran's formula has been used for sampling. According to the calculations of this formula with 95% confidence level for the statistical population of more than 10 thousand people, using Cochran's formula calculation software, a statistical sample of 370 people is obtained, which is the basis for the distribution of questionnaires in field studies of the present study.

Reliability

Cronbach's alpha coefficient method was used to calculate the reliability of the questionnaire. To measure the initial reliability of the present research questionnaire, first 30 questionnaires were distributed and gathered, then using Cronbach's alpha of SPSS software for the prototypes, 89% was obtained, which shows a very good reliability of the questionnaire. Additionally, after collecting all the research questionnaires and removing the questionnaires that were not completed carefully, 346 questionnaires were finally confirmed and the Cronbach's alpha coefficient for all questions of the questionnaire was 77%, which shows the appropriate reliability of the research tool. Also, the reliability of the questionnaire for the constructs of social network opportunities and threats are calculated separately. Accordingly, the reliability of opportunities construct, which includes the first 12 questions of the research questionnaire, was 87% and the reliability of threats construct, which includes the next 13 questions of the research questionnaire, was 67%, which shows the relatively good reliability of both constructs.

Validity

To determine the validity of the content of the research questionnaires, at first it is attempted to use as much as possible the standard variables, the validity of which has already been determined and confirmed in theoretical research. In addition, the face validity method was used; So that seven professors and experts of the university were asked about the questionnaire and it was modified and approved based on their opinions.

Before the test phase of hypotheses, it is necessary to ensure the accuracy of models for measuring exogenous and endogenous variables. In this research, the work has been done through confirmatory factor analysis. Confirmatory factor analysis is used to examine the relationship between latent variables (obtained factors) and observed variables (questions). CFA expresses the degree of discrepancy between predicted and empirical factor structure (Prudon, 2015). In the following, the validation criteria of the mean variance extracted and the goodness-of-fit index of have been used.

Table 2 shows the reliability indicators for all research variables. With the help of the extracted mean variance index, it was found that all studied variables have averaged extracted variance higher than 0.5. The combined reliability index is greater than 0.7.

Table 2. Model fit indices

The coefficient of determination	Combined reliability	average variance extracted	Latent variable	$\sqrt{R^2}$	$\sqrt{AVE}$	GOF
E-Learning	0.764	0.72	0.915			
Transfer ethical values	0.745	0.435	0.906			
Fill leisure time	0.749	0.81	0.928			
Orgonizing social groups	0.754	0.679	0.936			
The possibility of dialogue	0.733	0.309	0.929	0.653	0.779	0.839
Familiarity with cultures	0.744	0	0.963			
Transfer unethical values	0.725	0.552	0.918			
Abuse	0.531	0.564	0.849			

The goodness index shows the fit between the quality of the structural model and the measured model. A higher index of 0.4 indicates a good fit of the model. The value of the fit index is equal to 0.653 and is greater than the value of 0.4 and shows the proper fit of the model. In simpler terms, the data of this research have a good fit with the factor structure and theoretical basis of the research, and this indicates that the questions are in line with theoretical structures.

Demographic Data

Explaining and examining the demographic data of the sample provides readers and researchers with a clear picture of population. In addition, it helps us to give the results of this research if it is intended to generalize the results of the study.

Based on the analysis of demographic components on the dependent variables, the values of the adequacy limit are more than 0.05. Therefore, the null hypothesis (the hypothesis of equality of the average of views of groups) is confirmed. Accordingly, there was no significant difference in the views of demographic groups about the threats and opportunities identified in social networks.

Table 3. Demographic data of the sample

Valid percent	Frequency	category	Variables
Gender	Female	225	0.65
	Male	121	0.35
Marital status	Married	38	0.11
	Single	308	0.89
Degree	Bachelor	180	0.52
	Master	134	0.39
	PhD.	32	0.1
Average hours of social network use per day	Less than an hour	70	0.20
	Between one and two hours	96	0.27
	Between two and three hours	88	0.25
	More than three hours	92	0.26

Motivation for Students to Use Social Networks

As shown in the Table 4, the most motivating factor for respondents to use social networks is communication with friends with a value of 0.81. Also, the percentage of other motivational factors for using social networks is shown in the table.

Table 4. Motivational factor to use social networks

Priority	Variable	Frequency
1	Connecting with friends	81%
2	Entertainment	55%
3	Scientific learning	43%
4	Read the news	42%
5	Find old friends	35%
6	More communication with relatives	34%
7	Join interest groups	32%
8	Curiosity	19%
9	Find new friends	17%

NORMALITY TEST OF STATISTICAL SAMPLES

Kolmogorov-Smirnov test compares the distribution of an attribute in a sample with the distribution assumed for society; That is, it compares the frequency of a sample with the expected frequency of the assumed distribution type for the community. Therefore, this test is a method to detect the normality of the frequency distribution of observations collected. In this test, two claims are made as follows and its correctness is checked:

H0: Data distribution is normal.
H1: Data distribution is not normal.

The result of calculating this test for all research questions is as follows.

Table 5. Kolmogorov-Smirnov test

N	301
Average	3.5700
Standard Deviation	0.41175
Absolute	0.046
Positive	0.025
Negative	-0.046
Static test	0.046
Asymp. Sig. (2-tailed)	C,d200

Given that the significance level of the Kolmogorov-Smirnov test for all questions is more than 0.05, and considering the value of Kolmogorov-Smirnov, the hypothesis is confirmed, in other words, the distribution of data is normal. As can be seen from the results of this test, the distribution of variables follows the normal statistical distribution and parametric distribution tests are used to analyze it.

Testing Research Hypotheses

Due to the normal distribution, a one-sample t-test with a test value of 3 and a 95% confidence interval (5% error) was used to explain and interpret the research variables. Therefore, for all 11 identified criteria, the following two hypotheses are designed and their accuracy is measured.

H0: criterion has no positive and significant effect on students.
H1: criterion has a positive and significant effect on students.

It is a test that is used to determine if an unknown population mean is different from a specific value. The statistic is calculated based on the devision of mean difference by the standard error. The 95% confidence interval is an estimate of the boundaries between the correct difference mean that occurs in 95% of all possible random samples. The table below shows the results of a one sample t test for each or all of the criteria.

As can be seen in the table below, only the Sig. (2-tailed) for the criterion of 'transfer of ethical values' is more than 0.05 and its null hypothesis is confirmed, which means that this criterion does not have a positive and significant effect on students. However, the Sig. (2-tailed) for the other 10 identified criteria is less than 0.05 and the null hypothesis is rejected; therefore, it can be said that these 10 criteria have a positive and significant effect on students.

Table 6. Single sample t test results for criteria

Variable	Test value=3					
	T value	df	Sig. (2-tailed)	Mean difference	95% Confidence Interval of the Difference	
					Lower	Upper
E-Learning	4.480	344	0.000	0.18696	0.1049	0.2690
Transfer ethical values	1.114	341	0.266	0.5556	-0.425	0.1536
Fill leisure time	10.010	345	0.000	0.44798	0.3600	0.5360
Organizing social groups	15.253	343	0.000	0.65552	0.5710	0.7401
Possibility of conversations and dialogue	0.762	342	0.000	0.34694	0.2530	0.4409
Familiarity with cultures	7.720	337	0.000	0.35503	0.2646	0.4455
Tranfer unethical values	21.017	337	0.000	0.80276	0.7276	0.8779
Abuse	27.821	337	0.000	1.00690	0.9357	1.0781
Disseminate misinformation	10.485	338	0.000	0.30531	0.2480	0.3626
Internet addiction	25.017	331	0.000	0.90663	0.8353	0.9779
Malicious communication	17.420	341	0.000	0.67251	0.5966	0.7485

As shown in Table 6, a total of five social media opportunity variables were included in the theoretical literature and research background including e-learning, leisure time filling, social group organizing, possibility of conversation, and familiarity with cultures, as well as the five variables of social media threats including the transfer of unethical values, abuse, dissemination of misinformation, Internet addiction, and malicious communication have a positive and significant effect on students. Also due to the rejection of the criterion of ethical value transfer, it can be said that the respondents do not recommend the use of social networks to lay the groundwork for ethical values among students, and these networks will not be able to transfer ethical values including socialization and attention to human and moral values. Therefore, these ethical values must be transmitted through other means, such as families or face-to-face cultural programs.

Ranking of Research Variables

Friedman test was used to rank the criteria obtained for each category of opportunities and threats. First, to rank the opportunities of social networks, the hypotheses of this part of the research are statistically designed as follows:

H0: Social media opportunity criteria are equally important.
H1: Criteria for social media opportunities are not equally important.

Table 7. Test statistics

N	330
Chi-Square	160.025
Df	5
Asymp.sig.	0.000

To accept or reject this claim, Friedman test was used, the results of which can be seen in the table.

Considering that the value Asymp.sig. for opportunity criteria is less than 0.05, so the null hypothesis is rejected and there is a significant difference between these

Table 8. Results of ranking social networking opportunities

Priority	Opportunity	Mean rank
1	Organizing social groups	4.31
2	Fill leisure time	3.78
3	Dialogue	3.54
4	Fimiliarity with cultures	3.52
5	E-learning	3.09
6	Transfer ethical values	2.76

criteria. Accordingly, the rankings obtained for the criteria of social networking opportunities are as follows:

Moreover, to rank the threats of social networks, the hypotheses of this part of the research are designed to be statistically expressed as follows:

H0: Criteria for social media threats are equally important.
H1: Criteria for social media threats are not equally important.

Table 9. Test statistics

N	311
Chi-Square	222.086
Df	4
Asymp.sig.	0.000

To accept or reject this claim, Friedman test was used, the results of which can be seen in the Table 9.

Due to the fact that the value of Asymp.sig. for the criteria of threats is less than 0.05, so the null hypothesis is rejected and there is a significant difference between

Table 10. Results of ranking social network threats

Priority	Threats	Mean rank
1	Abuse	3.68
2	Internet addiction	3.34
3	Transfer unethical values	3.22
4	Disruptive communication	2.71
5	Publish misinformation	2.04

these criteria. Accordingly, the rankings obtained for the criteria of social network threats are as follows:

As examined in the research findings, all research variables were tested and the results of the hypothesis test showed that the five variables of social networking opportunities from the perspective of students (including organizing social groups, filling leisure time) possibility of conversation and dialogue, familiarity with cultures, e-learning), and all five variables of social media threats (including abuse, Internet addiction, transfer of unethical values, malacious communication, dissemination of misinformation) from the respondents' point of view, have positive and significant influence on students and only the effect of the variable of transferring ethical values that has been considered in the opportunities has been rejected by the students.

DISCUSSION

In terms of subject area, there is a lack of comprehensive research to examine the dimensions of opportunities and threats of social networks. Additionally, in terms of spatial scope, the present study was conducted at a university. Based on the obtained results, the importance of the opportunities in using social networks for the students is as follows in order of priority:

Organizing Social Groups

Just as the philosophy of real social networks is to form and link social groups based on religious, economic, political, and social commonalities, many social networks on the Internet are motivated by the organization of virtual social groups based on different commonalities. The members of these virtual communities, with the connections they have with each other, generally seek to pursue a common goal in the real world, whether political, social or cultural (Soleimanipoor, 2010). In universities and educational centers, it is also possible to take a step towards the growth of the university and the prosperity of startups by creating interdisciplinary social groups and pursuing the common goals of the members with indirect supervision of the university. Through virtual social groups, disciplinary constraints can be removed and interdisciplinary goals can be created for those interested.

Fill Leisure Time

The Internet is the most prominent symbol of this age, which has the most fundamental share in virtual leisure. Releasing a person from work, economic, and personal, family, educational, and social obligations through cyberspace creates virtual leisure. New types of emotional, aesthetic and cultural partnerships are among the main features of new media, especially cyberspace.

Possibility of Conversation

Social networks facilitate the sending of audience feedback and the cooperation and coordination of users with each other and encourage them to participate in discussions. These networks have blurred the line between the media and the audience. Most social networks are open for members to participate and receive feedback; they encourage voting, commenting and sharing information. Rarely there is a barrier to produce and access content on these websites. Traditional media used to publish and send content to the audience, but on social media there is a space for two-way conversation, and the flow of communication has changed from one-way to two-way. Using this feature of social networks, academic and scientific discussions and trainings can not be focused only on the time allotted for teaching in the university, and the training can be continued trans-temporally and according to the needs of students and professors.

Familiarity With Different Cultures

Nowadays, social networks are the cradle of various human civilizations and cultures. The existence of different languages in social media allows the presence of all members of society to expose the culture of their society to the public. The fact that young people can connect with their peers in other countries of the world, makes these media a place where they can communicate, introduce, and share their cultures and customs to others. In addition, in these networks, new ideas for the expansion of society are introduced and discussed. Organizations can also expose their culture and perspective to all communities.

E-Learning

Undoubtedly, social networks play a very effective role in the development of specialized and general education. Although due to the lack of scientific supervision of many Internet contents they have not yet reached an acceptable level of scientific validity, social networks are one of the areas of the Internet where countless users spontaneously train and transfer their specialized and general knowledge. Using virtual educational social networks, students can extend the scope of their learning process beyond the classroom at any time they need to ask questions and connect with a professor or other students in the same field. In other words, the biggest service of social networks in the field of education is e-learning.

Table 11. Practical strategies of opportunities

Priority	Opportunity	Practical solutions
1	Organizing social groups	• Using social networks for student activities as a group and team. • Use social media to raise awareness and encourage students to participate in a variety of social activities, such as marches, elections, Environment, celebrations, mourning. • Using the social media platform to form research groups.
2	Fill leisure time	• Using social networks to gain useful content and increase support • Utilizing social media to introduce tourism to students • Familiarize students with useful recreational and scientific groups
3	Dialogue	• Use of social networks to exchange scientific and non scientific views suitable for students • Use social networks to expand students' scientific communication with professors.
4	Fimiliarity with cultures	• Use social networks to strengthen the culture and values • Using social networks to acquaint students with the different cultures • Using social networks for cultural influence
5	E-learning	• Use of social networks to increase learning and scientific abilities • Use social media to share innovative ideas in social groups

Table 11 presents practical strategies of opportunities.

Besides based on the results obtained in the present study, the most important current threats in the use of social networks for students are in order of priority as follows:

Abuse: Users on social networks always post information about themselves that is likely to pose a risk of abuse. Some abusers also have opportunities to increase their benefits through social media. Education is of great importance in oder to eliminate this threat.

Internet Addiction: Internet addiction is facing a new face. The proliferation of personal computers and the rise of Internet connections at home and at work have led to the rise of online addiction. It includes addiction to chat rooms, pornography, online gambling, and online shopping. Internet addiction, like other addictions, isolates the addict from his family and those around him. Behavioral addictions, such as Internet addiction destroy a person's health, relationships, emotions, and ultimately their soul. It is so common among some young people and students that even in the classroom and during education distracts their focus.

Transfer of unethical values: Inspite of all the facilities social networks provide to users, they always put users at risk of unethical values due to their ease of access.

This sometimes takes place indirectly and without the awareness of users, which gradually attacks the individual's values and norms.

Malicious communication: Due to the fact that people with social media membership can hide their main character and can communicate with others through their virtual personality, the possibility of creating destructive and unhealthy relationships among users, especially the young community is very high. Sometimes young people become so engrossed in their virtual personality that over time they distance themselves from their real personality and become fond of their virtual personality.

Dissemination of misinformation: Recently, due to the prevalence of social networks among people, especially the youth, information is circulated quickly and very easily among users. However, the general public does not have the power to recognize the accuracy of information. Due to the fact that news and information are not controlled and monitored in cyberspace, users without the necessary qualifications and expertise in that field, can publish it quickly by intervening and changing the content of the information.

The practical solutions to deal with these threats has been determined as Table 12.

Table 12. Practical solutions for dealing with threats of social media

Priority	Threat	Practical solutions
1	Abuse	• Preventing the espionage • Preventing economic deception and fraud • Prevention of violation of Intellectual Property Rights
2	Internet addiction	• Prevention of inactivity and decline of face-to-face ups communication in the effects of activities on social networks • Prevent wasting students' time by aimless use of social media • Prevention of physical ailments (back pain, vision problems, overweight) due to social media activities
3	Transfer of unethical values	• Preventing the weakening of identity and cohesion of students • Prevent the spread of immoral words due to anonymity on social networks • Preventing the violation of students' privacy
4	Malacious communication	• Preventing the possibility of the formation of malicious groups (trafficking, addiction, sabotage) on social networks • Prevent the spread of inappropriate communication on social networks
5	Publish misinformation	• Creating a culture about how to trust the information published on social networks • Informing about how rumors and fake news spread on social networks

CONCLUSION

The present study aims to investigate and identify the opportunities and threats of social networks from the perspective of students. It should be noted that these two factors are completely interdependent and there is a close relationship between them. If social media opportunities are not used properly, these opportunities will be lost or become a threat over time. Besides, with proper planning and diligent follow-up, social media threats can be turned into opportunities. For instance, organizing social groups as an opportuny can lead to malicious communication and the spread of unethical values. Also, filling leisure time as an opportunity can lead to Internet addiction as a threat. Relevant authorities should analyze the opportunities and threats of social networks so that they can exploit opportunities and reduce threats of social networks with long-term education. Opportunities such as organizing social groups and e-learning can be used to save time and money, and with culture improvement and education, threats can be turned into opportunities.

REFERENCES

Boyd, D. M., & Ellison, N. B. (2007, October). Social network sites: Definition, history, and scholarship. *Journal of Computer-Mediated Communication*, *13*(1), 210–230. doi:10.1111/j.1083-6101.2007.00393.x

Brooks, G., Heffner, A., & Henderson, D. (2014). A SWOT analysis of competitive knowledge from social media for a small start-up business. *Review of Business Information Systems*, *18*(1), 23–34. doi:10.19030/rbis.v18i1.8540

Hu, C., & Racherla, P. (2008). Visual representation of knowledge networks: A social network analysis of hospitality research domain. *International Journal of Hospitality Management*, *27*(2), 302–312. doi:10.1016/j.ijhm.2007.01.002

Kaplan, A., & Haenlein, M. (2010). Users of the world, unite! The challenges and opportunities of social media. *Business Horizons*, *53*(1), 59–68. doi:10.1016/j.bushor.2009.09.003

Prudon, P. (2015). Confirmatory factor analysis as a tool in research using questionnaires: A critique. *Comprehensive Psychology*, *4*(10), 1–19. doi:10.2466/03.CP.4.10

Sahoo, H., and Krotov, V. (2018). The value map for social networking. *JCS, 26*(3, 4), 248-267.

Soleimanipoor, R. (2010). Social networks, opportunities and threats. *Rahavarde Nour Journal, 31*, 14–19.

Toffler, A. (1980). *The third wave*. William Morrow.

Chapter 4
The Phenomenon of Counteracting for Information Manipulation:
Ukranian Aspect

Nadezhda Lebedeva
https://orcid.org/0000-0003-4095-2631
International Personnel Academy, Ukraine

ABSTRACT

The highest degree of impact is observed nowadays from the bodies that finance the media. The information community of journalists and television companies are the tools for influencing society. As a result, the picture shown to the audience does not coincide with reality, so the people don't trust the media. Thus, there is a need to find alternatives to what viewers see on the screen of official television channels. This demand also creates a supply, which, having convincing facts and evidence of its innocence, forms an audience. The purpose of the chapter is to consider a practical attempt to counteract the process of manipulation of public consciousness. To achieve this goal, the author of this chapter set the following research tasks: to study the available scientific sources on the topic of manipulative influence on people, to compare the facts provided by the official media, and the means of the YouTube network, and to find a logical explanation for the emergence of the internet party in Ukraine.

DOI: 10.4018/978-1-7998-8235-0.ch004

INTRODUCTION

At the beginning of the twenty-first century, there is a global reappraisal of the role of the media. New information technologies are developing. States provide the world community with an information picture following their own economic and political objectives. As a result, there is a revision of information exchange strategies. It is common knowledge that the media influences all socio-political practices. Journalists form the necessary attitudes for the audience.

But it is not habitual to talk about the technologies of using the mass media for destructive purposes. This is a problem for people and society.

In 2012, Igor Prokopenko's book "Storming Consciousness. The Truth About Manipulating Human Consciousness" was published. In this book, it is told about how the special services of different countries are developing the theory and practice of mass brainwashing of people; train specialists, so-called "slippers", who, being thousands of kilometers away, can enter the minds of, for example, the chief of the General Staff of the country's Armed Forces. Famous scientists comment on the sensational results of unique experiments taking place in secret laboratories.

"The struggle for control over people's minds is not going to either subside or stop - it is only getting worse. New participants appear in it: militants, intelligence officers, etc. And unlike nuclear weapons, the proliferation of which is monitored by several international organizations, weapons of invisible war are spreading out of control." (Prokopenko, 2012, p. 12).

According to Lozovsky (2011), "the main subjects of influence on the media are the state and its many structures, including law enforcement; financial and industrial groups; political associations and parties; public organizations; specialized advertising, PR, consulting enterprises; social groups. They have their characteristics and resources of influence, such as the audience of periodicals, radio and television channels, and the shop corporation itself, the journalistic community" (Lozovsky, 2011, p. 3).

The above mentioned associations have different impacts on the mass media. Low impact is observed among social groups that do not have direct access to the mass media. "The most equipped subjects of influence are the state, its federal and regional structures, municipalities. The arsenal of methods is wide: from direct force pressure with the involvement of experts in the field of firefighting, tax inspection and police, sanitary and epidemiological station, control and audit department and prosecution to the use of various kinds of political technologies. The significant potential of influence is concentrated among financial and industrial groups" (Lozovsky, 2011, p. 6).

Their specificity: the acquisition of their newspapers, radio stations, TV channels with the ensuing political and creative consequences, which can be observed in Ukraine on the example of the closure of several television channels, selective sponsorship and distribution of advertising budgets; hiring journalists to perform specific tasks, which are also used in the television field of the Ukrainian information space.

The information community of journalists and television companies is a tool for influencing society. Due to different points of view, external oligarchic influence, the phenomenon of information wars arises, conflicts between the media and journalists for political reasons. Thus, the influence of power structures on television channels leads to the fact that the picture shown to viewers, for example, in news programs does not coincide with reality, so the audience does not trust the media more and more. As a result, there is a need to find alternatives to what people see on the screen of official television channels. This demand also creates a supply, which, having convincing facts and evidence of its innocence, forms an audience.

In the study by Gorina (2016), "the means of communication actively defend their independence to all political directions (the media are supposedly absolutely neutral and honest, so readers can fully trust them and rely on objective information), defend their rights to free choice of information are recognized as a powerful source of manipulation and propaganda. Of course, not only journalists manipulate the consciousness of society. Advertising, cinema, theatre, circus, literature, mass events, the Internet, computer games, educational programs in schools, and so on also have manipulative potential. But in terms of the effectiveness of manipulation, it is the mass media that occupy the first place in society. What is the specificity of their manipulations expressed?" (Gorina, 2016, p. 10)

Lozovsky (2011) approached the problem of understanding the essence of manipulative influence on the media using a systematic approach. The scientist established interconnections and interdependencies between all subjects participating in information exchange through the mass media.

The basic reasons for manipulating the media are associated with their ever-increasing role in solving many socio-political and socio-economic problems through the organization of information flows, the production and dissemination of meanings, while simultaneously influencing a significant part of the population. Lozovsky (2011) identifies subjective and objective circumstances that allow influencing the content of the media.

The authorities and business view the media as a tool for achieving their own goals and a source of income, controlling and directing the flow of information. The use of the media as one of the instruments of political technologies leads to the restriction or lack of access of citizens to the required volume and quality of information to satisfy the public interest. They are trying to prevent the dangers associated with developing technologies of manipulative influence on the media by improving legislation in the media sphere, as well as developing forms of public control over their activities.

The purpose of the chapter is to consider a practical attempt to counteract the process of manipulation of public consciousness. To achieve this goal, the author of this chapter sets the following research tasks:

- to study the available scientific sources on the topic of manipulative influence on people;
- to compare the facts provided by the official media, and using the you-tube network;
- to find a logical explanation for the emergence of the Internet party in Ukraine.

BACKGROUND

Scientific Approaches for Manipulation Research

According to Kozlova (2010) manipulation of public consciousness was viewed as a problem of organizing domestic political life and is associated with the reproduction of totalitarian regimes. The problems of interaction between the media and the authorities were considered in the works of Agapova (2017), Volgutova (2014), Malinova (2004), Morozova and Magamedli (2019), Singaevskaya (2020), Torgovanova and Shabanova (2016), Tutarashvili and Gushchina (2015), Khvatova, Timofeeva and Gulenko (2014), Shcheglova and Makarycheva (2020).

The word "manipulation" (from the French le main - hand) is used in a wide variety of contexts to refer to actions leading to the creation of an illusion. A classical manipulator (lat. Manipulare - to lead with the help of hands) is a Master-of-puppets, a person who controls puppets as if creating the illusion of their life. The result of the manipulation of people's consciousness are illusions that serve as a guide to action and thus, as it were, also turn people into puppets. However, to describe the illusions that have arisen in many of the public consciousness in the pre-civil society, the concept of "manipulation" is difficult, probably, it simply cannot be used. Manipulation of public (or mass) consciousness is defined as covert control (Kozlova, 2010, p. 113).

According to Singayevskaya (2020), in defining manipulation as an act of influencing people or controlling them or things with dexterity, especially with a dismissive connotation, as latent control or processing, the leading emphasis shifted to a technological view when approaching this phenomenon. In addition, the activities of entire institutions and state formations are also mentioned. This is used concerning the media and political events aimed at programming the opinions or aspirations of the masses, the mental state of the population, etc. The final goal of such efforts is to control the population, and its obedience (Singaevskaya, 2020, p. 72).

When such a system is established, as it proved by Ermakov (1995), the basis for the initiative of an individual with full rights and responsibility in economic and political relations - civil society, its institutions are destroyed, and the individual becomes a functional element of life support of the totalitarian order.

In the mechanism of totalitarianism, there are four types of manipulation of the process of replacing an individual personality in individuals: 1) value disorientation, 2) cultivation of an imaginary interest in totalitarian orders, 3) instilling one-thinking, 4) turning into an enemy. In other words, manipulation covers all the main motivation of a person's life - his value orientations, individual interests, thinking and beliefs. Together, these methods represent the existential dimension of the way of life in a totalitarian society and are built based on a general denial of the diversity of forms of individual existence (Ermakov, 1995, p. 126).

Kara Murza (2017) in his book "Manipulation of consciousness. XXI century" divides the human audience perceiving information into two types. He writes:

People, regardless of their ideology and political preferences, are divided into 2 types. Some believe that, in principle, a person is a big child, and the manipulation of his consciousness (for his good) by enlightened and wise rulers is not only acceptable but also preferable. For example, many experts and philosophers believe that the transition from coercion, especially with the use of violence, to the manipulation of consciousness is a huge step in the development of mankind.

Others believe that human free will, which presupposes the possession of an unclouded mind and allows making responsible choices (albeit erroneous), is a tremendous value. This category of people rejects the legality and moral justification of the manipulation of consciousness. As a result, this part of citizens considers physical violence to be less destructive (if not for the individual, then for the human race) than the "zombie" robotization of people (Kara-Murza, 2017, p. 5).

According to Gorina (2016), manipulation is a type of psychological influence aimed at secretly, covertly changing the opinions, attitudes, behaviour of the addressee in the interests of the manipulator, requiring skill from the manipulator so that the changes occurring to the addressee are unnoticed, unconscious (Gorina, 2016, p. 5).

Many media outlets are adjusting to the vertical of power. Lozovsky speaks of the Russian media, focusing on the fact that this process is not yet fully completed in Russia, but is very active. "Leading federal TV channels, for example, became the mouthpiece of the ruling party without any special worries. The same process is observed at the regional and municipal levels" (Lozovsky, 2011, p. 28). The scientist also notes the lack of political subjectivity of the media during the election period, which represents the greatest scope for manipulating journalists and public opinion. It is interesting to notice the scientist's observations regarding "PR", "PR specialization", "conflict of interests", "the dominance of information and political technologies". According to the Ukrainian scientist Sotnykov (2018):

"It is an indisputable fact that the media are an integral part of modern reality with its inherent contradictions, conflicts and trends that they reproduce. That is why the flow of information received by society is not homogeneous, as used by manipulators. The media have a significant impact Society does not form a homogeneous mass, it consists of different social groups and strata, each of which has its own moral and ethical values, so the media serve only as a means of communication between a person and society, thus satisfying an important emotional function. The influence of the media is modified by the influence of the family, educational institutions and other institutions of power. However, these same institutions note the influence of the media" (Sotnykov, 2018, p. 210).

Yakovlev & Lyulkin (2015) say that nowadays almost everyone can get into the focus of media attention, but its intellectual and ethical components are big problems. The appearance of a person who has got into circulation and the meaning of his information is false and as a result of the imposition of such information, given truthfully, people lose their critical judgment and the ability to form their own opinion. Such a situation is aggravated by information and communication technologies for manipulating consciousness, which is impossible to resist. Manipulation today is gaining a global scope and, constantly improving. It becomes more complex (Yakovlev & Lyulkin, 2015, p. 86).

As a result of the manipulation of consciousness, the real and the fictional are mixed, therefore, one of the beneficial constructions, scientists call the myth that hides knowledge and subjugates a large number of people. "Today, artificially created and imperceptibly introduced myths deform reality, hide the true state of affairs, distracting people from reality and focusing on cultural (political, economic, religious, scientific and other) meanings that are beneficial to creators and their customers" (Yakovlev & Lyulkin, 2015, p. 86). Ableev and Kuzminskaya (2015) talk about political mythology and demonization strategies. The works of Vasiliev

(2016), Znamenskaya (2015), Ibragimov (2015), Krainova (2013), Sazhia (2013), Sharkova (2020), Shustina (2016) are devoted to the media and electronic sources.

The author of this chapter fully agrees that the new electronic infrastructure, including media, television and virtual reality, is transforming reality into a media one, which is often far from the truth. As a result, people think that they have their own opinion and pseudo-thinking is formed in them.

A result of Ermkov (1995) – spontaneous manipulations are compromises of individuals with social order (Ermakov, 1995, p. 107).

Gureeva notes the fact that false information that is provided to us in the works of mass culture harms the population. It, by manipulating the opinion of people, sets them up for this or that attitude to any situation, which can lead to a violation of stability in society, to unrest and protests (Gureeva, 2019, p. 140).

Manipulation is common in most social practices. In the information space, the manipulation of the consciousness of the masses is carried out using control over the information media. Being a hidden influence on the mass consciousness, manipulation is aimed at the formation of the inertia of the masses. According to Chernikova (2015), the main task of information is to satisfy the needs of the mass population. An information product intended for perception by the masses is called mass information, which is a variety of information perceived by the audience without much difficulty. This kind of "news" does not imply active mental activity, deliberation, analysis, critical comprehension (Chernikova, 2015, p. 142-143).

It is well known that the most effective way to manipulate the minds of the masses is television. Television top managers are primarily interested in the rating, the number of viewers who are currently watching a television program. "As a result, we are witnessing how the media are playing an increasingly destructive role – they exacerbate political conflicts, deepening the gap between "friends" and "aliens", creating negative stereotypes of "aliens" and even demonizing them. Manipulation of public opinion, which has become a most important function. The media, from a hidden influence on the audience, is turning into a more explicit one and is taking on more and more aggressive forms" (Ozyumenko, 2017, p. 204).

Aggression in the media manifests itself in two directions, both with the political opponent and about the audience. As a result, Ozyumenko (2017) defines aggression in media discourse as "an expression of open hostility, hostility to the referent and a purposeful impact on the consciousness of the addressee (target audience) with the aim of its ideological subordination" (Ozyumenko, 2017, p. 204).

Information aggression is aimed not only at the ideological enemy but also at its people - they are convinced of the presence of an enemy with whom it is necessary to fight. And this is not accidental, since what is written in newspapers, is shown on television and the Internet, to a large extent the assessment of events by society depends, and its result is fateful political decisions for specific countries. That is why the influence on the minds and feelings of people by the authorities is becoming more and more aggressive and is carried out both through the manipulation of public opinion and through an open belief, which ultimately is also subordinated to the goals of manipulating public consciousness. (Ozyumenko, 2017, p. 205).

Tibinko (2011) in the study "Manipulation in Political Discourse" says that an important role in determining the country's image is played by the way it is presented by political leaders. Speaking politicians have the opportunity to reach out to both the international community and the citizens of their country. A certain worldview is being formed.

MAIN FOCUS OF THE CHAPTER

Information Technology as an Alternative to Mainstream Media

The scientific work of Nasyrova and Zamyatina (2013) discusses the blog in detail. "In the Internet space, such a concept as a "blog" has appeared. A blog is an Internet event log, an Internet diary, an online diary) - a website whose main content is regularly added posts containing text, images or multimedia. The use of blogs is one of the tendencies of the influence of information technology on the consciousness of people. Namely, in such blogs, both truthful information is published, and "blogging" is carried out – artificial or false inflating of information reasons' opinions" (Nasirova & Zamiatina, 2013, p. 258). The manipulation of public opinion through virtual communities is described in the work of Vasiliev (2016). This study is in consonant with the article by Zhukovets (2013) on the methods and techniques of manipulating public opinion used by sectarian-type organizations. Ibragimov (2015), Krainova (2013), Makarychev (2019), Sazhin (2013), Sladkova (2006), Sharkova (2020) considered the technologies of Internet manipulation in the network space of politics.

Information wars are modern tools in the struggle for the mass consciousness of people. They are carried out by distorting facts or presenting them in such a light as to cause the behaviour of an adversary or a consumer inadequate to the real state of affairs through the imposition of the perception of facts, events, beneficial to the influencing party. The global Internet network significantly affects the formation of moral norms that differ from those adopted in society.

Exploring the communication technologies of media manipulation and information security issues, Gorina (2016) writes that manipulation to create opinions and attitudes is carried out most often through print and television.

In most cases, when talking about social conflicts, the media may insist that their purpose is simply to inform readers about what is happening. At the same time, they provide negative information, information about acute conflicts, and thereby form a certain mood, assessments in the viewer, and induce any action. Newspapers, magazines, television try to please as many people as possible at once. "Expanding its audience with the help of headings, thematic bands, author columns, the media touch upon both generally significant, interesting problems for everyone, and very private, narrow ones, arousing strong, constant interest. Although people are sure that they choose what they want, but on, in fact, they do not choose, but take what is offered to them" (Gorina, 2016, p. 9).

The result of Gorina's scientific work is that media fulfil a social order, demonstrating the negative phenomena of lifc and involve the masses in the process of manipulation. Readers of newspapers and viewers of TV news replicate manipulative information. The information is distributed to a huge audience. The media are addictive, they become like a drug, especially television. The author of this chapter allows herself to add the YouTube service and smartphones to the existing list.

Ukrainian Phenomenon

The events in Ukraine in February 2014 marked the beginning of large-scale socio-economic changes in the existence of the Ukrainian society and state. They entailed the loss of the territories of Crimea, the outbreak of hostilities in the east of Ukraine, and a huge number of human victims. President Petro Poroshenko promised the people to end the war, but after the elections, the military conflict only intensified. For more than five years, people have been suffering, the country's economy is falling. President Poroshenko went to the polls for a second term, but ... he lost them. The reason is not only the dissatisfaction of the people but also the informational videos of the blogger. A blogger intervened in the presidential election campaign! What is it? Manipulation of public consciousness or resistance to manipulation? In the information field, where a huge amount of fake information is accumulated, the search for truth becomes relevant. The hypothesis of this chapter: using critical thinking, a method by contradiction to prove or disapprove the results of Anatoliy Shariy's activities.

RESULTS AND DISCUSSIONS

In the article "Why are you persecuting Anatoly Shariy?" The question that destroys Petro Poroshenko" Sidorchik (2019) writes: "Shariy's videos made him popular among Ukrainians who were disappointed in the Poroshenko regime, or were initially his opponents. The Ukrainian authorities, trying to neutralize the influence of the journalist on the masses, began to call him "the Kremlin propagandist". True, they could not cite at least one real fact proving Shariy's cooperation with Russia. At the end of 2018, the confrontation between Shariy and official Kiev reached a new level" (Sidorchik, 2019, para. 4)

As an illustration of the article is a video that is sent by the injured girl (https://www.youtube.com/watch?v=IuoYFO99YWg&t=2s), when, during a rally in the Kirovograd region, the President of Ukraine began to find out where the girl lives, and as a result, openly hit her. After the girl left the rally, police officers approached her and rudely demanded: "to go with them". However, she refused, and the police did not dare to detain her by force.

It is also known that the court-ordered Poroshenko to refute the words that "Shariy is not a Ukrainian journalist" and publish it in a government newspaper (Information Agency, 2019). Another high-profile investigation by Shariy was the exposure of the consul in Hamburg, which resulted in his suspension from the work (Correspondent, 2019).

The activities of the blogger Anatoliy Shariy cause conflicting reactions on the part of the media. The research question is: "Is Shariy's activity counter-manipulation?"

So, let's compare the excerpts from the biography of the blogger from Wikipedia (Table.1).

As it can be seen from the table: the article of the Ukrainian Wikipedia is larger and has a negative connotation of the person and activities of the journalist. The article from the Russian Wikipedia is smaller in volume with a neutral description about Anatoliy Shariy. The most objective information is given in the English version of Wikipedia (https://en.wikipedia.org/wiki/Anatoly_Shariy).

What are about the blogger's videos? So look at any of the 7111 videos on his channel. Shariy's video dated October 22, 2018 (14:16) 543,836 views (https://www.youtube.com/watch?v=t60G3NQrdC4)

The gas price for the population increased by 23%, which will entail an increase in other tariffs and prices, but the authorities were able to substantiate that the higher the tariffs, the fewer subsidies the population needs. Deputy Denisenko explains: "All the obligations to raise tariffs were taken back in 2008 - it is not us, we are not to blame. We will provide subsidies to those who are entitled to subsidies. Everyone who cannot pay, who has a small pension". (https://www.youtube.com/watch?v=t60G3NQrdC4)

Table 1. The biography of the blogger from Wikipedia

Ukrainian Wikipedia	Russian Wikipedia
Anatoliy Shariy (born August 20, 1978, in Kyiv) is a pro-Russian propagandist, video blogger, politician, and former journalist of Ukrainian descent. He has a video blog on YouTube, as well as on pro-Russian TV channels First Independent, KRT, NASH, 112 Ukraine, ZIK and NewsOne, associated with pro-Russian politicians Viktor Medvedchuk, Yevgeny Muraev and Vitaly Zakharchenko. Former activist of the homophobic organization "Love against homosexuality". In the video blog, Shariy relays Russian anti-Ukrainian propaganda, including the discrediting of the Ukrainian language, coat of arms, flag, anthem, and publishes misleading information that discredits the Ukrainian army, the Ukrainian government, and Ukraine in general; criticizes Russian unsystematic politicians in opposition to Putin. According to the SBU, Shariy creates his videos to discredit Ukraine in the interests of the Russian secret services. On February 16, 2021, the SBU declared Sharia suspected of treason, and on February 25, the SBU declared him wanted by the state. In 2011, Shariy attacked a visitor to Kyiv's McDonald's by shooting him with a pistol, which led to the opening of criminal proceedings against Shariy in Ukraine for attempting on a person's life. To avoid punishment, Sharii fled Ukraine in 2012 and has been hiding from Ukrainian law enforcement abroad in the EU ever since. In 2012, he received the status of a "political fugitive" in Lithuania. In 2017, Sharia was charged with sexual harassment of a minor, which led to a criminal case against him in the Netherlands and Ukraine on charges of paedophilia. Since January 2012, Shariy has been wanted in Ukraine in two cases involving an attempt on another person's life at a McDonald's restaurant, but in 2019-2020 he was removed from the wanted list in both cases for unknown reasons. In 2019, Shariy founded and became the de facto leader of the pro-Russian Sharia Party, which is most likely a project of another pro-Russian OPZZh party. Members and leaders of the Shariy Party participated in Russian pro-Putin organizations. In August 2020, the OPZH elected the Sharia Party as its main ally in the local elections in Ukraine 2020. During the 2020 local election campaign, Shariy's party distributed campaign materials with a map of Ukraine without Crimea. Shariy has Ukrainophobic views, supports the regime of Putin and Russian terrorists who occupied part of the Donbas and Crimean regions of Ukraine. Since 2019 he has been living in Roda de Bara, Spain.	Anatoly Anatolyevich Shariy (Ukrainian Anatoly Anatoliyovich Shariy; born August 20, 1978, Kyiv, Ukrainian SSR, USSR) is a Ukrainian politician, journalist, video blogger, businessman. Chairman of the political party "Party Sharia" since June 6, 2019. Founder of the Internet publication "Shariy.net". Author of publications on organized crime in Ukraine in 2008-2011, a political refugee in the European Union. Since 2013 - the author of a video blog aimed at systematic criticism, initially materials in the Ukrainian media (less often - Russian and Western), related to the events in Ukraine after the Euromaidan, later - to criticize the actions of the Ukrainian authorities (first President Petro Poroshenko, after 2019 - the actions of President Volodymyr Zelensky and his office). On February 16, 2021, the Security Service of Ukraine announced Sharia suspicion of committing a crime under two articles of the Criminal Code of Ukraine - part 1 of Art. 111 (High treason) and Part 1 of Art. 161 (Violation of the equality of citizens depending on their race, nationality, religious beliefs, disability and other grounds). February 25, 2021, put on the state wanted list.

This is exactly the information that interests ordinary citizens: the deterioration of their well-being, increasing in prices and taxes, declining the quality of life, the conditions of the communal sphere, the problems of schools, health care and the language. According to Krainova's research (2013), if earlier the main means of transmitting information to people were traditional print publications and electronic means of communication, then the beginning of the new century was marked by the active development of Internet technologies. They qualitatively changed the nature of politics and gave it virtual characteristics. "Thanks to new opportunities, mass political communication has increased the speed of dissemination of information, reaching the consumer in the shortest possible time. The large volume of transmitted information, the brevity and the memorable imagery of messages increased the intensity of the impact on the audience. The blogosphere, electronic media, social networks, portals, forums and websites - Internet communications are constantly being updated and have an increasingly significant impact on the political space. Internet communications give an impetus to the development of civil society, promote publicity and openness of political processes" (Krainova, 2013, p. 61). The Internet plays an important role in the development of civil society, expanding the possibilities of social control of power through network technologies.

"The Internet has become a platform for the production of alternative opinions and a sphere for the formation of special public education - an electronic civil society, which is in a position of opposition to state structures. The fact of alienation of the Internet audience from the actions and decisions of authorities and recognition of its legitimacy is aggravated by the fact that traditional communication channels (printed and electronic mass media) - are losing their relevance as the main and only source of information. Engagement of newspapers, magazines, television, radio, widespread in the public consciousness understanding of the absence of free and independent media provokes political withdrawal active audience in the Internet space, which opens up unlimited opportunities for self-expression (Krainova, 2013, pp. 62-63).

This is also characterized by the fact that "in electoral studies, a significant degree of distortion of the real picture of party-political priorities in Ukraine was revealed, which, of course, is nothing more than a form of implemented political technologies for manipulating the mass consciousness, which fundamentally contradicts the main democratic principles and conditions for the development of civil society" (Khrienko A.P., & Khrienko Al.P., 2008, p. 105). It is also noted that the manipulators of the official media use the patterns of mass psychology, such as the "spiral of silence". The idea behind this technique is that by referring to fabricated opinion polls. Citizens are convinced that the majority of society supports a political position pleasing to the manipulators: fears of being in with social and psychological isolation or for purpose of self-defence not to express their opinion or to change it. Such an impact has a great influence on the forced adaptation of people to the proposed conditions or on alienation, which the respondents, as a rule, hide in the polls behind the answers "I find it difficult to answer" (Sladkova, 2006, p. 8). The fact that Shariy's activities are countering manipulation is proved by the fact that the members of the European Parliament defence for the blogger.

From the video "Speech to Members of European Parliament (MEPs)" (https://www.youtube.com/watch?v=cTrQFf2IlXw), which received 457,860 views on April 14, 2021. Tatiana Zhdanok, a member of the European Parliament, calls Shariy as an "objective blogger." Since 2019, the blogger is the head of the Shariy Party, which passed to the city councils of Ukraine: Kharkov, Krupyansk and Chuguev (Kharkov region), Kramatorsk, Mariupol, Zaporozhye, Nikolaev, Odessa. Sharia channel has 3738703816 views, 7111 videos._The channel was registered on May 13, 2013, has 2,440,000 subscribers. In 2012, after a journalistic investigation in the authorities of Yanukovych, he received refugee status in the European Union, but with the change of power, another problem arose - neo-Nazism. Shariy has investigations into the activities of groups in the country, which differ in their ideology similar to the fascist (above mentioned the disclosure of the activities of the consul in Hamburg, which led to his dismissal).

Shariy criticized the language law, but representatives of European countries also expressed dissatisfaction with this law. For example, the article "Law on education: where will language passions lead in Zacarpathia?" (Popovich, 2017) or "Law on language: in the service sector is now only Ukrainian?" (Zhuravleva, 2021), "Schools in Zacarpathia: A child should study subjects in their native language"(GordonUA).

"A knife in the back"- this is how the head of the Hungarian Foreign Ministry described the law on education, which the Verkhovna Rada of Ukraine adopted on September 5 and which begins the reform of the educational sphere in Ukraine. Transcarpathia called it "the return of Stalin's times". "And these are just a few of the many bright comments on the bill. The Speaker of the Parliament and the President of Ukraine have not yet signed the document, but they have already positively assessed the document (Popovich, 2017 para.1-3).

The site Shariy.net was included in the top ten most-cited Russian-speaking, according to the Brand Analytics Analytical Center. On the first line of the rating was the website of the opposition politician Alexei Navalny. "When compiling the rating, its authors processed 786,975,681 Russian-language posts posted per month in social media. Users used 1,061,956,374 links to external resources, including 128,285,910 "short links" (like t.co, fb.me, goo.gl, etc.) in their posts. Data sources for message analysis - VKontakte, Twitter, Odnoklassniki, My World, Facebook,

Instagram, YouTube, G +, various blogs, news articles, forums, comments, thematic sites and groups for discussions" (https://sharij.net/2074905/04/2015), (sharij.net Competitive Analysis, Marketing Mix and Traffic - Alexa.). Shariy's videos are gaining more and more popularity. I. Koval stops as for Shariy's activities in the article by Deutsche Welle about the five best speakers of the Russian-speaking YouTube who talk about politics (https://p.dw.com/p/2eQQ1, 11.06.2017). UNIAN ranks Shariy 12th out of 25 (https://www.unian.net/society/2246389-reyting-ukrainskih-liderov-mneniy-v-sotssetyah-vakarchuk-obognal-poroshenko.html) in the rating of Ukrainian opinion leaders in social networks.

Using data from the Top of 20 Russian-speaking YouTube bloggers from Brand Analytics (https://www.sostav.ru/publication/fevralskij-top-20-russkoyazychnykh-youtube-blogerov-ot-brand-analytics-36208.html) in social media in February 2019 of the year (https://www.sostav.ru/03/18/2019) and Top-20 Russian-speaking YouTube bloggers 2020 (https://vc.ru/social/141738-top-20-russkoyazychnyh-youtube-blogerov-iyun-2020-totalnyy-lestpley-no-chellendzhery-ne-sdayutsya) the author of this chapter compiled a graph:

Figure 1. Increased interest in information activities A. Shariy
Source: compiled by the author of the chapter

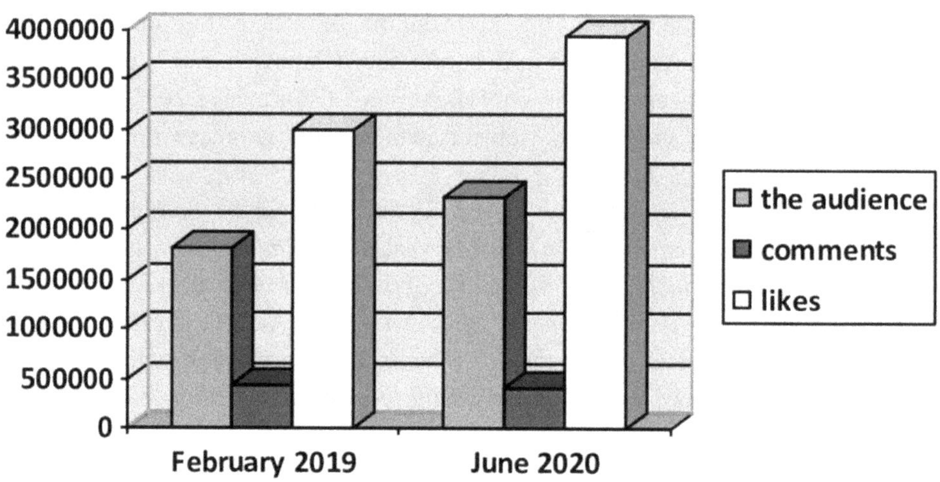

Now turn to the webinar with the MEPs, where, in addition to Shariy, several other respected experts speak: Online Forum: "Ukraine - Challenges for Constructing Democratic Plurality Confirmation" (https://www.youtube.com/watch?v=Vkl8JqN-wP8)

Three members of the European Parliament are here: Tatiana Zhdanok (a member from Latvia, being a member of Green's European free alliance group), Helmut Shultz (long-standing MP from Germany & the Lincoln the left group in the European Parliament) and Miroslav Vitovsky from Slovakia, who is non-attached. Also invited are V. Pogribinskiy, V. Muravitskiy. Ruslan Cotsaba, Anatoliy Sharij are invited as well.

Helmut Sholtz noted existing problems of a dangerous confrontation in the east of Ukraine, unresolved tasks in society, in the social development of the Ukrainian state, and the importance of the European Parliament better understand the specific situation in Ukraine, how best to find a prospect for the life of the Ukrainian state ...

Miroslav Radochevsky criticized the actions of President Zelensky and opposed the ban on the media, because this is freedom of speech, and any media resources can be prohibited only by the people of Ukraine, but there can be no legal prohibitions emanating from the legal system for any media if they do not disseminate information about murder or terrorism.

Mr Michail Pogrebinski who is a political expert a very famous both in Ukraine and other countries as political expert: "We chose a new person who was far from politics and people hoped that he would go the other way. But I also doubt that this person, who has no political experience and became a puppet in the hands of people who are pushing him in the same"...

According to Pogrebinsky, a caste society is being created and people who participated in the Maidan or the anti-terrorist operation, or who call themselves activists, immediately receive the protection of the authorities.

Thus, we see that not only Shariy speaks about the problems in Ukraine. There are many people with a similar point of view. In a democratic society, it is normal to have your point of view. On December 20, the Vesti edition publishes the Top-100 of the most influential people and phenomena in Ukraine. According to Vesti, where Shariy occupies the 34th position (Vesti, 2019). "Anatoly Shariy, the phenomenon of the last parliamentary elections, whose "nominal" party gained 2.23% from scratch, has settled on the 34th line of the rating. Thereby confirming the thesis that parties and party affiliation have ceased to be an exclusively political category, stepping into the world of marketing and even if the influence of the journalist, blogger and politician Anatoly Shariy on decision-making remains dubious, on the other hand, who else will be able to assemble a massive colourful rally "for" or "against" an event in a matter of hours, and the participants they will come not for the sake of money, but for the idea, clothed in a form accessible to them. "According to the publication, the blogger achieved the impossible. He is not only organized his viewers into a party but also received a result of 2.23%, which allows it to qualify for state funding. This did not happen, because a law was passed that did not allow the Shariy Party to receive funding, but the blogger continued his actions: representatives of his party went to several cities and regions to local authorities, which is reflected on the website of the Central Election Commission (https://www.cvk.gov.ua/pls/vm2020/pvm002pt001f01=695pt00_t001f01=695.html)

Ukrainians Filatov and Shariy topped the rating of the most popular bloggers of the Russian-speaking Facebook to the Verkhovna Rada of Ukraine on July 21, 2019: Shariy's party gains more than 7% (Yarovaya, 2015). Southeast Ukraine is disappointed in Zelenskiy and is ready to support Shariy (Oleg Filin, 2020). The publication in "Ukrainska Pravda" [Ukrainian Truth] on February 4, 2021 notes that 4 parties confidently pass into the Parliamentary rating: seven more parties can overcome the passing barrier, taking into account the error. These are the "Ukrainian Strategy of Groisman" (4.8%), the Radical Party (4.7%), the party "Strength and Honor" (4.5%), "For the Future" (4.4%), the party "Golos" (3.5%), the Sharia party (3.4%), the Svoboda party (3.1%). Other parties have significantly lower support. In particular, 2.4% of voters are ready to support Vitali Klitschko's party, and 1.4% are ready to support Nash Krai [Our Region] (https://www.pravda.com.ua/rus/news/2021/02/4/7282282/)

Already on May 20, 2021, "Ukrainska Pravda" [Ukrainian Truth] publishes a new rating (https://www.pravda.com.ua/rus/news/2021/05/20/7294185/) "A fresh rating of parties has appeared. If elections to the Verkhovna Rada were held next Sunday in parliament would pass 5 parties, 7 more parties have a chance to get into the Rada, taking into account the error Source: poll of the Sociological Group "Rating", conducted on May 16-18 Details: The parliamentary rating is headed by the party "Servant of the People", which is ready to support 24.8% of those who will vote and have made their choice.

For the party "European Solidarity" - 13.5%, "Opposition Platform - For Life" - 13.2%, "Fatherland" - 11.8%. In particular, the party "Strength and Honor" is supported by 5.0%, Radical party - 4.1%, Vitali Klitschko's BLOW - 4.0%, Muraev's party "Nashi" - 4.0%, the party "Ukrainian Strategy of Groisman" - 3.8%, VO "Svoboda" - 3.7%, "Golos" - 3.3%, the Shariy Party - 3.1%. The rating of other political forces is less than 2%.

Evgeny Nazarenko (2019) devoted his article "The Miracle of Anatoly Shariy's Party: How to Successfully Step from YouTube into Politics". He writes that the head of the sociological group "Rating" Aleksey Antipovich explained who the voters of the "Party of Shariy" are: "On the one hand, these are pro-Russian voters, and on the other hand, these are the voters of the former "Party of Regions", "Opposition Platform", "Opposition Bloc". But at the same time, they are also voters who do not perceive social status. The gap between the poor and the rich is this is all the protest for which the Servant of the People voters also voted. He has a direct speech, very understandable theses, "without cuts", not intellectual statements, as is the case with many politicians. The head of the "Rating" sociological group added that TV still beats the Internet. But some of the people, as in the case of the "Party of Shariy", are exclusively its Internet subscribers (Nazarenko, 2019).

What do the deputies from the Shariy Party do? They act exclusively in the interests of their constituents. For example, a video dated July 18, 2021. At 11 minutes 29 seconds, a deputy of the Kharkiv City Council from the Shariy Party (https://www.youtube.com/watch?v=eitpSwj8Sto) Davito Matcichenko shows a video report on the work done. He was approached by the employees of the tram depot in Kharkiv. It turned out that the problematic Oktyabrskoye depot has two managers: an actual one and its shadow patron. Transport enterprises of the city have huge wage and tax debts.

Deputy of the Zaporizhzhia City Council Sergei Nikulin at the 12th minute 57th second of Shariy's video "Putin's Article. Hee-hee and ha-ha?" (07/14/2021) https://www.youtube.com/watch?v=cSQ2AEnUHbA) says that due to the incompetence of utilities, several apartments were left without gas. The residents turned to the Shariy Party for help. The deputies, in turn, made public utilities fulfil their obligations. As a result, people can again use gas for which they regularly paper.

Deputy of the Kharkiv City Council Nikita Rozhenko at 11 minutes 52 seconds of A. Shariy's video "Tikhanovskaya successfully visited the states" (20.07.2021) reports that an appeal was received from a resident of Kharkiv that after the scheduled repairs of the heating network, utilities did not put the territory in order: for a whole year, there was a dug trench near the house. Workers of the heating main forgot to bury a hole after laying communications. The deputy from the party sent out appeals to those responsible, and after the party's work, the communal services fulfilled their obligations: they dug a ditch and defrauded the path.

In this case, there is a natural reaction from the authorities, the confirmation of which we find in the study of Agapova (2017), and also the technology of public opinion management, which Singayevskaya (2020) speaks of, is being introduced – the formation of an image of the enemy is pro-Russian revenge.

Thus, we see that not only Shariy speaks about the problems in Ukraine. There are many people with a similar point of view, there are subscribers and followers of Shariy, there is his party. In a democratic society, it is normal to have your point of view. The following question arises: "Could the MEPs pay attention to the person spreading lies?" The answer to this question is found in an article by a Spanish-language authoritative publication, which provides official data from the Catalan police. The article also deals with the attacks of ultra-right groups on members of the Shariy Party. On May 20, 2021, the Spanish newspaper "El Pais" published an article that a Spanish court is investigating the persecution of the leader of the "Party of Sharia", journalist and blogger Anatoly Shariy by Ukrainian neo-Nazis. The article describes cases of attacks on his home, as well as death threats on the

Internet. In addition, the material "El Pais" describes the pressure on Anatoly Shariy by the Ukrainian authorities.

A Spanish judge is investigating threats and hate crimes committed by the leaders of the National Corps, an ultra-right party formed from the Azov battalion, a paramilitary organization that fought against Donetsk separatists and served as a source of inspiration for white supremacists everywhere.

In one of the consolidated reports, which was accessed by El País, the Catalan police conclude that the spouses are "being persecuted for their journalistic activities and for belonging" to an opposition party (Jesus Garcia, 2021, para.5,7).

To the pressure from the neo-Nazis, there was also a judicial offensive by the Ukrainian authorities. A criminal case has been opened in Ukraine on charges of high treason and incitement to ethnic hatred, writes El País.(Jesus Garcia, 2021, para.17).

The charges, under which a journalist can receive an imprisonment of up to 20 years in prison, are based on the content of a series of interviews and videos posted on the Internet. (Jesus Garcia, 2021, para.18).

"Before making a decision, the judge is awaiting a report from the Catalan police, but already considers the journalist to be a protected witness. The head of the Office for Civil and Political Rights of the Generalitat of Catalonia, Adam Mayo, sent a letter stating that the Sharia family meets the conditions for granting them asylum in Spain, El País reports". (Jesus Garcia, 2021, para.25).

Turning to the scientific research of Ermakov (1995), the author finds that the totalitarian system is based on a one-party system. It "prohibits democratic institutions, liquidates the real rights and freedoms of citizens, militarizes the economy, and violently organizes public life on the principles of a state of emergency, carries out terror and repressions initiated from above against the opposition and dissidents" (Ermakov, 1995, p. 104). Such manipulation as turning into an enemy performs several important functions. Singayevskaya (2020) writes that a such manipulation is a convenient form of switching the discontent, irritation and aggression of people against the authorities and living conditions to others, as well as getting rid of persons unwanted by the authorities. In addition, the authorities, artificially transferring the aggression, rebellious energy and hatred accumulated by the forced masses to the enemy, prevented possible social explosions. It would be good if Avakov's resignation and his replacement by a member of the ruling party is just a coincidence. (Avakov's resignation News July 15: Avakov's dismissal, free entry to the EU https://www.

pravda.com.ua/rus/news/2021/07/15/7300682/. Victoria Kolomiets Rada dismissed Avakov). He held this position for over 7 years.

FUTURE RESEARCH DIRECTIONS

If to compare the number of subscribers in YouTube Shariy and news channels of the leading Ukrainian media, which have official coverage throughout the country, it is showed by figures that Shariy, having only YouTube (2,440,000 subscribers), has been able to create competition, and this is already the opposition of the media to the authorities (1 + 1 TV channel - 2.28 million subscribers, ICTV - 910 thousand, STB - 192 thousand). The author of this chapter has done the histogram that reflects competition with official TV channels in YouTube:

Figure 2. Shariy channel's competition with official TV
Source: completed by the author

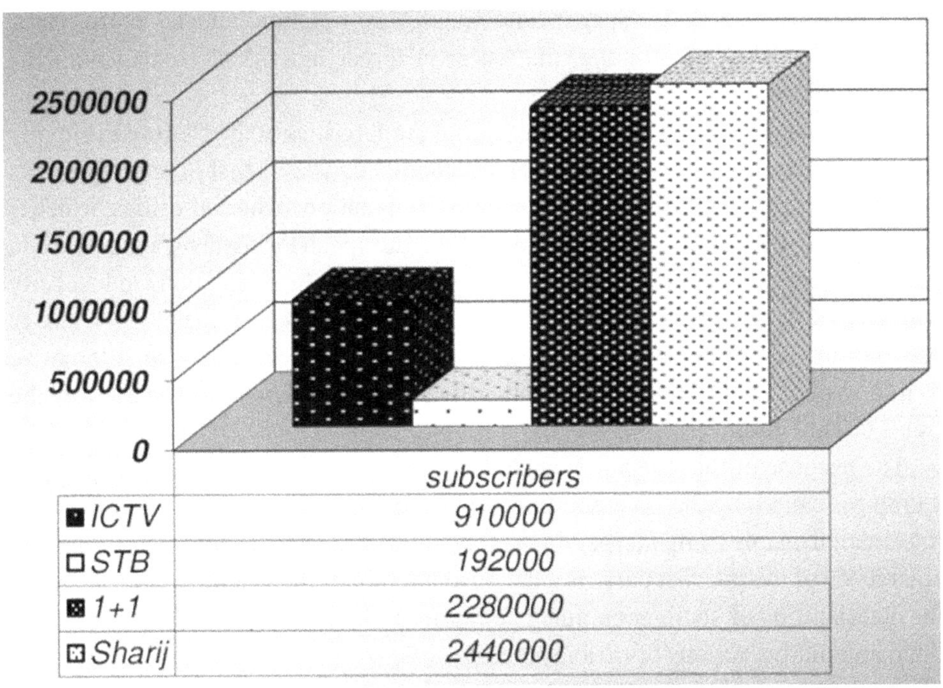

The quantitative superiority of the Shariy channel is evident in the number of subscribers, which is a competition for official channels. This is already a counteraction to the information that is broadcast by these media. (TV channel 1 + 1 - 2.28 million subscribers, ICTV - 910 thousand, STB - 192 thousand. How will the events unfold next? Will Shariy get into parliament? All this can become the content of further scientific research: compare the official election data, build appropriate graphs. If the blogger's party gets into the Ukrainian parliament, then we can say that there is an alternative to information manipulation - this is the truth of life, which is broadcasted by the free YouTube resource.

CONCLUSION

Manipulation of the consciousness of the masses continues to be television, which gives rise to the prohibition of objectionable TV channels. Aggression in the media manifests itself both about a political opponent and with the audience that supports him. In social conflicts, the media may claim that their purpose is to inform readers and viewers about what is happening. At the same time, they form a certain mood of aggression and, therefore, a negative picture of the world. But an individual, daily or periodically reading newspapers and magazines, watching television programs, remains with them one-on-one, that is, is in direct individual contact with the journalistic text.

After analyzing and comparing the facts of the activities of the Ukrainian blogger Anatoly Shariy, his party, the author of this chapter considers that Shariy represents an alternative opinion to the official media and opposition to the authorities, which is confirmed by the opinion of the deputies of the European Parliament, an increase in the number of views and subscribers, as well as the results of elections to local city councils' advice, which is also reflected in the official sources. If the blogger's party gets into the Ukrainian Parliament, then it may be said that there is an alternative to information manipulation - this is the truth of life, which is broadcasted by the free YouTube resource.

The purpose of this chapter is achieved: the emergence of the Internet party in Ukraine is caused by the disappointment of some of the citizens. They receive news information mainly from Internet sources and think critically. It can be proved that the emergence of the Internet party is a practical attempt of the electorate to counteract the deterioration of socio-economic conditions in the country and a protest against the manipulative actions of official sources.

REFERENCES

Ableev, S. R., & Kuzminskaya, S. I. (2015). Manipulation of Mass Consciousness: Political Mythology and Demonization Strategy. *Bulletin of the Moscow University of the Ministry of Internal Affairs of Russia*, (5), 172–176.

Agapova, E. A. (2017). On the role of the media in manipulating public consciousness. *Humanities and Social Sciences*, (5), 2–8.

Amineva, E. S. (2018). Techniques and techniques for manipulating public consciousness in the weekly "Arguments and Facts". *Philological sciences. Questions of theory and practice*, *1-2*(79).

Belousov, A. B. (2012). Edward Bernays: From Public Opinion Manipulation to Consent Engineering. *Policy. Political Studies*, (4), 143–148.

Bernays, E. (2012). Manipulation of Public Opinion: How and Why. Policy. *Political Studies*, (4), 149–159.

Boyarkin, V. V., & Boyarkina, L. A. (2012). Manipulation of Public Consciousness: Present and Future. In *Proceedings of conferences SIC Sociosphere* (No. 1, pp. 51-53). Vedecko vydavatelske centrum Sociosfera-CZ sro.

Chernikova, V.E. (2015). Manipulation of mass consciousness as a phenomenon of the information society. *Philosophical Sciences. Theory and practice of social development, 3,* 141-144. DOI: doi:10.22363/231291822017211203220

Ermakov, Yu. A. (1995). *Manipulation of a Person: Meaning, Techniques, Consequences*. Yekaterinburg: Publishing house Ural, University.

Garcia. (in press). *Un juez investiga el acoso de neonazis ucranios a un activista oculto en España*. https://elpais.com/espana/catalunya/2021-05-20/un-juez-investiga-el-acoso-de-neonazis-ucranios-a-un-activista-oculto-en-espana.html

Gordon. (2019). *Posol Vengrii ob ukrainskom yazyke v shkolah Zakarpat'ya: Rebenok dolzhen izuchat' predmety na rodnom yazyke* [Ambassador of Hungary on the Ukrainian language in schools in Transcarpathia: A child should study subjects in their native language]. https://gordonua.com/news/politics/posol-vengrii-ob-ukrainskom-yazyke-v-shkolah-zakarpatya-rebenok-dolzhen-izuchat-predmety-na-rodnom-yazyke-1468964.html

Gorina, E. V. (2016). Kommunikativnye tekhnologii manipulyacii v SMI i voprosy informacionnoj bezopasnosti [Communication technologies of media manipulation and information security issues]. Ekaterinburg: Izd-vo Ural. un-ta, Russia.

Gorshkova, L. A. (2019). Functioning of euphemisms in newspaper and journalistic discourse in the process of manipulating public opinion. Media in the modern world. 58th Petersburg Readings, 173-175.

Gureeva, M. A. (2019). Manipulirovanie soznaniem i povedeniem lyudej v sisteme massovoj kul'tury [Manipulation of consciousness and behavior of people in the system of mass culture]. Sociology in the modern world: Science, education, creativity. Izd-vo Alt. un-ta.

Ibragimov, L. K. (2015). Internet manipulation technologies in the network space of politics. *The Contours of Global Transformations: Politics, Economics, Law*, *8*(2).

Kara Murza, S. (2017). *Consciousness manipulation. XXI century*. Lites.

Khlopkov, K.A. (2009). The importance of mass media in the manipulation of mass consciousness. *Bulletin of the Krasnoyarsk State Pedagogical University by V.P. Astafieva*, (2).

Khrienko, A. P., & Khrienko, Al. P. (2008). Electoral ratings as a tool for manipulating public opinion. *RGGU Bulletin. Series "Philosophy. Sociology. Art Criticism,"* (2), 99–106.

Khvatov, K. Y., Timofeev, A. I., & Gulenko, P. I. (2014). Development and Application of Technologies for Manipulating Public Opinion: A Historical Review. Topical issues of development of the Russian economy, 45-52.

Kolosheina, M. G. (2020). Ugrozy ekonomicheskoj bezopasnosti i ih minimizacia [Threats to economic security and their minimization]. *Sovremennye tekhnologii v nauke i obrazovanii-STNO-2020*.

Kovalik, E. V., & Gubin, A. I. (2019). Aktual'nost' razvitia mediakommunikacii [Relevance of media communication development]. Penzenskij gosudarstvennyj universitet, g. Penza.

Kozlov, K. N. (2019). Mechanisms of manipulation of public opinion in modern politics. In Society and Power: History and Modernity (pp. 475-479). Academic Press.

Kozlova, O. N. (2010). Manipulyaciya soznaniem i sub"ektnost' v XXI veke [Manipulation of consciousness and subjectivity in the XXI century]. *Vestnik RGGU. Seriya. Filosofiya. Sociologiya. Iskusstvovedenie*, (3 (46)), 113–130.

Krainova, K. A. (2013). The Internet as a means of political manipulation in modern political governance. *PolitBook*, (2), 60–67.

Larionova, D. P. (2015). Information as a social weapon. *Electronic Bulletin of the Rostov Social and Economic Institute*, (3-4), 1082–1086.

Levashov, V. I. (2011). Manipulation of public opinion in the election campaign. *Metropolitan Management*, (3), 98–106.

Lozovsky, B. N. (2011). Kto i kak manipuliruet zhurnalistami. Manipulyativnye tekhnologii vliyaniya na sredstva massovoj informacii [Who and how manipulates journalists. Manipulative technologies of influence on the media]. Izdatel'stvo Ural'skogo Universiteta.

Makarychev, V.N. (2019). Marketing and manipulation of public opinion. *Advertising: Theory and Practice*, (4), 302-308.

Malinova, O. (2004). Public opinion and public policy models. *Public policy: collection of articles*. Norma. https://www.civisbook.ru/files/File/Malinova_obsh_mn.pdf

Morozova, J., & Magamedli, N. (2019). Media as a subject of public opinion manipulation. *Topical issues of education and science development in modern society*, 247-251.

Nafieva, N. R. (2019). Manipulation of public counsciousness as a news media. *Electronic Scientific Journal,* 35-36. https://sibac.info/archive/journal/student/5%2849_1%29.pdf#page=36

Nasyrova, O.A., & Zamyatina, E. V. (2013). Mass consciousness manipulation is one of the ways to manage people in the field of information technology. *Actual Problems of Aviation and Cosmonautics, 2*(9), 258-259.

Ozyumenko, V. (2017). Media Discourse in an Atmosphere of Information Warfare. *Manipulation to Aggression. Russian Journal of Linguistics, 21*(1), 203–220. doi:10.22363/2312-9182-2017-21-1-203-220

Popovich, Z. (2017). *Law on education: where will language passions lead in Zacarpathia?* https://www.bbc.com/ukrainian/features-russian-41265262

Prokopenko, I. S. (2012). *Storm of consciousness. The truth about manipulating human consciousness*. Eksmo.

Sazhin, N. O. (2013). Manipulation of public opinion on the Internet. In *Materials of the International Congress of FSBEI HPE "SibADI" Architecture. Building. Transport. Technologies. Innovation* (pp. 279-285). Academic Press.

Sharkova, I. V. (2020). *Methods of manipulating public opinion in modern mass media and social networks*. Modern Media and the Media Market.

Shcheglov, A. V., & Makarychev, V. N. (2020). Manipulation of public opinion. *Economic Security Bulletin*, (1), 285–288.

Shustina, I. V. (2016). *Speech means of manipulating public opinion in modern political advertising*. Man in the Information Space.

Singaevskaya, M. V. (2020). Public Opinion Management Technologies. *Sociology*, (2), 71–80.

Sladkova, O. B. (2006). Manipulation of public consciousness in the information society. *Observatory of Culture*, (6), 4–12.

Sotnykov, A. V. (2018). Manipulation in mass media: Components and resistance. *Research Journal of Drohobych Ivan Franco State Pedagogical University. Series. Philology (Linguistics)*, *9*, 208–210.

Staroverov, V. I., & Levashov, V. I. (2009). Manipulating Public Opinion: Sociological Aspects of Analysis. *Sociology of Power*, (4).

Sur, E.I. (2012). Manipulation: concept, main features and structure. *Actual problems of the humanities and natural sciences, 3,* 143-146.

Tibinko, N. D. (2011). Manipulation in political discourse. *Bulletin of the Chelyabinsk State University*, *3*(218), 134-137.

Torgovanova, O. N., & Shabanova, A. E. (2016). Manipulation of public opinion in political discourse (on the example of Barack Obama's speech). *Bulletin of Tver State University. Series. Philosophy*, (4), 93–98.

Tutarashvili, R. Y., & Gushchina, L. V. (2015). Manipulation of public consciousness within the framework of political discourse: the role of the media in manipulating public consciousness, the main types of manipulative technologies. *International Research Journal*, *3-2*(34), 85-87.

Vasiliev, A. A. (2016). Manipulation of public opinion through virtual communities. *Christian Reading*, (5), 207–222. doi:10.24411/1814-5574-2016-00074

Volgutova, A. V. (2014). Mass media and power: Specificity of public opinion manipulation. *Ogarev-Online*, (5 (19)), 6.

Yakovleva, E. L. Lyulkin S. N. (2015). Manipulation of information as a violation of human rights. *Балтийский гуманитарный журнал, 3(12)*, 85-88.

Zhukovets, O. Yu. (2013). Methods and techniques for manipulating public opinion used by sectarian-type organizations. *Humanities and Social Sciences*, (5).

Zhuravleva, O. (2021). *Law on state language: in the service sector now only Ukrainian*. https://www.dw.com/ru/zakon-o-gosjazyke-v-sfere-uslug-teper-tolko-ukrainskij/a-56225227

Znamenskaya, T. A. (2015). The use of metaphors as a means of manipulating public opinion in English-language publications about Ukraine. *CETERIS PARIBUS*, (1), 67–69.

KEY TERMS AND DEFINITIONS

MEP: A Member of the European Parliament (MEP) is a person who has been elected to serve as a popular representative in the European Parliament.

PR: Is an abbreviation for public relations.

Chapter 5
Counteracting Online Health Misinformation

Mahshid Ebrahimi
Independent Researcher, Germany

ABSTRACT

The use of internet and new media technologies provide new ways of communicating and online searching for health information. False health-related information as a result of the lack of reliable scientific sources is intentionally or unintentionally created and disseminated and can have negative effects on people's health. The purpose of this study is to identify strategies for counteracting online health misinformation from the perspective of health professionals using content analysis approach. From the analysis, strategies for dealing with the effects of misinformation include training of health staff at all levels, improving public awareness, and filtering or fact-checking. It is revealed that the most important way to cope with health misinformation in cyberspace is to enhance public awareness, which can reduce its detrimental impact to a great extent.

INTRODUCTION

Health information refers to any health-related knowledge (Mahmoudi and Taheri, 2015). It is a type of information that people need to use for themselves or other family members. Health information defined by U.S. National Library of Medicine includes information about general health, drugs and supplements, specific populations, genetics, environmental health and toxicology, clinical trials and biomedical literature (Zhao and Zhang, 2017). The process engaged in by humans to change their state of knowledge through a set of actions: information needs, seek information, evaluate

DOI: 10.4018/978-1-7998-8235-0.ch005

and select information, and finally use the information is called information seeking (Sultana, 2016). Prior to the development the Internet and information technology, printed information sources, libraries, and information centers were used. About four decades ago, with the introduction of computers in data processing and retrieval, and over the past few years, a dramatic change has taken place (Chowdhury & Chowdhury, 2003). The Internet provides:

- Possibilities to communicate via electronic mail (e-mail), mailing listserv, news groups, chat boxes, Wide Area Information Server (WAIS) and the World Wide Web (WWW),
- Electronic resources, such as electronic books (e-books), electronic journals and electronic reports. Institutional repositories/ archives,
- Various programs such as search engines to help users search and find their required information, and social media as a significant online medium for the exchange of health-related information and advice.

Interest in the Internet as a means of communication for obtaining health information is growing rapidly (Tustin, 2010). The sheer volume of information and its availability through the Internet makes people looking for health issues online. Reports show that 44% of people have changed their decision about how to treat the disease after comparing it with online search results (Ghenai, 2017).

As most people use the Internet as a source of health information, the issue of source credibility and trust in websites is important. High quality information does not necessarily indicate trust. For example, a person may understand the desired quality of a message, but due to external factors, such as previous negative experiences do not trust the source and therefore do not act on it. Trust is defined as reliability, and a subjective judgment is whether or not an electronic resource on online health information is worth trusting (Diviani et al., 2015). Searching and sharing information about health and medicine has never been easier in human history, but much of the information available and shared on the Internet is inaccurate and even dangerous.

Thus, finding reliable information requires verifying the large amount of information published through social networks, which has become a complex computational task. Therefore, some studies have examined solutions to deal with misinformation published in virtual disclosure. Such research can be traced back to studies of Dordevic et al. (2016), Sommariva et al. (2018), Seymour et al. (2015), and Nambisan (2011). This research shows the high importance of this issue and the need for further research in this regard. Health professionals are one of the most important sources for developing solutions to deal with online health misinformation. Therefore, the purpose of this study was to identify justified solutions to counteract with online health misinformation from the perspective of health professionals.

LITERATURE REVIEW

Misinformation is harmful to the well-being and health of millions of people and poses a serious threat to public health. The development of sustainable and sound strategies to reduce and combat misinformation is particularly important in the field of covid-19 vaccine distribution. Recently, distrust of the vaccine, due to the dissemination of misinformation, has consistently led to reduced immunization and increased mortality in the United States and the world due to lack of vaccination (Xiang and Lehmann, 2021).
To deal with the effects of misinformation, it is necessary to (Ali, 2020):

- Implement a risk-taking social participation and national communication program that may include details of all recommended public health measures.
- Prioritize two-way communication to gather public feedback and ongoing monitoring.
- Partner with community-based public health care networks, ie non-governmental organizations (NGOs), media platforms, businesses, education providers, health care services and others.
- Promote health care measures using different communication platforms in accordance with national health care containment recommendations.

Accurate dissemination of medical research is crucial in combating misinformation. Evidence suggests that research findings are often represented as larger, better, or worse than in reality or gave a false or misleading account of the nature in press releases and news media. It is important that research findings are presented accurately, impartially and in a balanced way in the biomedical literature. Medical journals may be able to help correct misinformation. Many journals are currently actively teaching and publishing research through social media. Journals can communicate directly with the public by setting up more accurate and accessible summaries of important research findings. In addition, magazine editors can review articles that address controversial health issues (Trethewey, 2020).

One possible solution is to deliberately and carefully review social media posts by experts. Processes of fact-checking can be used in each individual social media context. Further research is needed to identify the most effective ways to examine the health claims on social media. To maximize the effectiveness of the fact-checking process, corrective information should be obtained from reputable expert sources, and specific health messages should be simple. Another way to deal with medical misinformation in virtual media is to reach specific audiences, which is possible through collaboration with social media influencers or keynote leaders. For example, collaborating with bloggers in a particular field of medicine on specific health promotion campaigns may facilitate the dissemination of accurate health information to target audiences. In addition, it may also be helpful to consider new ways to interact directly with people to facilitate open dialogue on controversial health issues. By helping ordinary people develop important scientific skills and health literacy, they can question the validity of health information shared on social media. Because, people with lower health literacy are more likely to trust health information sources on social media and blogs. The threat posed by medical misinformation requires an active and participatory response from key stakeholders, including physicians. Physicians contribute to reduce the medical misinformation by selecting and disseminating evidence-based content to the public through social media (Trethewey, 2020).

There are two targets for each corrective message on social media, 1) the person who shares the misinformation, and (2) the community of people who see the misinformation or correction. These two targets may have different levels of correction resistance. However, even people who share misinformation can be modified, especially in the influence of a close tie. The ability of correction from various sources - algorithms within the platform, expert organizations, and other social media users to reduce health misperceptions is shown in studies (Vraga and Bode, 2020). In addition to correcting the information provided, evaluation of that information is important. Credibility is an important assessment to consider because it shapes how people respond to messages. The more credibility of a message creates the more people to accept it as true (Bode and Vraga, 2017). The ability to validate information from scientific journals is perhaps the most common retaliation against misinformation. Journal information is usually provided by explicitly identifying sources and conflicts of interest, and is regulated through peer review (Merchant and Asch, 2018).

Researchers must defend the available evidence against challenges to the validity and interpretation of their research and, at times, take the lead in ensuring that basic messages do not compete with the correct message. Three factors increase the risk of misinformation. One is the rapid reduction in the cost of publishing information. The second is to increase the users' ability to select information heard. Third, misinformation has no limits and can be strategically designed to spread (Merchant and Asch, 2018).

Misinformation is a public health concern, and health care professionals can correct misinformation on social media. When correcting misinformation on social media, health care professionals perform authentication (for example, internal authentication e.g., author review, cue review, and subject review and external authentication e.g., journal articles and websites of health care institutions) followed by corrective actions (ie, preparation for correction and publication of correction) (Bautista et al., 2021).

METHODOLOGY

The present study is a qualitative study conducted in 2020. In this study, data was collected through in-depth semi-structured interviews with 7 health professionals. Sampling was done by purposive method and snowball and the criterion for determining the number of samples was the theoretical saturation of the data. Participants entered the study with their consent, and ethical standards including anonymity, confidentiality of information, the right to withdraw at any time, and obtaining the necessary permits were observed. The place and time of the interviews were determined according to the interviewee. At the beginning of the interview, explanations about the study and its objectives were given orally and accurately. The duration of each interview varied between 30 and 45 minutes. During or at the end of each interview, by reviewing the main points or a summary of the participants 'answers, an attempt was made to confirm the accuracy of the data, and in case of ambiguity in the interpretation of the participants' answers, they were asked to explain more for having transparency.

Initially, 3 interviews were conducted to formulate questions and details of the main interviews. These interviews were recorded and, while being implemented, the framework of semi-structured interview questions was designed and its face and content validity was assessed with the opinion of two professors of health care and nursing management. After preparing the interview questions by referring to the sample people, the interview was conducted and thus sampling continued until data saturation, which was interviewed with a total of 7 participants.

Data analysis was performed by MAXQDA software. Conventional content analysis method was used in data analysis. Based on this method, the following steps were taken in order, implementing a word-for-word interview tape immediately after each interview, re-reading the text to gain a general understanding of its content, dividing the text into semantic units, extracting a summary of semantic units and coding, classifying primary codes into subcategories and categories based on comparing their similarities and differences, and finally extracting terms as an expression of the content hidden in the data.

In order to determine the accuracy and validity, sampling with maximum diversity and long-term involvement of researchers with data was performed. Participants were also assured that personal information would be kept confidential and that they would be given the freedom to leave the research. To ensure the reliability of the data, data review was used by members of the research team and they checked the accuracy of the coding. In order to provide data transfer capability, a detailed description of the topic, characteristics of the participants, data collection method, interview questions and data analysis method were provided to enable others to follow the research path. This study has also been approved by the relevant authorities with a specific code of ethics.

RESULTS

Participants in this study were 7 people including 5 women and 2 men faculty members, experts and health professionals. Their average work experience was 14 years. After analyzing the data obtained from the interview, 106 initial codes were extracted in relation to the strategies for dealing with misinformation in online health information, which with the aggregation of similar codes, the final number of initial codes was reduced to 100 codes. The extracted codes were placed in 14 items according to the number of codes and the priority of the experts.

Table 1. Themes and sub-themes for the explanation of the strategies to deal with online health misinformation

Themes	Sub-themes
Strategies for dealing with the effects of misinformation	• Training of health workers at all levels, • The effect of face-to-face training on people, • Informing the public about the impossibility of trusting all cyberspace information, • Broadcast educational ads, • Insert a filter to prevent the spread of misinformation, • Information verification, • Value reading and support it, • Increase public awareness of misinformation, • Accurate response by experts, • Learn how to think, • Consider some items in making decisions, • Establishment of organizations responsible for educating people in the field of cyberspace, • Creating culture in this regard, • Creating critical thinking culture in society.

Sub-themes of increasing public awareness in the field of misinformation, public awareness of the impossibility of trusting all cyberspace information and information verification, respectively, accounted for the most extracted codes. The analysis of the interviewees showed that training health workers and then educating people by them is one of the most important things to increase accurate information in cyberspace. In the field of training, face-to-face training has a greater impact on learning the right information. Regarding public awareness of the impossibility of trusting cyberspace information, most experts believed that the general public should not trust health information without a credible source.

Regarding the broadcasting of educational advertisements, the interviewees stated that the use of media for educating and using educational applications are the effective ways to increase accurate information in cyberspace. Regarding the placement of a filter to prevent the dissemination of misinformation, one of the interviewees believed that a filter should be placed to prevent the dissemination of misinformation. In the field of information verification, the review of conversations showed that the information observed in cyberspace should be verified, which can be done by specialized books or questions from experts. Regarding the value of reading and its support, one of the interviewees stated that obtaining the required information from books instead of cyberspace would be an effective step towards increasing the correct information.

Regarding the increase of people's awareness about misinformation, the analysis of the interviewees showed that by increasing the broadcasting of educational programs and designing sites that answer people's questions, their awareness about misinformation can be increased. Regarding accurate response by experts, experts stated that people should consult with physicians about the information needed, and physician-centric media should be designed to correct misinformation by experts. Another important way to increase accurate information in cyberspace from the perspective of research participants was to learn how to think. Regarding the consideration of several items in the decision, the interviewees believed that in order to make the right decision, various factors such as personal characteristics should be considered. Also, organizations should be formed to teach how to use cyberspace properly, and their subdivisions should be present in hospitals and health centers. Creating a culture was another important factor in increasing the correct information in the virtual space from the participants' point of view. According to one of the interviewees, increasing the literacy of health information critique makes people able to use information.

DISCUSSION

Due to the increase in the dissemination of health misinformation in cyberspace, the present study was conducted with the aim of identifying solutions to deal with online health misinformation from the perspective of health professionals. From the results of the study, which was done qualitatively and in the form of content analysis, a main theme called strategies for dealing with the effects of misinformation and 14 sub-themes including training of health workers at all levels, the impact of face-to-face training on people, community awareness to the impossibility of trusting all cyberspace information, broadcasting educational advertisements, putting a filter to prevent the dissemination of misinformation, verifying information, valuing and supporting reading, increasing public awareness about misinformation, accurate response by experts, learning how to think, considering several items in decision-making, forming organizations responsible for educating people in the field of cyberspace, creating a culture in this regard, and creating a culture of critical thinking in society.

Dordevic et al. (2016) in a study conducted in the United States identified key variables on the spread and combat against online misinformation. Seymour et al. (2015) performed a study in the United States with the aim of examining Internet epidemics and the social spread of health misinformation and concluded that due to the vastness of online information and the inaccuracy of many of them, solutions are needed to address misinformation.

Vraga and Bode (2017) conducted a study at an Atlantic university and stressed the need to quickly correct health misinformation published by specialized organizations. In another example, Park et al. (2012) conducted a study in Korea and concluded that organizations should be actively involved in social media and be accountable to people at all times, not just in times of crisis. Also, due to the speed of dissemination of misinformation, they should be ready to respond within a few hours, not a few days. In collaboration with professionals to reduce misinformation about health, Brady et al. (2017) reported in a study in the United States that given the possibility of abuse through social media is very high. It is possible to make sure of the verification of the information being published on the social media by the help of experts. Grech and Masukume (2017) in a study in Iceland found that due to the growing number of misinformation, experts should correct misinformation so as not to lose public confidence in science.

On the relationship between health literacy levels and information received, Paige et al. (2017) conducted a similar study in the United States and concluded that experts should publish health information in channels and valid communication sources based on health literacy and socio-demographic factors of the audience. Another strategy is to train health workers at all levels, which has a great impact on reducing health misinformation in cyberspace. Sommariva et al. (2018) conducted a study in the United States and concluded that health educators need to understand the content of fake news on major public health topics in order to better reduce their effects. Waszak et al. (2018) in another study on Polish-language social media, noted the importance of conducting an extensive training campaign on social media misinformation. Education and thus increasing public awareness are key strategies to reduce the effects of disseminating health misinformation. Valero and Oliveira (2018) in their study of fake news in Spain, concluded that knowledge and education are the best and most important weapons against the spread of fake news.

Due to the increasing dissemination of health misinformation in cyberspace, action to prevent the destructive consequences of such information seems necessary. In this regard, the formation of a health messaging council is useful in order to train and implement strategies to promote public health literacy and with the aim of increasing the speed of information, improving the quality of information, taking care of the continuity and communication of health information in different time periods and dimensions, maintaining and promoting stakeholder support of the program. The council prepares the material in two parts for presentation to the media: health information page and health-oriented news and events page. The council selects and appreciates the top media in the coverage of health information and news annually, and also determines and uses the cost-effective strategies for transmitting health information in accordance with the level of literacy of the people. Strengthening the status and function of such structures can help organize health information in cyberspace. The findings of this study can also be used as a guide for these measures. Due to little research on the subject, the present study has been conducted. This study could be the beginning of more research in this area.

CONCLUSION

Due to the increasing use of virtual space and increasing the dissemination of health information in this space, there is a need to manage published misinformation. The purpose of this study was to identify strategies for counteracting online health misinformation from the perspective of 7 health professionals with the use of content analysis approach. According to the findings of this study, strategies to increase public awareness in the field of misinformation, public awareness of the impossibility of trusting all cyberspace information, and verification of information were the most extracted codes, and this shows the high importance of these strategies. Therefore, from the point of view of the interviewees, the most important way to deal with misinformation in cyberspace is to increase public awareness in this field. The suggested strategies of this study can be used as a guide to deal with online health misinformation.

REFERENCES

Ali, S. (2020). *Combatting against Covid-19 & misinformation: A systematic review*. Human Arenas., doi:10.100742087-020-00139-1

Bautista, J. R., Zhang, Y., & Gwizdka, J. (2021). Healthcare professionals' acts of correcting health misinformation on social media. *International Journal of Medical Informatics, 148*(104375). Advance online publication. doi:10.1016/j.ijmedinf.2021.104375 PMID:33461008

Bode, L., & Vraga, E. K. (2017). See something, say something: Correction of global health misinformation on social media. *Health Communication*, 1–10. doi:10.1080/10410236.2017.1331312 PMID:28622038

Brady, J. T., Kelly, M. E., & Stein, S. L. (2017). The trump effect: With no peer review, how do we know what to really believe on social media? *Clinics in Colon and Rectal Surgery, 30*(04), 270–276. doi:10.1055-0037-1604256 PMID:28924401

Chowdhury, G. G., & Chowdhury, S. C. (2003). *Introduction to digital libraries*. Facet Publishing.

Diviani, N., van den Putte, B., Giani, S., & van Weert, J. C. (2015). Low health literacy and evaluation of online health information: A systematic review of the literature. *Journal of Medical Internet Research, 17*(5), e112. doi:10.2196/jmir.4018 PMID:25953147

Dordevic, M., Safieddine, F., Masri, W., & Pourghomi, P. (2016). Combating misinformation online: Identification of variables and proof-of-concept study. *15th Conference on e-Business, e-Services and e-Society (I3E).*

Ghenai, A. (2017). Health Misinformation in Search and Social Media. In *Proceedings of the 2017 International Conference on Digital Health* (2-10), New York, NY: ACM.

Grech, V., & Masukume, G. (2017). Fake news of baby booms 9 months after major sporting events distorts the public's understanding of early human development science. *Early Human Development, 115*, 16–17. doi:10.1016/j.earlhumdev.2017.08.007

Mahmoudi, H., & Taheri, A. (2015). Relation between information literacy and health literacy of students in Ferdowsi University of Mashhad. *Human Information Interaction, 2*(2), 31–41.

Merchant, R. M., & Asch, D. A. (2018). Protecting the value of medical science in the age of social media and "Fake News". *Journal of the American Medical Association, 320*(23), 2415–2416. doi:10.1001/jama.2018.18416 PMID:30453315

Nambisan, P. (2011). Information seeking and social support in online health communities: Impact on patients' perceived empathy. *Journal of the American Medical Informatics Association: JAMIA, 18*(3), 298–304. doi:10.1136/amiajnl-2010-000058 PMID:21486888

Paige, S. R., Krieger, J. L., & Stellefson, M. L. (2017). The influence of e-health literacy on perceived trust in online health communication channels and sources. *Journal of Health Communication*, *22*(1), 53–65. doi:10.1080/10810730.2016.1250846 PMID:28001489

Park, J., Cha, M., Kim, H., & Jeong, J. (2012). Managing bad news in social media: A case study on Domino's pizza crisis. *Proceedings of the Sixth International AAAI Conference on Weblogs and Social Media*, 282-289.

Seymour, B., Getman, R., Saraf, A., Zhang, L. H., & Kalenderian, E. (2015). When advocacy obscures accuracy online: Digital pandemics of public health misinformation through an antifluoride case study. *American Journal of Public Health*, *105*(3), 517–523. doi:10.2105/AJPH.2014.302437 PMID:25602893

Sommariva, S., Vamos, Ch., Mantzarlis, A., Đào, L. U. L., & Martinez Tyson, D. (2018). Spreading the (fake) news: Exploring health messages on social media and the implications for health professionals using a case study. *American Journal of Health Education*, *49*(4), 246–255. doi:10.1080/19325037.2018.1473178

Sultana, A. (2016). Information seeking behaviour of academics of Maulana Azad national Urdu University in the digital environment. In S. Dhanavandan (Ed.), Transition in librarianship (pp. 245-252). Dominant Publishers annd Distributions Pvt ltd.

Trethewey, S. P. (2020). Strategies to combat medical misinformation on social media. *Postgraduate Medical Journal*, *96*(1131), 4–6. doi:10.1136/postgradmedj-2019-137201 PMID:31732511

Tustin, N. (2010). The role of patient satisfaction in online health information seeking. *Journal of Health Communication*, *15*(1), 3–17. doi:10.1080/10810730903465491 PMID:20390974

Valero, P.P., Oliveira, L. (2018). Fake news: una revision sistemática de la literatura. *Observatorio*, 54-78.

Vraga, E. K., & Bode, L. (2020). Using expert sources to correct health misinformation in social media. *Science Communication*, *39*(5), 621–645. doi:10.1177/1075547017731776

Vraga, E. K., & Bode, L. (2020). Correction as a solution for health misinformation on social media. *American Journal of Public Health*, *110*(53). https://ajph.aphapublications.org/doi/abs/10.2105/AJPH.2020.305916 PMID:33001724

Waszak, P.M., Kasprzycka-Waszak, W., & Kubanek, A. (n.d.). The spread of medical fake news in social media – The pilot quantitative study. *Health Policy and Technology, 7*(2), 115-8. doi:10.1016/j.hlpt.2018.03.002

Xiang, D., & Lehmann, L. S. (2021). Confronting the misinformation pandemic. *Health Policy and Technology, 10*(3), 100520. doi:10.1016/j.hlpt.2021.100520 PMID:34002131

Zhao, Y., & Zhang, J. (2017). Consumer health information seeking in social media: A literature review. *Health Information and Libraries Journal, 34*(4), 268–283. doi:10.1111/hir.12192 PMID:29045011

Chapter 6
A Model of Human Factors in Cyber Security

Maryam Ebrahimi
https://orcid.org/0000-0001-5837-8864
University of Bayreuth, Germany

ABSTRACT

Data has become the new trading currency in today's competitive environment. The human factor is still seen as a significant threat through social engineering channels, despite the advanced technological controls implemented by organizations. Companies can implement appropriate technical solutions, but they are still unable to control the human factor. The aim of the chapter is to better understand the role of human factors in information security. For this purpose, it provides a model that focuses on human-security elements including management commitment, skills, experiences, self-efficacy of human resources, and security culture and training as the vulnerable factors in information security issues. Quantitative methodology and statistical technique are used for analysis. Thus, the main contribution of this research is to present a model of human resource factors in information security that can be applied in several case studies, and the results can be compared.

INTRODUCTION

In today's business, information is recognized as a company's capital and the protection of information and information systems of the organization is one of the important pillars of its survival. The globalization of the economy has created global competition and many companies for the sake of the presence in the global arena have to cooperate with other companies. Thus, the classification, valuation

DOI: 10.4018/978-1-7998-8235-0.ch006

and protection of information resources of the organization (both in the information system and members of the organization) is very vital and important.

Given the modern national economies that are completely dependent on information technology for survival, today the need for information security and information systems is inevitable (Schou and Trimmer, 2004). Numerous national surveys have adapted a large number of attacks on the organization's intelligence resources (Bagchi and Udo, 2003; Gordon et al., 2004; CERT, 2004). Between 1998 and 2003, the number of accidents reported to the US Computer Emergency Response Team almost doubled each year, to which must be added the 529,137 accidents reported in 2003 alone. Management must pay close attention to security in order to maintain and protect organizational information and information systems.

FBI and Crime Scene Investigation in 2008 in respect of cybercrime and security showed that viral attacks were a major cause of financial loss, and that hacking-related incidents had become increasingly common in recent years. Although most respondents to this survey believed in the importance of end-user awareness, many organizations did not provide the necessary training resources. According to the National Cyber Security Alliance in Symantec Home User Study in 2008, 68 percent of users surveyed said they kept sensitive information such as personal, financial and health records on their home computers, 74 percent said they used the Internet for activities such as banking, stock trading, and browsing their personal medical information. In other words, people constantly have access to their banking, financial, and medical records from their computers, which are themselves vulnerable to cyber security threats. Accordingly, organizations have recently been exposed to information security risk, whereby they take preventive measures to maintain organizational information security and control risk. Today, employees use different locations to access organizational information through their mobile phones. Changes in working conditions, especially in crises such as Corona, allow employees to access organizational information by working remotely from their homes. Email-based communication with its attachments is another threat to inbound and outbound traffic (Hazari et al., 2008).

Information security knowledge is essential for all employees or users according to their needs. A lot of information about information security is available through books, the Internet, magazines, etc., but people do not use this information because (Mittal et al., 2010):

- This is a very difficult and time - consuming to obtain specific useful information from the mass of information.
- Users may not be aware of the importance of information security, since they feel that this is the work of information security staff or the IT department.
- There is lack of motivation in acquiring information security knowledge.

- Information security experts are reluctant to share their knowledge with users.
- There is a communication gap or social gap between users and experts.
- Users may not know who specializes in a particular security issue.
- Users are very busy with their regular tasks.
- There is no infrastructure for communication.
- There is a geographical distance between users and professionals.
- Much of the knowledge is experience-based, either implicit and requires coding to share, or a platform for sharing.

Therefore, there may be several reasons for not being aware of security threats and their solutions. But the result is terrible in terms of security incidents, which can lead to information leaks, unavailability, compromise on integrity, etc., and can have major damage in terms of reputation, customer loss, and loss of direct surveillance.

In this study, a conceptual framework has been presented that shows human resources factors influence information security in an organization. The rest of this chapter is organized as follows. Existing literature is reviewed in Section 2, the conceptual model is developed on the basis of the literature in Section 3, the methodology is presented in Section 4, the statistical results of the proposed model are provided in Section 5, and the paper is concluded by some future works in Section 6.

LITERATURE REVIEW

In the 1980s, MIS Quarterly published the results of a review of key issues given to a number of members of the Society of Information Management and a group of IT executives. During the 1980s, security was ranked as a low-ranking issue and never ranked higher than 12 (Knapp et al., 2005). In the 1994 survey, security was removed from the list of the top 20 issues. However, in the 2003 survey, security and privacy fluctuated so much that they were identified as the third most important issue among the survey participants. Table 1 shows a summary of how security issues were ranked during the years 1980 to 2003.

Table 1. Ranking results from the issue of security

Year	Rank
1980	12
1986	18
1989	19
1994	Removed
2003	3

Source: Knapp et al., 2005

Examining the table above, it seems that IT executives today see security as one of their major issues. Information is a set of data that has meaning and purpose; therefore, information is any meaningful data such as printed, paper, electronic, audio and video information and can even include oral discourses between people. The word "security" means protection against attack by an aggressor internally and externally (Khan, 2017). Information security is the process of protecting information against unauthorized activities including access, use, disclosure, disruption, alteration, study, inspection, recording, or destruction. In this definition, the word unauthorized refers to being undesirable and harmful. Accordingly, if authorized persons do not have access to relevant information, undesirable action has been taken and is detrimental to organizational decisions. Today, one of the priorities of managers is to increase information security in organizations (Ransbotham and Mitra, 2009).

Information security issues are usually based on three basic concepts. These three concepts are the main and fundamental factors for achieving information security, which are described below:

- **Confidentiality:** There are two types of data: data that is being transmitted and moving on the network and data that is archived (data that is located on devices such as servers, clients, etc.). Confidentiality means that only authorized individuals and devices can view sensitive or classified information, and others have no access to this data. The main way to protect data is to encrypt it before sending. Another option can be to use a separate network to send confidential information (Information should only be available to relevant people.)
- **Integrity:** Information integrity means that only authorized individuals and systems can make changes to the data (Information must be sound and free of tampering.)
- **Availability:** It relates to data and systems. If the network or its data is not available to authorized users (for reasons such as denial-of-service (DoS or routine network crashes) it can cause serious problems for the organization and users who rely on the network. System failure, including data, applications, devices, and networks, typically reduces an organization's revenue (Information must be available to those in need when needed.)

When it came to data protection, CIA triangle might sound a bit vague. A much simpler solution to change mindset is to have the mindset of a hacker. Hackers intend to do three things with information:

- **Disclosure:** It is against confidentiality. Companies must evaluate and categorize their information. This rarely happens. Employees must always be aware in order to protect a company's information. For example, information can be classified in these three categories: (1) Top secret-disclosure will cause a lot of serious damage to the company (Company closure); (2) Secret-disclosure will cause significant damage to the company (reduction of the company's stock and layoffs); (3) Confidential-disclosure brings shame to the company negative effects on the media; and (4) Public information. Companies need to look at what information disclosure is important to them and their customers. They can then prioritize what information needs the most protection, make it harder, and so on.

- **Destruction:** It is the opposite of integrity. After reviewing important information and determining how vital it is, it is possible to define what happens if it is tampered with or destroyed. Organizations must have solutions to both of these problems. They have to ask themselves what more information an enemy tends to destroy or change.
- **Denial or unavailability:** It is the opposite of availability. The first thing that comes to mind by the word availability is DDoS attacks (attacks that cause a set to crash). DDoS attacks in many cases cause significant damage to a business. Especially for the online businesses, it would have a harder effect, as obviously this is a problem if customers cannot use websites, but in many cases leaking or disclosing their personal information will cause them to no longer use the website.

Figure 1. DDD and CIA dimensions
Source: Rapid 7, 2021

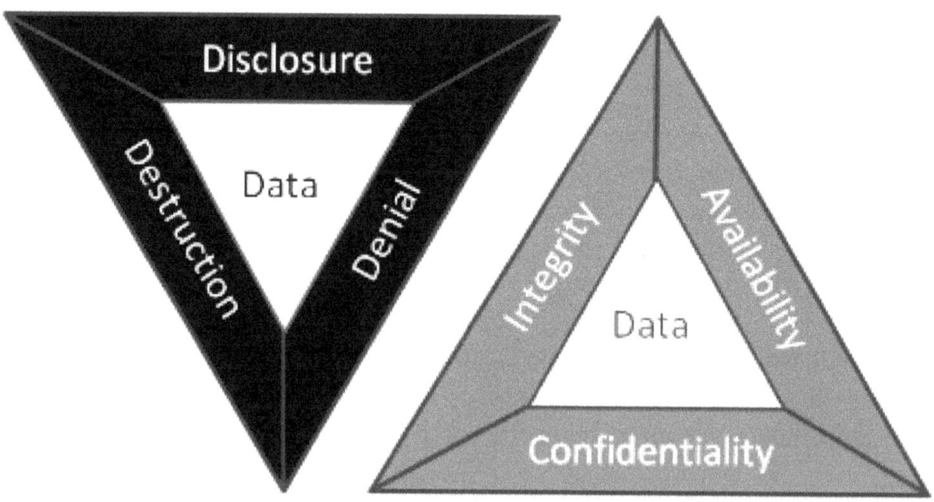

STRIDE Model

To classify threats, STRIDE model was developed by Microsoft. Threat categorizing in this model is done by classifying the type of exploitation used by the attacker or aggressor. In addition, because it detects countless attacks and is a simple yet comprehensive method of identifying a threat, it is recognized as the best approach to create a threat level. Six classes of STRIDE model is as the followings (Shostack, 2014; Meier et al., 2003):

- **Spoofing** is trying to gain access to the system using a false identity (to pretend to be someone else.)
- **Tampering** refers to the unauthorized modification of data (changing information.)
- **Repudiation** is users' ability (legal or otherwise) to deny that they have performed certain actions or transactions (to deny an act.)
- **Disclosure of information** is unwanted private exposure of data (to reveal information to unauthorized ones.)
- **Denial of service** is the process of building an inaccessible system or application (Damaging service for other users.)
- **Elevation of privilege** occurs when a user with limited privileges assumes the identity of a privileged user for privileged access to an asset (to have access while being unauthorized.)

ISO Model

The ISO standard (ISO 7498-2) lists five major effects of security and service threats as a reference model (Jouini et al., 2014):

- Destruction of information and other resources,
- Corruption or modification of information,
- Theft, removal or loss of information and other resources,
- Information disclosure,
- Interruption of services.

Human Factors

So far, most of the research in information security has been in the field of technical issues, and as a result, most of the researches in the field of information security have had technical attitudes and views (Magklaras and Furnell, 2002; Carley, 2000; Gonzalez and Sawicka,2002; Theoharidou et al., 2005; Hinson, 2003) .

Haiynd (2004) stated that in most of the research that has been done in the field of information security of information systems, there has been a technical view and approach, and information security experts are more looking for technical tools such as antivirus, firewalls, etc. to solve problems. Hinson (2003) stated that information security encompasses both technology and the individual. But most organizations see technical solutions as the immediate answer to their security problems. While there are many barriers to a purely technical approach, such as technology is error-prone, the technical solution is costly, security technologies regardless of their effectiveness can be misused or disrupted by users, thereby losing their usefulness. Many factors such as imposing more priority on production and less on security, cost-benefit factors, including understanding of personal gain and loss, conflict between Personal and organizational goals are recognized as affecting factors on compliance with security measures (Gonzalez and Sawicka, 2002).

In the field of information security, few studies have been conducted in which models have been experimentally tested and the limitations and structures related to human behavior and factors or organizational and managerial structures have been used, and if research in this area is done, the behavior of the people is not taken into account; rather, behavioral consequences have been considered (Kotulic and Clark, 2004; Solmsa and Solms, 2005). Numerous experts in the field of information security have emphasized the lack of serious empirical research in these areas (Bagchi and Udo, 2003; Bento and Bento, 2004).

Solms (2006) examined the four waves of information security. The first wave is the technical wave, which deals with providing technical solutions to security issues. The second wave stated that information security has a strong management dimension. Those dimensions, such as policy and management involvement, are very important in this area. The third wave refers to a need for standardization of information security in the company and consists aspects such as the best management practices, the establishment of an appropriate culture of information security, and the measurement and monitoring of information security. The fourth wave is about developing the crucial role of how information security is managed. All of the above must be put together to ensure that the confidentiality, integrity and availability of the company's information assets is maintained at all times. As it is known, from the first wave onwards, management issues in information security have become more prominent, and based on the latest wave of information security, the role of top management, user education and awareness, and security policy are mentioned as its foundations.

Jouini et al. (2014) in their proposed model of security threat classification refer to human-made actions. This class includes threats created by human actions such as insiders or hackers to harm or risk in systems.

Table 2. Human-made security threats

External/Internal	Human	Malicious/ Non malicious	Accidental/ Intentional	• Information destruction • Information corruption • Theft, loss of information • Illegal use • Information disclosure • Denial of use • Elevation of privilege

Source: Jouini et al., 2014

Metalidou et al. (2014) discussed human factors which influence information security.

Table 3. Human factor affecting information security

Lack of Motivation	It is essential for the adoption of secure behaviours and practices.
Lack of awareness	It is relevant to a lack of general knowledge about Attacks
Belief	It refers to the users' beliefs for security policies and actions.
Behavior	It refers to users' behaviors and user-involving approach for the security protection.
Inadequate Use of Technology	It emphasizes the need of continuous human cooperation and the effective use of technologies.
Computer security risks	Risk factors such as social engineering, denial of service, etc.

Source: Metalidou et al., 2014

Colwill (2009) examines some of the key human factors affecting information security. Of the total data losses reported by the UK government since the HRMC incident, only 5% are due to technology issues while 95% are for the sake of cultural factors or individual behavior. The trust and loyalty of employees is sacred. It is declared that organizations with a high percentage of long-term staff have seen more security by strengthening trust in the organization and its willingness to protect the future of employees. These conditions are supported by transparent structures, long-term careers and reward schemes. The resulting organizational culture facilitates the establishment of personal relationships with other employees and their management, and helps to raise levels of trust, loyalty and personal interdependence.

Knapp et al. (2004) presented issues in the field of information security, they pay attention to human and organizational issues. Today, the success of information security largely depends on the effective behavior of employees. Correct and constructive behaviors by users, system administrators, and others can greatly increase the effectiveness of information security; while misbehaving and destructive behaviors can actually hinder its effectiveness.

Vuuren (2016) mentioned social engineering is considered as a common channel for hackers to exploit a vulnerable human environment. Using a combination of social and technical relations of trust, an attacker can manipulate a trusted resource to access to fully protected programs and systems. Human factors such as accountability, leadership/employee behavior, visibility and transparency, knowledge and training, communication and collaboration, understanding and acceptance, awareness, education and trust are discussed as human-security elements.

Figure 2. ITST Model
Source: Vuuren, 2016

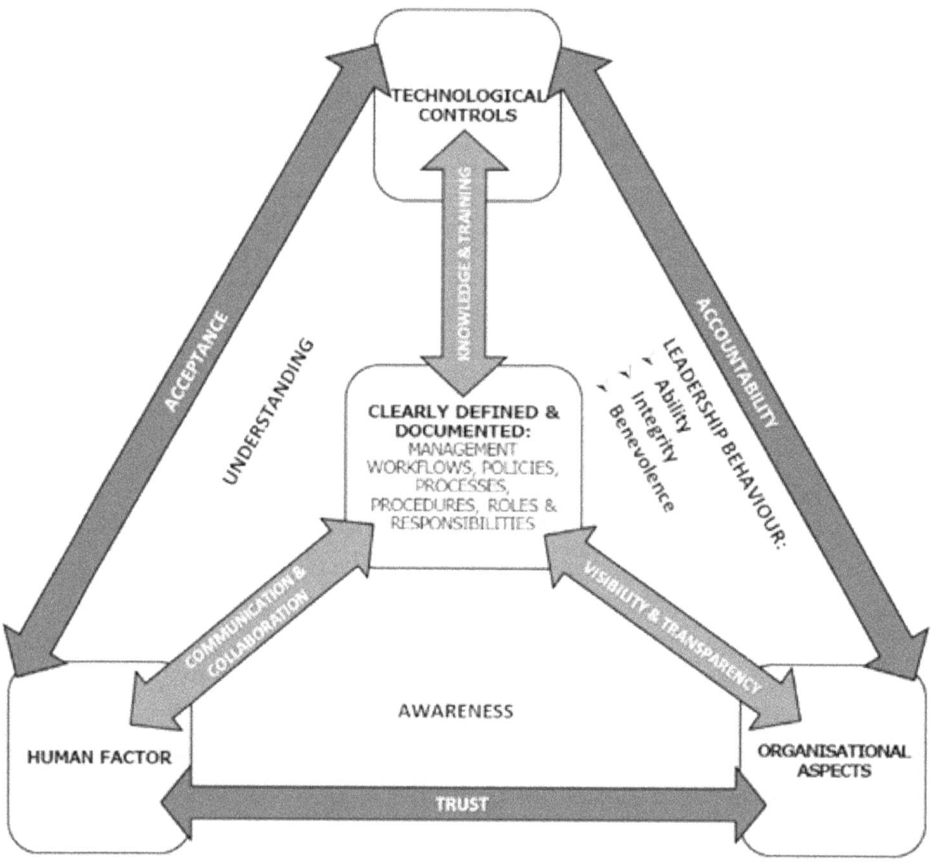

Figure 2 shows the ITST model, which shows the relationship between human trust and security that exists between the three elements of IS implementation, both acting as security and vulnerability controls. In this model, one of important factor presented is trust which refers to the sense of security or security confidence staff have in their company environment.

In a research entitled "detection of anomalies in the network using the illustration of security warnings" conducted by Nasr Mohammadi (2013) some factors are examined which include the experiences, culture, and skill of human resources. Goharian (2015) performed a study entitled "designing an intelligent system for detecting and controlling security risks in the Web 2.0 environment" which examines the experiences and skills of human resources. Kim et al. (2014) in a study entitled "an integrated behavioral model to follow Information security policies" explored the factors that affect the organization's employees' adherence to information security policies. In this study, the effect of factors such as self-efficacy, attitude, and beliefs about compliance costs on the willingness to follow the policies of information security systems was investigated.

CONCEPTUAL MODEL

The present study, in line with the studies conducted, has identified the human factors that affect the effectiveness of information security in the organization. These factors include top management support, human resource training, human resource skills, human resource experience, information security culture, and self-efficacy. Therefore, the research model is as follows.

Figure 3. Research model

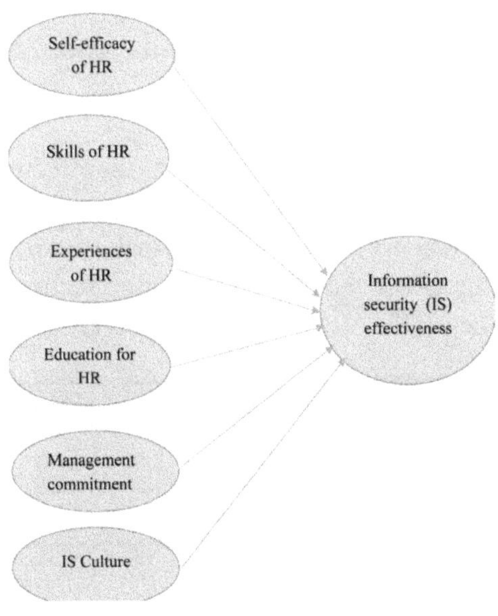

Table 4. Research indicators

No.	Variable	Indicator	References
1	**Self-efficacy of HR**	• Experiences regarding information security • Information security training • Personal judgments related to information security	(Phelps, 2005; Bandura, 1986)
2	**Skills of HR**	• Individual knowledge in the field of information security • Apply information security considerations	(Magklaras and Furnell, 2005)
3	**Experiences of HR**	• Expertise of individuals • Computer skills • Duration of involvement in information security issues	(Phelps, 2005)
4	**Management commitment**	• Involvement of the manager in information security activities • Personal agreement on policies • Prioritize information security	(Knapp et al., 2005; Kearns, 2006)
5	**IS culture**	• Attitudes towards information security • Information security values • Traditions related to information security	(Knapp et al., 2005; Schlienger and Teufel, 2003)
6	**Education for HR**	• Information security training programs Information Security Training Tools	(Knapp et al., 2005; Salanova et al., 2000)

RESEARCH METHODOLOGY

In line with the research model, the following sub-hypotheses according to the main hypothesis that human resources factors affect the effectiveness of information security are analyzed.

Sub-hypothesis 1. Top management support affects the effectiveness of information security.

Sub-hypothesis 2. Education for human resources in the field of information security has an effect on the effectiveness of information security.

Sub-hypothesis 3. The skills of human resources affects the effectiveness of information security.

Sub-hypothesis 4. Human resource experiences affect the effectiveness of information security.

Sub-hypothesis 5. Human resource self-efficacy affects the effectiveness of information security.

Sub-hypothesis 6. Information security culture affects the effectiveness of information security.

The method of collecting information and data required for this research has been done in two ways:

A) Library method: The library method has been used to collect the materials and theories needed to write the research literature through related books, articles, dissertations, and the Internet.

B) Field method: The data of this research was collected through a questionnaire. After reviewing the theoretical literature, the presented models, and using the dimensions and indicators extracted that form the conceptual framework of the research, a researcher-made questionnaire was obtained and after having the expert opinions of respected professors, the final questionnaire was developed to collect field data.

The statistical population of this research includes the employees of a company in the field of information technology, which according to the statistics taken from this organization in 2020 is less than 500 people and based on Morgan table, the number of statistical samples is 200 people selected through simple random sampling.

Validity and Reliability

Using face validity, the questionnaire was provided to the expert professors to confirm the content validity and for a more comprehensive review, the questionnaire was distributed among several employees of the company. Regarding construct validity, the average variance extracted (AVE) is used in SmartPLS software and the acceptance condition is that the average value should be more than 0.5. The results are shown in Table 5.

Table 5. AVE measured for research variables

Variable	AVE
Self-efficacy of HR	0.67
Skills of HR	0.64
Experiences of HR	0.64
Management commitment	0.71
IS culture	0.69
Education for HR	0.63

In a pilot study, 30 questionnaires were distributed among the company's employees. The composite reliability (construct reliability) and Cronbach's alpha coefficient values for all variables were calculated using SmartPLS software and they are more than 0.7. It is worth noting that the CR of each variable is higher than its AVE; therefore, the questionnaire has convergent validity. Additionally, the total Cronbach's alpha coefficient value is 0.95, indicating the appropriate reliability of the questionnaire. The results of reliability are presented in Table 6.

Table 6. The reliability of the variables

Variable	Cronbach's alpha	Composite reliability
Self-efficacy of HR	0.83	0.89
Skills of HR	0.81	0.84
Experiences of HR	0.80	0.85
Management commitment	0.81	0.87
IS culture	0.80	0.86
Education for HR	0.80	0.82
Total	0.95	

Descriptive Statistics

The descriptive statistics of the variables are provided in Table 7.

Table 7. Averages and standard deviations of the variables

Variable	Average	Standard deviation
Self-efficacy of HR	3.26	0.83
Skills of HR	3.15	0.84
Experiences of HR	2.93	0.82
Management commitment	2.75	0.90
IS culture	2.61	1.03
Education for HR	3.30	0.81

For the analysis of central tendency, or the average, of data sets of each variable, it is found that the highest mean is related to education for HR with a value of 3.30 and then self-efficacy of HR with a value of 3.26.

Normality Test

To check the normality of data distribution, the results of the Kolmogorov-Smirnov-Test are presented in Table 8. As a rule of thumb, a variable is not normally distributed if "Sig." < 0.05; therefore, all variable have a normal distribution.

Table 8. The results of the K-S-Test of the variables

Variable	Statistic	df	Sig.
Self-efficacy of HR	0.02	200	0.41
Skills of HR	0.07	200	0.09
Experiences of HR	0.07	200	0.15
Management commitment	0.014	200	0.51
IS culture	0.007	200	0.11
Education for HR	0.08	200	0.07

Hypothesis testing

For hypothesis testing SEM is used. SEM is a very general and robust multivariate analysis of the multivariate regression family that is used to create a general linear model to test a set of regression equations simultaneously. It is used to analyze complex data structures and investigate causal relationships (Ebrahimi, 2021).

Table 9. Coefficients of the hypothesis

Independent variable on dependent	Standard coefficient	t-statistic	Result
Self-efficacy of HR on information security effectiveness	0.29	5.678	Affect
Skills of HR on information security effectiveness	0.022	7.129	Affect
Experiences of HR on information security effectiveness	0.048	4.250	Affect
Management commitment on information security effectiveness	0.144	4.593	Affect
IS culture on information security effectiveness	0.180	3.627	Affect
Education for HR on information security effectiveness	0.343	2.934	Affect

According to Table 9, the positive effect of each six variables on Information security effectiveness is confirmed.

DISCUSSION

According to the research results, human resource skills should be increased to increase information security effectiveness in the organization. This finding is consistent with Wood's research findings in 2000 that skills are essential to employees, and Hinson (2003) who believes human resource skills are essential.

To increase the effectiveness of information security, human resource self-efficacy in the organization must be increased. This finding is consistent with Wood's research findings in 2000 that individuals' self-efficacy is effective in building the safe virtue of the organization, and also with Vroom and Solms's findings in 2004 on the importance of increasing human resource self-confidence.

To increase the effectiveness of information security, the experiences of human factors in the organization should be increased. This result is based on the findings of Nasr Mohammadi (2013) based on the importance of human factors experiences and Goharian (2015) who believes that increasing direct and indirect experiences in individuals increases information security in the organization.

To increase information security effectiveness, a security culture must be created among employees. This result is in line with Shayan's research findings in 2008 based on the importance of security culture, and Pakdaman's findings in 2009 which considers security culture as a necessity of any organization that intends to create information security.

To increase information security effectiveness, staff training should be provided. This result is consistent with the research findings of Shayan (2008) based on the need for education, Pakdaman (2009) based on the need for education for individuals, and Knapp et al. (2004) which considered the need for education to create information security.

To increase the effectiveness of information security, top managers must support staff. This result is consistent with the research findings of Pakdaman (2009) based on the need to support senior management, Vermeclen and solms (1999), who believe that the existence of top management support is essential for the effectiveness of information security in the organization, and Smith (2004) based on the importance of top management support and Knapp et al. (2004) based on the need for top management support in organizations.

CONCLUSION

In this study, an information security model was proposed which is based on human resources factors. For the analysis of the model in an organization, statistical method of structural equations (SEM) was applied. Data was collected through a researcher-made questionnaire with the use of simple random sampling from 200 participants. The validity and reliability of the questionnaire were tested, the hypothesis was modeled and examined. The model can be applied in several case studies and the results can be compared.

Practical suggestions can be proposed as the followings:

- The organization should plan and implement training courses to create a culture of information security.
- The organization must develop and implement a system for information security.
- A team in the organization responsible for information security in the organization should be created.
- Managers are advised to invest more in the field of information security.
- Using the experiences of other companies in information security should be considered.
- The organization must develop trainers in the field of information security.
- Appropriate criteria for staff recruitment in the company should be developed so that new staff, in addition to have more cooperation in the field of information security to facilitate the change of organizational culture.

Suggestions for future studies:

- The model presented in this research is almost a complete model that includes management and human structures related to information security, but other structures such as risk management structures that this model does not include can be added.
- Researchers can study the model presented in this research by using different examples of different cultures or industries to better identify its effect in different fields.
- In the field of the possibility of other relationships between the variables of this research, they can do another research.
- Conducting comparative studies of successful countries in the field of information security in terms of human resources.

REFERENCES

Bagchi, K., & Udo, G. (2003). An Analysis of the Growth of Computer and Internet Security Breaches. *Communications of the AIS*, *12*(46), 684–700. doi:10.17705/1CAIS.01246

Bandura, A. (1986). *Social foundations of thought and action: A social cognitive theory*. Prentice-Hall.

Bento, A., & Bento, R. (2004). Empirical test of a hacking model: An exploratory study. *Communications of the AIS*, *14*(32), 678–690. doi:10.17705/1CAIS.01432

Carley, K. M. (2000). *Information security: The human perspective*. Department of Social and Decision Sciences, Carnegie Mellon University.

Colwill, C. (2009). Human factors in information security: The insider threat- Who can you trust these days? *Information Security Technical Report*, *14*(4), 186–196. doi:10.1016/j.istr.2010.04.004

Computer Emergency Response Team (CERT). (2004). *CERT Statistics*. Retrieved from https://whatis.techtarget.com/definition/CERT-Computer-Emergency-Readiness-Team

Ebrahimi, M. (2021). Analysis of the impact of customer relationship management on innovation acquisition using agent-based modeling. In A. Amini, S. Bushell, & A. Mahmood (Eds.), *Driving innovation and productivity through sustainable automation* (pp. 1–28). IGI Global. doi:10.4018/978-1-7998-5879-9.ch001

Goharian, H. (2015). *Designing an intelligent system for detecting and controlling security risks in the web environment 2* (Master Thesis). Tarbiat Modares University.

Gonzalez, J., & Sawicka, A. (2002). *A framework for human factors in information security*. Retrieved from http://www.wseas.us/e-library/conferences/brazil2002/papers/448-187.pdf

Gordon, L. A., Loeb, M. P., Lucyshyn, W., & Richardson, R. (2004). *The 9th annual CSI/FBI computer crime and security survey*. Computer Security Institute.

Hazari, S., Hargrave, W., & Clenney, B. (2008). An empirical investigation of factors influencing information security behavior. *Journal of Information Privacy & Security*, *4*(4), 3–20. doi:10.1080/2333696X.2008.10855849

Hinson, G. (2003). *Human factors in information security, Innovative information security awareness programs*. Notice Bored.

Jouini, M., Rabai, L. B. A., & Aissa, A. B. (2014). Classification of security threats in information systems. *Procedia Computer Science*, *32*, 489–496. doi:10.1016/j.procs.2014.05.452

Kearns, G. S. (2006). The effect of top management support of SISP on strategic IS management: Insights from the US electric power industry. *Omega*, *34*(3), 236–253. doi:10.1016/j.omega.2004.10.008

Khan, S. A. (2017). A STRIDE model based threat modelling using unified and-or fuzzy operator for computer network security. *International Journal of Computing and Network Technology*, *5*(1), 13–20. doi:10.12785/ijcnt/050103

Kim, S. H., Yang, K. H., & Park, S. (2014). An integrative behavioral model of information security policy compliance. *TheScientificWorldJournal*, *3*, 1–12. doi:10.1155/2014/463870 PMID:24971373

Knapp, K. J., Marshall, T. E., Rainer, R. K., & Ford, N. (2005). *Managerial dimensions in information security: A theoretical model of organizational effectiveness*. Management Information Systems Department College of Business, Auburn University.

Knapp, K. J., Marshall, T. E., Rainer, R. K. Jr, & Morrow, D. W. (2004). *Top ranked information security issues: The 2004 International Information Systems Security Certification Consortium (ISC) 2 Survey Results*. Auburn University.

Kotulic, A. G., & Clark, J. G. (2004). Why there aren't more information security research studies. *Information & Management*, *41*(5), 597–607. doi:10.1016/j.im.2003.08.001

Magklaras, G. B., & Furnell, S. M. (2005). A preliminary model of end user sophistication for insider threat prediction in IT systems. *Computers & Security*, *24*(5), 371–38. doi:10.1016/j.cose.2004.10.003

Meier, J., Mackman, A., Dunner, M., Vasireddy, S., Escamilla, R., & Murukan, A. (2003). *Improving web application security: threats and counter measures*. Microsoft Redmond.

Metalidou, E., Marinagi, C., Trivellas, P., Eberhagen, N., Skourlas, C., & Giannakopoulos, G. (2014). The human factor of information security: Unintentional damage perspective. *Procedia: Social and Behavioral Sciences*, *147*, 424–428. doi:10.1016/j.sbspro.2014.07.133

Mittal, Y. K., Roy, S., & Saxena, M. (2010). Role of knowledge management in enhancing information security. *IJCSI International Journal of Computer Science Issues*, *7*(6), 320–324.

Nasr Mohammadi, M. (2013). *Detection of anomalies in the network using the illustration of security warnings* (Master's thesis). Tarbiat Modares University.

Pakdaman, R. (2009). *Designing the structure and process of certification and accreditation of information and information security* (Master Thesis). Tarbiat Modares University.

Phelps, D. (2005). *Information system security: self-efficacy and security effectiveness in Florida Libraries*. PhD dissertation

Ransbotham, S., & Sabyasachi, M. (2009). Choice and chance: A conceptual model of paths to information security compromise. *Information Systems Research*, *20*(1), 121–139. doi:10.1287/isre.1080.0174

Rapid7. (2011). Retrieved form https://www.rapid7.com/blog/post/2011/07/19/the-attackers-triad/

Salanova, M., Grau, R. M., Cifre, E., & Llorens, S. (2000). Computer training, frequency of usage and burnout: The moderating role of computer self-efficacy. *Computers in Human Behavior*, *16*(6), 575–590. doi:10.1016/S0747-5632(00)00028-5

Schlienger, T., & Teufel, S. (2003). Analyzing information security culture: Increasing trust by an appropriate information security culture. *The 14th International Conference on Database and Expert Systems Applications (DEXA 2003)*.

Schou, C. D., & Trimmer, K. J. (2004). Information assurance and security. *Journal of Organizational and End User Computing*, *16*(3), i–vii.

Shayan, A. (2008). *Designing a comprehensive model of information security management in electronic banking* (Master Thesis). Tarbiat Modares University.

Shostack, A. (2014). *Threat modeling: Designing for security*. John Wiley & Sons.

Smith, J. (2004). Social cognitive theory of organizational management. *Academy of Management Journal*.

Solms, B. (2006). Information ssecurity – the fourth wave. *Computers & Security*, *25*(3), 165–168. doi:10.1016/j.cose.2006.03.004

Solmsa, B., & Solms, R. (2005). From information security to business security? *Computers & Security*, *24*(4), 271–273. doi:10.1016/j.cose.2005.04.004

Theoharidou, M., Kokolakis, S., Karyda, M., & Kiountouzis, E. (2005). The insider threat to information systems and the effectiveness of ISO17799. *Computers & Security*, *24*(6), 472–484. doi:10.1016/j.cose.2005.05.002

Vermeclen, C., & von Solms, R. (1999). Information security policy. Department of Computer Science.

Vroom, C., & Solms, R. (2004). Towards information security behavioral compliance. *Computers & Security*, *23*(3), 191–198. doi:10.1016/j.cose.2004.01.012

Vuuren, I. E. V. (2016). IT Security Trust Model—Securing the Human Perimeter. *International Journal of Social Science and Humanity*, *6*(11), 852–858. doi:10.18178/ijssh.2016.V6.761

Wood, C. (2000). An unappreciated reason why security policies fail. *Computer Fraud & Security*, *10*(10), 13–14. doi:10.1016/S1361-3723(00)10029-6

Chapter 7
Information Literacy and Its Effects on Spotting Misinformation

John Ryan
Independent Researcher, Canada

ABSTRACT

Facing diverse unverified and verified sources of information, users have to be considerably notified of the best accessible information sources to make informed decisions. The main purpose of this study is to determine the relationship between information literacy and the ability to detect fake news based on structural equation model using data from 300 samples selected through cluster sampling. It is indicated that there is a relationship between information literacy and the ability to spot fake news. Therefore, users should have prerequisite skills to distinguish between fake news and factual content by way of improving the quality of literacy programs of education institutions and promoting a culture of reading and critical thinking.

INTRODUCTION

Nowadays, we are witnessing a lot of advances in information technology and we are in contact with this advanced world every day in our workplace, school or everyday life. Access to and use of information or information literacy is very important, which refers to the ability to correctly identify information sources, access them, and use the target purposefully.

Since currently information is mostly transmitted through virtual social networks, these networks are most similar to human society and the individual is able to

DOI: 10.4018/978-1-7998-8235-0.ch007

communicate with a large number of other people (Katz & Aspden, 1997), regardless of temporal, spatial, political, cultural and economic limitations (Kraut et al., 2002); therefore, there is a close relationship between information literacy and social networks. Individuals are able to get a lot of information by joining a virtual social network. Transmitting information through virtual social networks is a normal thing and a large amount of correct and incorrect information is published daily through these communication channels between people with different levels of literacy.

Every day more and more unfiltered information is seen that people are skeptical about to ensure their credibility and should be able to use a tool to ensure. The issue of accuracy of information published and reproduced in virtual social networks is seriously questioned. Therefore, users in virtual social networks must be able to distinguish correct information from incorrect information, which, if not done, will impair the process of sending correct information to others. Today, the importance of information literacy is not hidden from anyone, so without it, it is not possible to find the right way through the huge amount of information and reach the destination. In addition to measuring the level of skill in users, the effects that are accompanied by the increasing transfer of information via these networks in society should be considered.

In this study, in order to better compare and more accurately investigate the effect of information literacy on the accuracy of information of social network users, according to the questionnaire, respondents have a general difference in publishing / republishing messages that divide them into two groups of one and two. Group one is the users who have not paid attention to the accuracy of the messages on social networks and have attempted to publish or republish the message, regardless of its accuracy, and group two are users who have paid attention to the accuracy of the messages and have published or they did not republish the message without considering its accuracy. It is possible to produce content on social networks, without any restrictions for different people with any kind of education and specialization. The important thing is to be able to understand these specific goals and intentions of people in the meantime.

It is very difficult for us to recognize and understand these messages in networks, so that it confuses users in order to accept the accuracy of this information, that is, people must be able to distinguish the correct information from the multitude of messages. Many of the messages that are circulated daily by social media users are a kind of rumor and are sent and broadcast for specific purposes, or at best it can be stated that they are false and are published without knowing their accuracy.

The following are the hypotheses of this research:

- **Hypothesis 1:** There is a significant relationship between the accuracy of information published by social network users who publish or republish news without regard to the reliability and accuracy of information and their information literacy.

- **Hypothesis 2:** There is a significant relationship between the accuracy of information published by users of social networks who do not publish or republish news regardless of the reliability and accuracy of information of social networks and their information literacy.
- **Hypothesis 3:** There is a significant direct relationship between the level of information literacy and the level of education of virtual social network users.

If users do not have enough literacy and knowledge to determine the accuracy of published information, they become passive recipients of media information and claims and then republish this sometimes fake undocumented information. Therefore, addressing the issue of information literacy should be considered as one of the most essential needs for social network users. Therefore, the purpose of this study is to investigate the effect of users' information literacy level on the accuracy of information published on social networks. To be more precise, the present study aims to answer the question of how much does the information literacy of users affect the accuracy of the messages posted by them in virtual social networks?

Some Internet users are members of several social networks that they visit daily and use most of their features, and others may be members of only one network and occasionally refer only to their personal page. Between these two groups, Internet users are in a wide range according to the amount and type of their use of social networks. Internet users are categorized in different ways according to how they encounter social networks. In this study, users are members of the Telegram social network and visit it at least once or twice a week and at least read various information messages or generate messages themselves or send incoming messages to others without change. Due to the diversity and multiplicity of users, used have examined in different groups and channels in the Telegram virtual social network.

LITERATURE REVIEW

Much research has been done on information literacy, social networks and related concepts, but the relationship between the accuracy of information produced or reproduced on social networks and the information literacy of their publishers has not been considered. Concepts such as information pollution have also been studied in the background, which are closely related to the accuracy of the information. For example, Chamberlian (2009) in a study by presenting Twitter as a channel for producing a lot of information and describing its intentional and unintentional role in polluting information, introduced it as a powerful tool in causing such a phenomenon to occur.

The research of Cuadrado-Garcia et al. (2012) is one of the rare studies that exmined the impact of social networks on information literacy and the ability to use technology on students. To conduct this research, they distributed educational videos as well as a questionnaire through the Tuenti social network among the students. The results of this research show that Tuenti and Facebook are the two most popular social networks among the students. Sending messages is the most common use of these websites among students. Regarding students' understanding of information literacy and technology, "the importance of the Internet for information", "the importance of new technologies" and "the importance of information" had the highest score. In contrast, "software use" is less understood by students.

Stec and Varlejs (2014) focus specifically on students' information literacy, and examined whether schools were able to have they trained students with the necessary skills to enter the university or not? The results of this study suggest that school librarians are rarely in a position to engage with teachers and that opportunities to assist students in information literacy skills are limited.

Some researchers have linked information literacy to the use of technology (Tapaloglu and Tekkanat, 2015) examined the two-way relationship between the level of literacy in information technology and the level of literacy in the use of information technology. The statistical sample of this study was 200 undergraduate students and students studying at Trakya University. In this study, students had no problem in "problem solving" skills. Another point is that according to the tests taken, there was no significant difference in the development of skills and the duration of use of information technology, which can be attributed to the fact that the development of skills is created through education.

In Parirokh and Moghadaszadeh (1999) research, the level of information literacy of graduate students of Ferdowsi University has been measured. This study showed that students are not equipped with information literacy skills and it is suggested that librarians should first master these skills and then teach students.

Some researchers have specifically focused on teaching information literacy and have tried to integrate information literacy with distance learning environments. The research of Nikkar (2008) is one of these studies that has reached interesting results regarding information literacy: the use of new technologies requires information literacy skills that must be combined with distance learning curricula and offer them to students in the form of credits.

The connection between information literacy and virtual environments and social networks has been considered in some internal studies. Ziaee Parvar and Aghili (2009) should be considered among the first researchers, who considered the extent of social network penetration and in their study was found that 78% Internet users in Iran are members of one of the types of virtual social networks and for most Internet users in Iran, virtual social networks, in addition to the function of making friends, also have the function of obtaining information and news. Making the connection between critical thinking and information literacy also draws attention in the background. For example, Moradi et al. (2014) in a study have found that there is a direct relationship between critical thinking skill and its sub-components with information literacy. Thus, enhancement of the information literacy among medical students depend on the process of critical thinking.

The formation of rumors on the basis of social networks should be considered as one of the immediate consequences of users entering social networks. Turkman and Shahabi (2016) specifically focused on the topic of "rumors and social factors affecting its acceptance" and found that the acceptance of rumor (dependent variable) has a significant relationship with independent variables (subject importance, subject ambiguity, rumor source). The source of rumors (people) with the beta coefficient (0.344) have the greatest impact on the acceptance of rumors. The study of individual components has also shown that there is a significant relationship between age and education with acceptance of rumors but between gender and occupation with acceptance of rumors no significant relationship was observed.

A review of a number of studies conducted on virtual social networks and information literacy shows that researchers focused on subjects such as information literacy, its relationship with virtual environments as well as information literacy training projects on the one hand and concepts including social networks, the rate of penetration and their effects. But there is a serious research gap in understanding the function of information literacy in social networks, especially in terms of impact on the accuracy of the content of information produced and reproduced in these networks. The present study seeks to address this issue and fill the gap of serious research in this field. The main hypothesis of this study is that the level of information literacy of users on the accuracy of messages posted by them on social networks (whether published or republished) has a significant relationship.

METHODOLOGY

This research, which is of an applied type, uses a two-part questionnaire to collect information. The first part includes the information literacy of users and the second part includes the accuracy of the information published by users on social networks. Due to the fact that in the field of information literacy, numerous researches have been done and there are standard questionnaires in this field, the questionnaire of the research of the Zerehsaz (2015) has been used. The dimensions of information literacy were divided into the following categories:

1. **Introductory information literacy skills:** Including elements related to identifying information needs (items 1 and 2 of the questionnaire), question/problem formulation (items 3 and 4 of the questionnaire), and evaluation of information resources (items 5 and 6 of the questionnaire).
2. **Fundamental information literacy skills:** Including elements related to retrieved assessment (items 7 and 8 of the questionnaire), information locating (items 9,10,11,12 of the questionnaire), information retrieval (items 13, 14, 10 of the questionnaire), information utilization (items 15 and 16 of the questionnaire) (Zerehsaz, 2015).

For the accuracy of the information, the three main indicators of documented content, content health, and expertise of the narrator were considered: the documentability of the content with 6 questions, the health index with 8 questions and the expertise of the narrator with 2 questions were represented.

The statistical population of this study included all users of the virtual social network. Due to the unlimited and uncertain nature of the statistical population, the present questionnaire was distributed virtually among users of 20 groups or channels. The online form was designed and sent to individuals through the freelinesurveys website. It is attempted to select members in various channels and groups so that it is possible to have all kinds of users in this social network. Out of 300 questionnaires sent to users, 210 questionnaires were returned, of which 35 questionnaires were unusable data due to the lack of coordination between the answers to self-assessment questions and objective questions; therefore, they were removed from the statistical sample and finally this study was performed with 165 correct data.

In order to determine the validity of the questionnaires from face content validity and to determine the reliability of the instrument, its alpha coefficient was calculated. Cronbach's alpha coefficient was 0.894 for the information accuracy section and 0.875 for the Cronbach's alpha information literacy section. Therefore, the questionnaire had the necessary reliability in two parts of literacy and information accuracy.

RESULTS

The data collection showed that 50% of the users of virtual networks have a master degree, 37% of them have a bachelor degree, 9.1% have a doctorate, and 2.4% have a diploma and 1.2% have an associate degree.

Figure 1. Demographic characteristics- Level of education

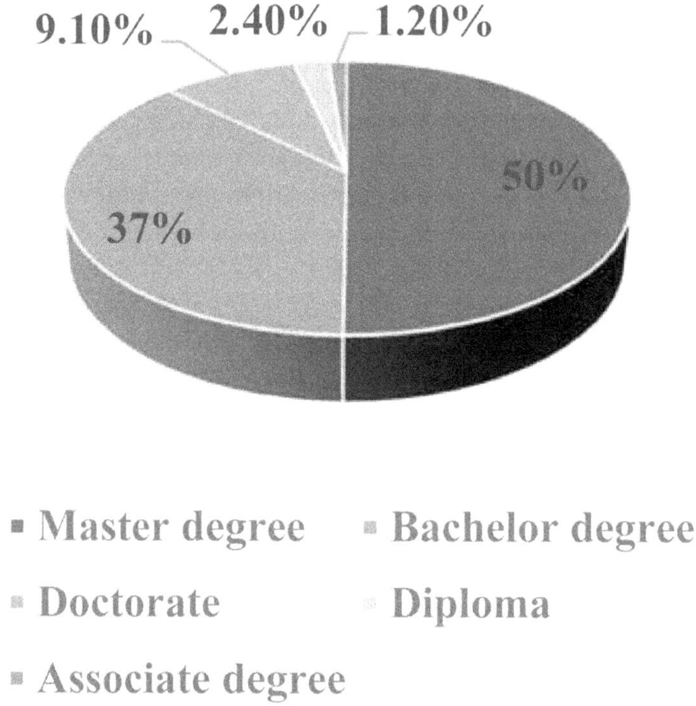

Statistical sample includes different people from different social spectrums (Figure 2). Students have the most users with 27%. Employees, librarians, teachers, and freelancers are next with 18, 7, and 5 percent, respectively. University lecturers, faculty members, physicians and nurses accounted for 4%. 3% of users are housewives, which is the same number of architects and civil engineers. 30% were managers, designers, as well as computer programmers and computer science specialists. Reporters make up 1.5 percent. Researchers, network specialists, soldiers and the unemployed were 1 percent. Less than one percent also belong to publishers or investment consultants.

Figure 3 shows the time users spend on the Telegram social network. According to the chart, 43% of people spend between one and three hours a day on these networks. 28% of people spend an hour or less, 15% of people spend more than 5 hours and 14% of people spend 3 to 5 hours a day on social media.

The number of posts reposted or published by social media users was assessed through a research questionnaire. According to Figure 4, 83.71% of people share between 1 and 15 posts on social networks daily. 8.322% of people produce or republish between 15 and 25 posts. 4.66 percent of people share more than 50 posts,

2.22 percent between 25 and 35 posts and less than one percent between 35 and 50 posts modestly produce or republish.

Figure 2. Demographic characteristics- Job

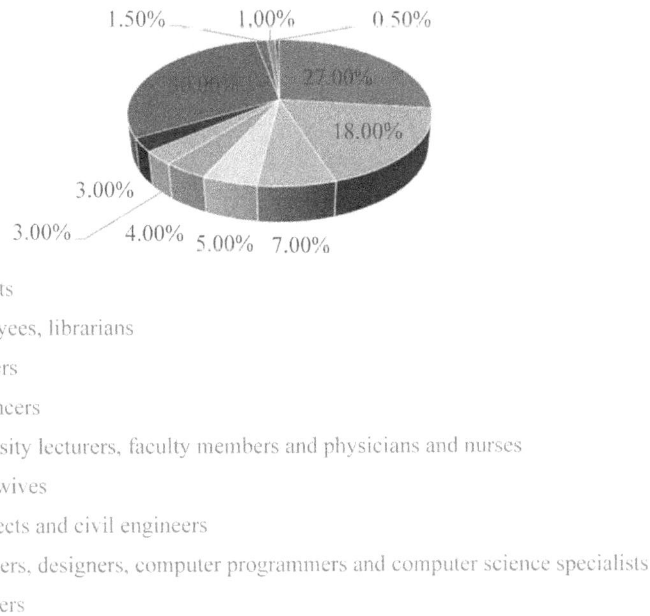

Figure 3. Demographic characteristics- Time spent in social media per day

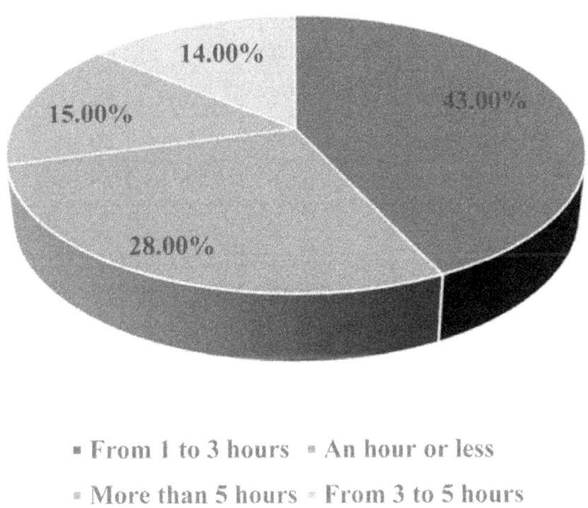

Figure 4. Demographic characteristics- Number of posts per day

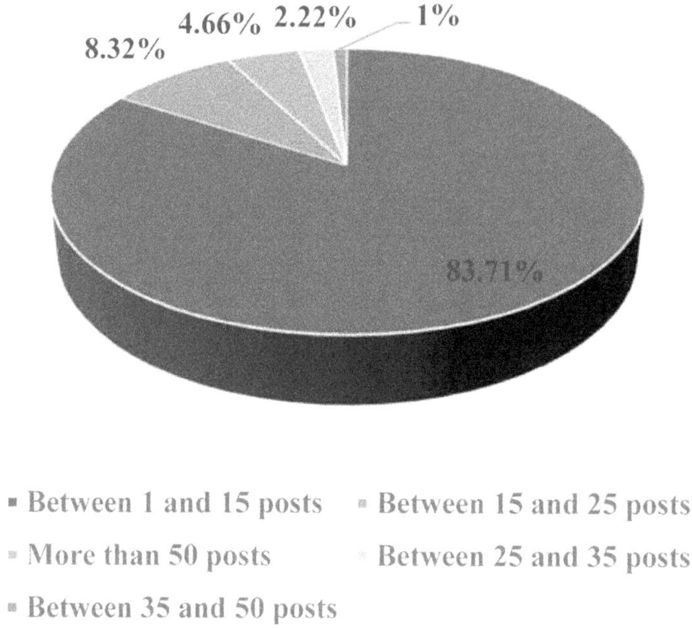

Information about the attention of users on the accuracy of information as well as user information literacy is given in Table 1.

Table 1. Users' attention on the accuracy of information in social networks and users' information literacy

Component	Indicator	Average
Accuracy of information	Documentability	3.72
	Health	3.73
	Messenger specialty	3.54

According to Table 1, all expressed variables are above average. In other words, users' attention to items related to the accuracy of the information, which includes documentability, health, and expertise of the messenger, has been more than desirable. Among these three indicators, the least attention is paid to the message conveying expertise with an average of 3.54.

Table 2. Users' information literacy rate

Component	Indicator	Average
Information literacy	Information use	3.76
	Identify information needs	3.74
	Formulate a question or problem	3.63
	Evaluate information resources	3.47
	Evaluate retrieved information	3.51
	Locating information	3.53
	Data recovery	3.60

Also shown in Table 2, the level of information literacy of users in all 7 indicators is higher than average. The index of information use has the highest average of 3.76, followed by the index of information needs with an average of 3.74. On the other hand, the evaluation index of information resources has an average of 3.47 and the lowest average.

Table 3 shows the average attention of users on information accuracy and information literacy in two groups of one and two. According to this table in group two, the average of the total accuracy of the information is 3.86, which, although higher than group one, is still in the average range. Regarding information literacy in group two, it is concluded that the average information literacy in group two is 3.61, but it is still in the middle ground. This means that people may not have high information literacy; however, they pay attention to the accuracy of the information published on social networks, and people's information literacy does not have a significant effect on the accuracy of the information published on social networks. In the following, it is reviewed the results of the hypotheses.

Table 3. Average attention of users on the accuracy of information in social networks and information literacy of users in two groups of one and two

Average of The	Value
The average of the total accuracy of the information in group one	3.48
The average of the total accuracy of the information in group two	3.86
Average of total information literacy in group one	3.57
The average of total information literacy in group two	3.61

Hypothesis 1: There is a significant relationship between the accuracy of information published by social network users who publish or republish news without regard to the reliability and accuracy of information and their information literacy

Due to the non-normality of the data, the nonparametric Spearman test was used. The results showed that there is a positive and significant relationship between the the accuracy of information published and information literacy of people who have attempted to publish or republish news without regard to the reliability and accuracy of the information, given that the correlation value is less than 0.50. This difference was less severe ($p < 0.01$).

Table 4. Spearman correlation coefficient test result for correlation between information literacy and information accuracy in group one

		Information accuracy Group (1)	**Information literacy Group (1)**
Information accuracy	Correlation coefficient	1.000	**0.296
	Significance (two-way)	0	0.009
	Number	76	76
Information literacy	Correlation coefficient	**0.296	1.000
	Significance (two-way)	0.009	0
	Number	76	76
Correlation at the level of 0.01 **			

Hypothesis 2: There is a significant relationship between the accuracy of information published by social network users who do not publish or republish news regardless of the reliability and accuracy of social media information, and their information literacy.

Pearson correlation test between information literacy and accuracy of information published on social networks for users who do not republish and send information without knowing the reliability and accuracy of the news, according to Table 7 is as follows between information accuracy and literacy in group two, there is a positive and significant relationship, but due to the correlation value which is less than 0.05, the difference between the two is less intense ($p < 0.5$).

Table 5. Spearman correlation coefficient test result for correlation between information literacy and information accuracy in group two

		Information accuracy Group (2)	Information literacy Group (2)
Information accuracy	Correlation coefficient	1.000	**0.254
	Significance (two-way)	0	0.019
	Number	85	85
Information literacy	Correlation coefficient	**0.254	1.000
	Significance (two-way)	0.019	0
	Number	85	85
Correlation at the level of 0.01 **			

Hypothesis 3: There is a significant direct relationship between the level of information literacy and the level of education of virtual social network users.

The relationship between information literacy of social network users and their level of education was also determined in this study through Pearson correlation test, based on which there is no significant difference between information literacy and users' level of education.

Table 6. Spearman correlation coefficient test result for the correlation between users' information literacy and their level of education

		Level of education	Information literacy
Level of education	Correlation coefficient	1.000	0.147
	Significance (two-way)	0	0.059
	Number	165	165
Information literacy	Correlation coefficient	0.147	1.000
	Significance (two-way)	0.059	0
	Number	165	165

DISCUSSION

In the research of Tapaloglu and Tekkanat (2015), the level of students' literacy regarding information technology and the use of this technology has been examined, according to which students are trained in technology-related skills at the basic information level and Internet and information skills at the high level. While they were not at a good level in problem solving skills. Another noteworthy point is that there is no significant relationship between the duration of technology use and the development of these skills. Students should be taught the use of technology and these skills can not be expected to increase in students through experience.

The status of information literacy of social network users based on the results obtained in this study is generally in the middle range and among the seven indicators of information literacy, which include identifying information needs, formulating a question / problem, evaluating information resources, evaluation of retrieved information, information locating, information retrieval, and information utilization, users are the most skilled in the information utilization stage and this index is among the users with an average of 3.76. Moradi et al. (2014) in a study entitled the relationship between critical thinking and information literacy in medical students have concluded that there is a direct relationship between critical thinking skills and its sub-components with information literacy.

Based on the results obtained in this study, there is a significant relationship between information literacy and information accuracy in both groups, but according to the test value in each group there is no high correlation between information literacy and accuracy of published information.

Turkman and Shahabi (2016). has reached significant results in a study on the subject of rumor and social factors affecting its acceptance. There is no significant relationship between the job and rumor acceptance.

Compared to the results of the study of Chamberlian (2009) entitled as Twitter, a path to information pollution, it should be noted that in this study, by examining the social network Twitter as one of the most popular and powerful virtual social networks in the world, it is used to spread misinformation among users. It is possible to use Twitter for various organizations to spread true and false information through unreal and popular accounts. As a result, social networks need to be aware of the dangers of rolling out information using these channels. There should be different strategies to ensure the distribution of correct information.

The Effect of Rapid Information Transfer on Social Networks

Toffler's theory is based on three historical periods (three waves or universal civilizations). The first wave of civilization, the agricultural revolution, the second wave, the emergence of industrial civilization, and the third wave will affect us all by disintegrating our families, shaking our economy, crippling our political systems, and shattering our values. In stating this theory, Toffler believes that during the third wave of diversification and rapid change of products, in fact, companies are trying to train customers and create false needs in people and thus make more profit by offering expensive and exclusive goods (Toffler, 1980).

According to Toffler's third wave theory, the decisions of individuals in this period are accelerated due to competition and information transfer. The rapid transfer of information through social networks makes people act faster in decisions, and this may affect the quality of the decision. All of these factors lead people to fall into the trap of misinformation with more tricks. Perhaps it is the case that in the virtual world there are so many attractions that people are busy for many hours during the day and finally for many years that they no longer even pay attention to important issues. The question is, what benefit can the busyness of users in these networks have for which individuals or groups? Cultural battles are battles for power in the information age. These battles take place mainly in or through the media, but the media does not have power. Power, as the ability to impose behavior, lies in information exchange networks and the skillful use of symbols that connect social actors, symbols, and cultural movements through symbols, speakers, and intellectual reinforcers.

Behavior Pattern of Users in Social Networks

It can be said that the use of media is used to promote and impose certain beliefs and cultures, and the media, especially social networks that have certain characteristics, are a good platform for individuals and groups who want to spread their information and ideas in the community.

Users of any social network are accustomed to its virtual environment. It should be noted that the pattern of behavior in social networks is more or less the same for users who by sending and transmitting information support groups seeking power. Users in this space, after creating profiles and membership steps, develop their space by participating in the space and with the help of the site's multimedia capabilities such as posting photos, text, content or links to external content. Sending or republishing messages to users has become a template. Users in social networks send and republish news and information by imitating each other, rather than thinking about them or paying attention to more important issues such as the purpose of sending this message or the consequences of republishing it.

The Impact of Virtual Social Networks on Behavioral Patterns and Values in Society

According to Albert Bandura's theory of social learning, most people do not learn what they need to guide and act in life simply from direct experience and observation, but most of it is learned indirectly, especially through mass media. The main claim is that most human behaviors are learned by observing the behavior of others and by modeling. Dissemination of various information in virtual social networks has become a model for users, regardless of the accuracy of the message. So that users can follow the pattern by observing the behavior (republish the message) from other people, and after having the desired feedback from different people, they have necessary motivation to repeat the action of republishing. The preference of doing so outweighs the issues such as the correctness of the content and their accuracy.

So it can be said that the media in general and now, virtual social networks in particular, have a great impact on the values, patterns and performance of people in society. This allows individuals and groups take advantage of this powerful platform, and it is the users who must be familiar with this process and have the information and literacy to deal with it.

CONCLUSION

According to the tables of the average of indicators of information literacy and information accuracy in the previous section, it can be concluded that social network users have more than average information literacy, in other words, close to relatively desirable. Also, users' attention to the indicators of accuracy of information published in virtual networks is higher than the average of their information literacy indicators and close to a relatively desirable area. This reminds us to pay more attention to both information literacy and users' attention to information accuracy.

Regarding groups one and two, it should be noted that people in group one with an average of 3.48 in terms of information accuracy on social networks and an average of 3.57 in information literacy are in a situation above average, and group two, in terms of information accuracy In social networks with an average of 3.86 and in the field of information literacy 3.61 in the above-average situation; but they are more than group one. As stated above:

The group two was expected to pay close attention to the accuracy of the information, stating that they paid attention to the accuracy of the information. Also, according to Table 2, it can be stated that users 'attention to information accuracy indicators has been in the medium range and among the three indicators of documentability, health and expertise of message transmitters, users' attention to message health in social networks with an average of 3.73 has highest attention and message expertise index with an average of 3.54 has received the least attention from users.

As mentioned previously, there is no significant difference between the information literacy of virtual social network users and their level of education. The level of education of individuals is not compatible with their information literacy. This means that people with higher education can not be expected to be at a high level in terms of information literacy, given that having information literacy is essential for all people, especially educated people, so it should be possible to learn this important skill. It should be taken more seriously in university courses and also devised measures to increase this skill among all sections of society.

REFERENCES

Chamberlain, P. R. (2010). Twitter as a vector for disinformation. *Journal of Information Warfare*, *9*(1), 11-17.

Cuadrado-Garcia, M., Ruiz-Mol, M., & Montoro-Pons, J. D. (2012). Academic contest and social networking to promote technology and information literacy among university students. *Procedia: Social and Behavioral Sciences*, *46*(10), 222–226. doi:10.1016/j.sbspro.2012.05.097

Katz, E. J., & Aspden, P. (1997). A nation of strangers? *Communications of the ACM, 40*(12), 81-86. doi:10.1145/265563.265575

Kraut, R., Kiesler, S., Boneva, B., Cummings, J., Helgeson, V., & Crawford, A. (2002). Internet paradox revisited. *Journal of Social Issues*, *58*(1), 49-74.

Moradi, R., Aliabadi, K., Khazayi, A., & Rasuli, B. (2014). The relationship between critical thinking and information literacy in medical students. *Teaching Strategies in Medical Sciences*, *3*(7), 141–147.

Nikkar, M. (2008). Information literacy training plan in distance learning environment. *Peyke Nour*, *6*(3), 43-51.

Parirokh, M., Moghadaszadeh, H. (1999). Information Literacy: A research on how to acquire information literacy. *Journal of the Faculty of Literature and Humanities*, (1-2), 318-334.

Stec, E., & Varlejs, J. (2014). *Factors affecting students' information literacy as they transition from high school to college.* School Library Media Research. Retreived 2016, May 31 from https://www.ala.org/aasl/sites/ala.org.aasl/files/content/aaslpubsandjournals/slr/vol17/SLR_FactorsAffecting_V17.pdf

Toffler, L. (1980). *The third wave*. William Morrow.

Topaloglu, M., & Tekkanat, E. (2015). Identifying the usage of information technologies and literacy levels. *Procedia-Social and Behavioral Sciences*, *182*(3), 574–583. doi:10.1016/j.sbspro.2015.04.784

Turkman, F., & Shahabi, Z. (2016). Rumors and social factors affecting its acceptance. *Socio-Cultural Strategy*, *5*(19), 191-216.

Zerehsaz, M. (2015). *Analysis of the relationship between psychological and skill capabilities of users with their guiding behavior based on the modified model of Marchionni information* (PhD thesis). Shahid Ferdowsi University of Mashhad, Faculty of Educational Sciences and Psychology.

Ziaee Parvar, H., & Aghili, S. V. (2009). Investigating the influence of social networks among Iranian users. *Rashaneh*, *20*(4), 23–42.

Chapter 8
Lies and Deceit vs. Social Capital

John Ryan
Independent Researcher, Canada

ABSTRACT

Misleading statements and outright lies by governmental figures might reduce economic growth rates and would result in a substantially lower level of economic well-being. The lie is the induction of false belief with the aim of misleading the audience in any way possible. Although a liar knows lying has its costs, he lies in the hope of gaining short-term benefits. Lies accumulated reduce trust, increase transaction costs in the business environment, create dysfunctional balances, all of which are factors in the decline of well-being. The aim of this study is to analyze the economics literature on lies in terms of lying's effects on harming social capital, destroying the expected functions of institutions, increasing transaction costs, and creating asymmetric information.

INTRODUCTION

Economic analysis of lie is possible because this action is influenced by conflicting motives as a result of the decision of economic agents. The extent to which a person lies depends on the cost curves and the ultimate benefits of lying. But above all, there is a need to provide a definition of a lie. Aquinas (1964) states that expressing a belief to others while that belief is wrong is enough to lie and there is no need to intend to deceive. Lying is wrong, and Aquinas states that one should never lie. There is a difference between not lying and being honest. Lying hurts the liar for the first time and destroys trust in society. Hence, there is never a harmless lie.

DOI: 10.4018/978-1-7998-8235-0.ch008

According to world definitions, there is no uniform agreement on the act of lying. In a general agreement, lying is practical along with the act of cheating to succeed or to ruin the belief and trust of others (Borchert, 2005). Smith (2004) has several definitions of lying. He believes that lying in any form is a mission to provide false information to others or to deprive them of real information (not telling the truth). He believes that keeping information secret is a lie.

Ekman (1985) has a definition of lying that is slightly narrower than Smith's. He does not differentiate between lying and cheating, but he believes that both are based on intention. Ekman states that hiding information with the intention of misleading others (that is, hiding information from others with the intention that others believe something is wrong) is a lie, and that any behavior outside of words and statements with the intention of misleading others is also a lie.

Vrij (2000) agrees with Ekman that lying does not always require the use of words. For example, an athlete's pretension to a sore leg or part of the body is a lie that does not require words. It also states that concealing information with intent is a lie. Vrij states that people lie when they do not inform others of their intention to lie.

Lies have different forms among researchers, the most obvious and famous of which is the big lie. The big lie is a term and technique first used by Adolf Hitler and represents the propaganda technique in the world of politics. In my battle (Mein Kampf), he said that people accepted Germany's defeat in World War I because influential Jews in the press used the technique. In his view, this method requires that the lie be so great that no one believes it as a lie. In other words, a person should be so rude as to shamelessly distort the truth. The first use of the big lie is documented in his famous sentence that in the big lie there is always the power of believability.

This is stated on page 51 of a report released by the US Office of Strategic Services on Hitler's mental history (Wikipedia):

'His first rule is never to let people down, never to admit mistakes, never to admit that the enemy may have a good character. Never leave room for an alternative, focus on one enemy at a time and blame him for every bad thing. People believe the big lie sooner than the small lie, and if you repeat the lie over and over, they will believe it sooner or later.'

Therefore, any form of inducing a false belief or preventing the publication of the truth that is done intentionally is the accepted definition of a lie in this chapter. Lies can be told at different levels of society: at the family level, at the work and business level, at the government level, between policymakers and the nation. Since the economic impact of each is different, and this study addresses the problem of lying from an economics perspective, lying refers to most of the issues that exist at the business level and between the government and the nation.

This study tries to review the literature of economics and suggest some cases that can explain some of the false consequences. Nowhere in economics has the problem of lies and its consequences have not been directly discussed, and what exists includes some theories that are directly related to the problem of lies, including theories of social capital, exchange rates, and asymmetric information. For this reason, the relationship between each theory and lie is examined in an independent section.

In this chapter, according to the definition of a lie, its economic and welfare consequences are discussed. First, there will be an economic look at the costs and benefits of lies and the issue of social capital. Then, the relationship between institutional functions in institutional economics and lies is presented.

COST-BENEFIT ANALYSIS

The act of lying, like any other act, has benefits and costs. An economic agent (individual, firm, or policymaker) can advance his plans by lying, gaining a better position in the contract, earning more money in the labor market, winning elections, and so on. It can create a cost for a person, such as distrust of those around him, exclusion from the environment of friends and acquaintances, etc. Lying, like other human actions, is influenced by human material motives. So that the benefits of lying lead a person to tell a lie and its costs prevent him from telling a lie. The intersection of the final cost curve and the ultimate benefit of the lie determines the number of lies told by each individual.

For example, point a in Figure 1 is where the final cost of the lie meets the ultimate benefits of the lie. If a person lies less than this level, telling one more lie can benefit more than the cost of lying. If he lies at a higher level than a, the last lie he said would cost him more than the benefits of that lie.

There are two reasons for the decline in the ultimate benefits of lying: First, the more a person lies and the more lies he or she has, the lower the benefits of the last unit of lie due to the loss of trust in others. Because a lie works when it is shown to be true by others. Second, if it is assumed that big lies have less benefit because they are unbelievable and a non-linear relationship can be established between big lies and lies, then it can be shown that by increasing the number of lies (big lies) the benefit of the last unit is also reduced.

Figure 1. The ultimate costs and benefits of lies

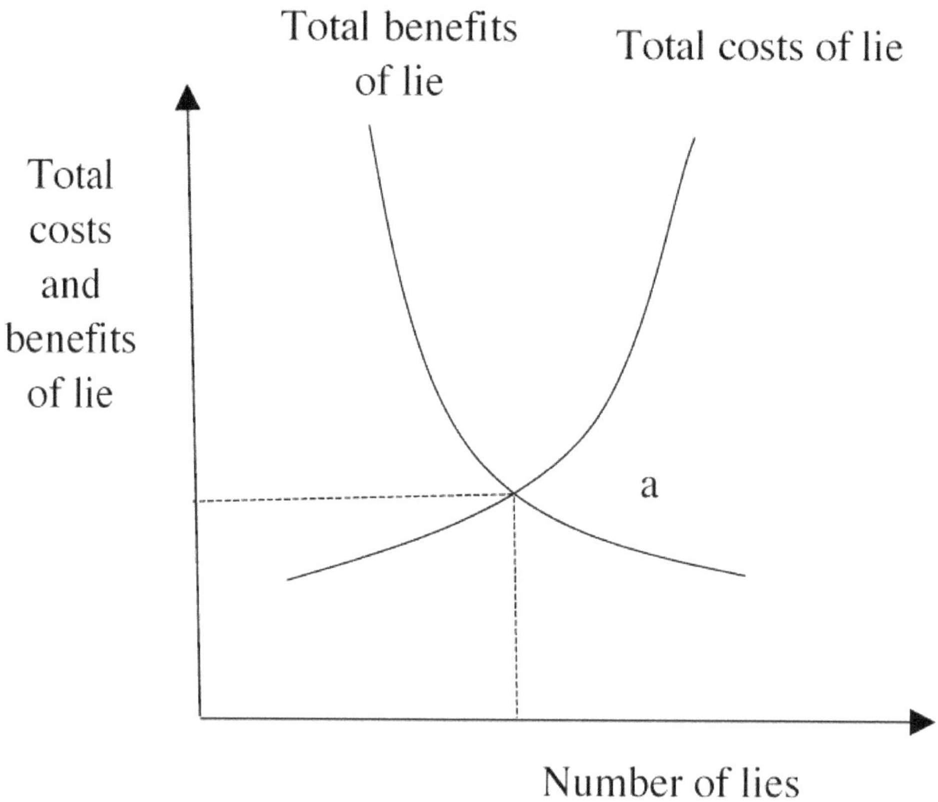

Apart from individuals in society, organizations and governments can also decide to instil misconceptions under the influence of lie benefits and costs. Although lying can bring benefits to its owners in the short term; but in the long run, because the lie is exposed, it affects its benefits. Here the short term depends on how long the lie is hidden. To show the dynamism in the above model, it can be said that by exposing the lie, the ultimate benefit curve of the lie is shifted to the left and bottom, and the final cost of the lie is shifted to the left and up. In the short run, regardless of time dynamics, one decides to lie at point a, but by exposing the lie and transmitting the final cost and final benefit curves, the state of change and the equilibrium point over time move toward the axis-y, where there is no tendency to lie and the person regrets lying.

The same is true of policymakers' lies about demand-side policies at the macro level. Given rational expectations, if the government at the outset - when the nation believes in it - falsely declares money to be less than real, it can reap the benefits of production and employment in the short term, but with as time goes on and expectations are adjusted, the real wages demanded by workers also increase, and the macroeconomic balance returns to full employment.

What has been said so far about costs of lying was related to external cost. For people who insist on certain moral principles and do not lie at all, there is another cost that affects their beliefs. Therefore, the cost of psychological (internal) is added to external cost of lying. The liar also pays psychologically and is worried and ashamed of lying. Initially, for a person who is not accustomed to lying, the final cost of lying or psychological (as opposed to the final external cost) is high, but over time it decreases as the number of lies increases. Figure 2 shows these curves side by side.

Figure 2. Internal final costs and external final costs of lie

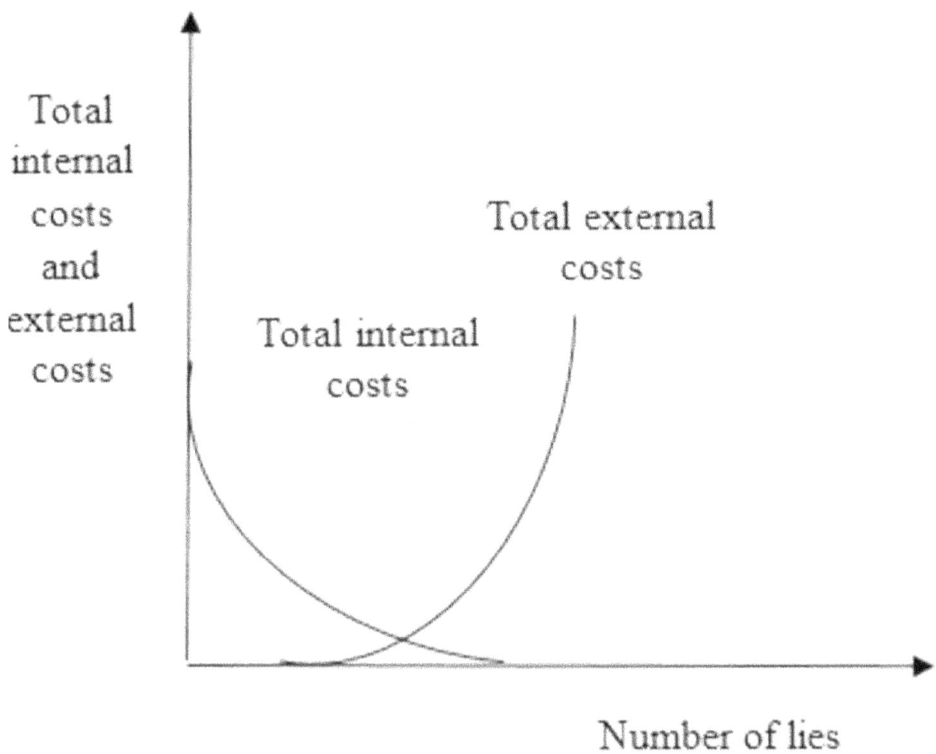

By summing the final external and internal cost of the lie, the total final cost can be obtained. Thus, the sum of the final costs of a U-shape is formed. In Figure 3, the total final cost curve with b is where the ethicist does not lie. In this case, one can analyze why some people do not lie or why religious or moral people lie less.

Because the internal costs plus the external costs for the person are so high that at first, he does not tend to lie. But since the final cost is declining, and assuming that the ultimate benefit of lying is linear descending, telling the first lie leads to a situation where the ultimate benefit outweighs the final cost, and this is where small lies turn into great lies over time. By continuing to lie, one reaches a state of equilibrium a, where the ultimate benefit and cost are equal.

Figure 3. Final benefits and total final costs

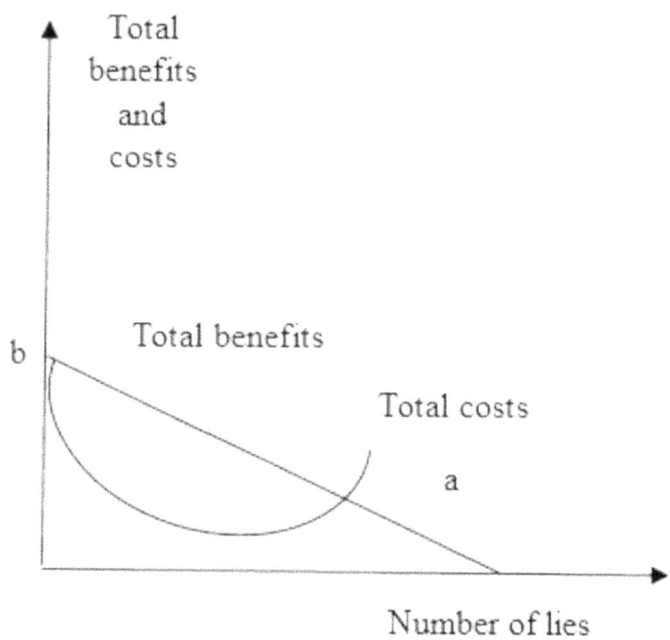

Lying not only imposes private costs on the individual, firm, or policymaker, but also imposes social costs that make the difference between the private and social equilibrium points. Since lying has negative external impact- for example, one person's lying undermines everyone's public trust - the final social cost curve is higher than the private final cost, meaning that even in the short term, where factors do not take in to account the long-term horizon, lying has no social economic justification. If social costs are added to private costs, the final cost curve in Figure 3 is shifted upwards by a large margin. So that no point of contact is formed between the two curves, which shows the fact that lying has no economic justification under any circumstances (Figure 4).

Figure 4. Total private and social costs

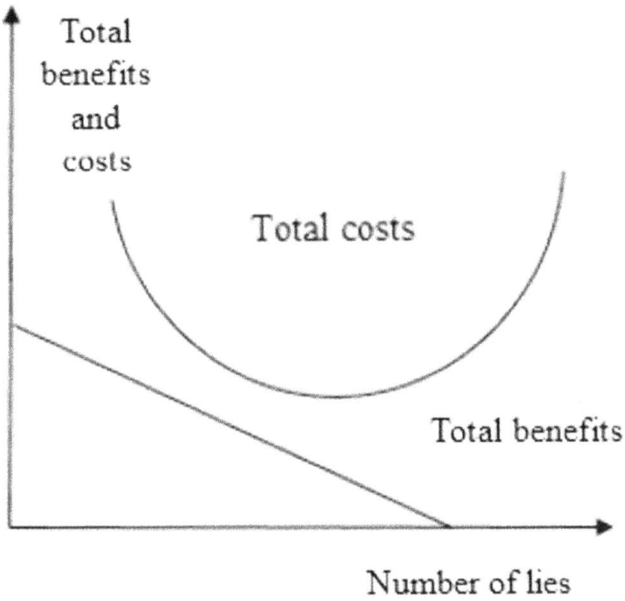

SOCIAL CAPITAL AND LIES

Social capital is something beyond physical and human capital. So that this capital is formed and accumulated from the social reaction between economic factors. Social capital is a complicated concept involving several dimensions and including cultural and social elements. Lately, it has become very common and attractive among relevant scientists. Its history goes back to classical economists. However, the concept of social capital as a thematic issue was only considered in the late 1980s and has since become the focus of many studies. In spite of the extensive literature, a single and universal definition of social capital cannot be found. This is often defined and measured in a pragmatic and non-systematic way. Theory of social capital is specifically derived from the concept of trusts, norms, and networks, and holds that "social relations are worthy resources." (Bhandari and Yasunobu, 2009).

Bourdieu (1986) differentiated three sorts of capital: economic, cultural and social. He declared that social capital refers to the sum of real or possible resources associated with having a stable network of established relations of reciprocal familiarity and recognition. That is to say, it refers to a belonging to a group. Coleman (1990) explained social capital from the perspective of its function. Social capital is a combination of entities, which have two shared features including a social structure and making easier the specified measures of persons in the structure. Entities include commitments, expectations, trust and information flow.

Fukuyama (1995) defined social capital in a simple way as the presence of definite group of informal values or norms common in a group for having a better cooperation. Lin (2001) defined social capital as investing in social relationships with anticipated gain in the market. Robison et al. (2002) illustrated that social capital refers to a understanding between people to create a mutual benefit, advantage, and privileged treatment for individuals more than what regraded as likely in an exchange relations.

Putnam (1993) defines social capital as follows: Social capital is composed of trusts, values, and networks that facilitate cooperation to achieve mutual benefits. What is certain is that trust is one of the cornerstones of all definitions of social capital. This is where lies begin their economic effects. Lying reduces trust (social capital) and will have a negative impact on the national economy.

Numerous studies have been conducted on social capital, religion, and ethics as well as their impacts on economic development such as (Glah and Vorhies, 1989; Grier, 1997; Paldam, 1999; McCleary and Barros, 2003). All of these studies have found evidence for the influence of religion and ethics on production and economic growth.

In addition to the impact that religious and moral beliefs may have on growth, studies have shown that household productivity and consumer behavior are also affected by these factors. For example, khan and Bashar (2008) has shown that religious and moral beliefs affect the ultimate productivity of human capital, and that increasing public trust leads to a reduction in crime in societies.

Studies on religion and moral principles and economic development are all part of the social capital literature. Because religion and moral principles create a positive overflow between individuals by creating a network between people who are committed to religion and moral principles in society, increases trust between people, and it binds all people to a common set of values. These three functions of religion and moral principles are the elements that underlie all definitions of social capital.

Knack and Keefer (1997) in a study entitled "does social capital have economic benefits?", in a cross-sectional study, examined the relationship between social capital and measurable economic performance. They have used two criteria of trust and social norms in measuring social capital. The results of this study, which was conducted on 29 countries, showed that membership in formal groups has no significant relationship with the index of trust and social capital. Also, according to the results of this study, trust and social norms are stronger and higher in countries with higher incomes and stronger institutions.

Some researchers, such as Paxton (1999), Stolle and Rochon (1998), and Knack and Keefer (1997) emphasize two main points. First, it is necessary to distinguish between social life and its potential effects on public trust and cooperation. Second, attention must be paid to heterogeneity between social groups; this is because the question of whether membership in groups and other social ties affects mutual cooperation and public trust, and thus the performance of government and the economy, depends on the purpose of the groups, the diversity and number of their members, and the intensity and nature of the activity of those groups. As Putnam (1993) pointed out, many groups give their members a spirit of cooperation, while others - categorized by profession, associational Type, ethnicity, and religion - increase trust among group members, however they encourage mistrust between non-members (Savignon, 2010).

Zak and Knack (2001) believes that there are channels through which increasing social capital leads to better government performance: 1. Social capital can increase government accountability, because the government must respond to citizens with broader demands. 2. Social capital can provide a platform through which the political preferences of the people can be channeled. Because people increase government accountability through participation in voting.

Knack (2002) examined the impact of various forms of social capital on government performance in another study named as "social capital and the quality of government: Evidence from the United States." In this study, he used indicators of social trust, public accountability, and social communication (such as activities in informal associations and communities) and evaluated their relationship with better government performance. The results of this study show that while the first two alternative indicators for social capital (i.e. public trust and accountability) have a positive relationship with government performance, but the third indicator (i.e. social relations) has no significant relationship with government performance. The results of this study rely on the accuracy of the use of social indicators, because social capital indicators are generally heterogeneous, the use of a general index - which takes in to account all aspects of social capital - may produce biased results.

Jankauskas and Seputiene (2007) examined the relationship between social capital (including trust, social norms, and networks) and government efficiency and economic performance. Using social capital indicators in 23 European countries, they tested the intensity of the relationship between social capital, government quality, and economic performance. The results of this study show that the indicators of social capital (including trust and networks) and the quality index of the government together with the performance of the economy - as measured by the indicators of GDP per capita, labor productivity and research and development expenditures are in direct relationships.

Casey and Christ (2002) tested the Putnam hypothesis that social capital improves economic performance and thus economic growth in the United States. The results of this study show that states with a high level of social capital have had successful experience in creating jobs, but the relationship between social capital and other indicators of social capital has not been confirmed. In other words, based on the results of this study, at least for the US empirical case, the validity of the results between the relationship between social capital and economic performance is still questionable and has not been confirmed with high confidence. Of course, on the other hand, the claim that social capital is beneficial to political economy cannot be easily dismissed. Finally, the authors emphasize the development of conceptual relationships between social capital and its economic consequences.

Some studies have also used some institutional variables to express the impact of government social capital on economic performance - and especially economic growth. These institutional variables include indicators such as civil liberties, political freedoms, the frequency of political violence, and the subjective ratings of political risk. One of the first studies in this field is the study of Kormendi and Menguire (1985) which examined the social capital of the government and economic growth. Using an intergovernmental study, they used an indicator called Gastil for Civil Liberties. In this study, researchers considered countries with a score of 1 or 2 as the countries with the highest degree of civil liberties and included it in their growth model as a virtual variable. The result of this study shows that the virtual variable has a positive and significant effect on economic growth.

TRANSACTION COSTS AND LIES

Institutional economics is a branch of economics based on the principles of neoclassical economics, with the difference that it has added the importance of institutions in its analysis. Institutions that have functions such as the rule of law, commercial law, property rights, security, and information dissemination. The difference between the institutionalism and the neoclassical approach is that it sees the assumptions of neoclassical economics in the context of institutions. For example, it sees rationality in a cultural and institutional context and analyzes it with the help of behavioral economics. The existence of asymmetric information, bounded rationality, the existence of transaction costs are among the items that have been further considered and analyzed in institutional economics. In institutional economics, two cases have been proposed as institutional functions in economics, which are: reducing the costs of transaction and eliminating information asymmetry.

As mentioned, lying reduces the accumulation of trust. If it is assumed that L is the amount of lies and N is the number of transactions between agents (network), the following relationship can be assumed for trust:

$$et = f(L,N) \tag{1}$$

Where e_t is the confidence level at time t. In the above relation, $f'_L<0$, $f''_L\geq 0$, $f'_N>0$, $\lim_{L=\infty} f(L,N)=0$. Each lie reduces the accumulation of trust, and the next lie reduces trust to a lesser extent. Of course, the assumption of the convexity of the trust function does not matter here, but this assumption and the assumption that the limit of the function of zero is zero, shows the fact that man can give a chance to those who have immersed themselves in infinity to lie again, in the sense that trust to them never becomes zero.

Figure 5. The relationship between trust and lies

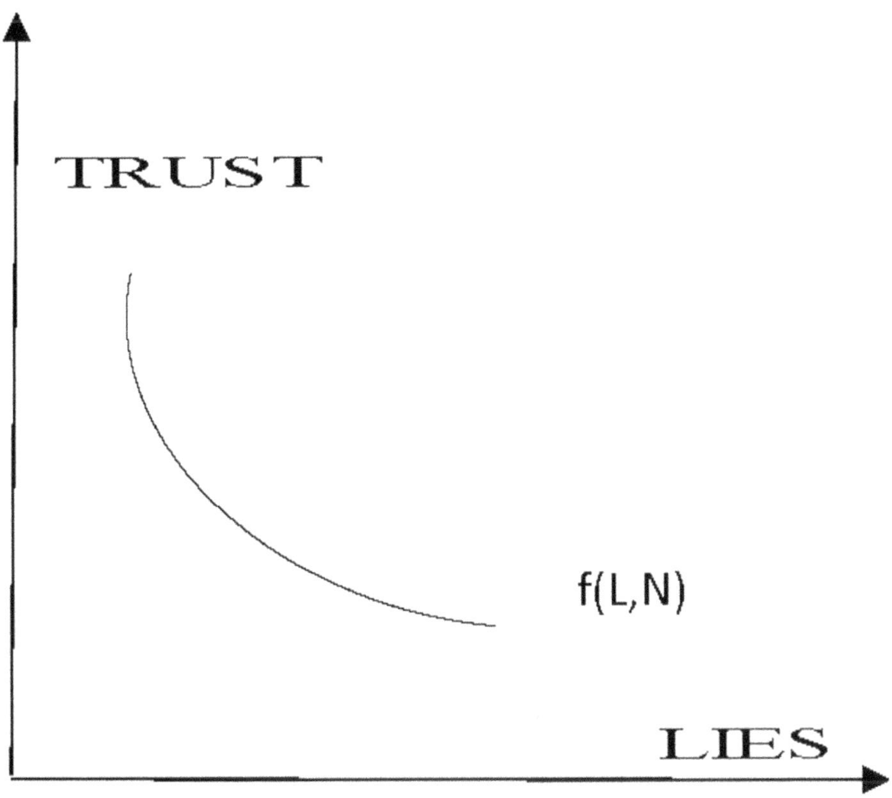

Decreasing trust increases the costs of transaction in the economy. Because every contract requires a minimum amount of trust and to achieve this level of trust the parties to the transaction are forced to pay. Also, lack of trust due to spreading lies leads to the formation of balance in the non-optimal (inefficient) situation.

ASYMMETRIC INFORMATION AND LIE

One of the basic assumptions in neoclassical theory is the existence of complete information. It is assumed that consumers have complete information about the characteristics of the product such as quality, durability, and etc. In addition, manufacturers will have complete information about the efficiency of the factors of production. Violation of the assumption of complete information can lead to decisions in conditions of uncertainty. The issue of asymmetric information in an economy is one of the conditions that violates the assumption of complete information. Some people can have more access to information than others for a variety of reasons, including expertise, knowledge, intelligence, talent, power, and etc. One of the factors that causes information asymmetry or aggravates the situation of information asymmetry is spreading lies or preventing the sharing of truth. One of the consequences of asymmetric information is that it helps to create balance somewhere other than condition of efficiency.

For the past three decades, the theory of markets with asymmetric information in the economy has been considered and various models have been proposed for it. Akerlof (1970) has clearly shown that asymmetric information can increase the possibility of adverse selection. The study shows that if different units obtain different information, how does this information asymmetry ultimately lead to the performance of markets? In this study, it is presented that the first formal analysis of markets with asymmetric information problems under adverse selection and also the application of this theory in developing countries is emphasized.

Signaling has been suggested as a solution to some of the problems of adverse selection. Signaling requires economic agents to provide observable criteria (which are costly) in order to convince other agents of their capabilities or the value and quality of their product in general.

Therefore, in case of lies or obstruction of the dissemination of the truth, there is an asymmetry of information, even if by reducing market inefficiency with the use of signaling, there are two issues: first, the signaling itself comes at a cost to society and results in increased transaction costs, that must be met to convince people of the extent to which honesty in speech should be appreciated by each person. The second issue is that the prevalence of lies in a society also reduces the level of trust in signaling by economic agents. Therefore, individuals (on the demand side of the product) have to pay a fee to ensure that the signs are sent, which ultimately leads to an increase in transaction costs (on the demand side).

DISCUSSION

Economic analysis of lies is because lies as a human behavior are influenced by conflicting motives as a result of the decision of economic agents. The extent to which a person lies is dependent on the cost curves and ultimate benefits of lying. But this is a comparative static state and is formed in the short run, while in the long run what remains of the lie are only costs. Because sooner or later the truth will be revealed. But since a person has myopia problem, he cannot see clearly in the long run and tries to lie. What remains of this action for the society is a decrease in public trust, social capital, and public welfare. Then, in the approach of institutional economics, the effect of lie on the functioning of transaction costs and asymmetric information was examined.

One of the functions of the institution in institutional economics is to reduce the cost of transactions. But lying, as a practice that undermines trust, increases the cost of transactions. The more lies are told, the higher the cost of gaining trust in the contract. Lying and dishonesty in behavior cause the phenomenon of information asymmetry in the economy. Information asymmetry is a phenomenon that leads actors to form an inefficient situation.

CONCLUSION

In this chapter, it is attempted to examine the part of the economics literature that could explain the consequences of lies. Social capital was evaluated first, because lying, as a behavior that reduces trust, reduces social capital, and since social capital reduces growth and prosperity, lies appear with negative economic consequences. What was introduced as a lie in this chapter is to instill a misconception in any way possible with the aim of misleading the audience. According to this definition, not only lie is spreading false beliefs, but also it is considered as an act that leads to the induction of a false belief. Therefore, not telling the truth is also regarded as a lie. A government that does not respect honesty in its policies reduces prosperity.

REFERENCES

Akerlof, G. A. (1970). The market for "Lemons": Quality uncertainty and the market mechanism. *The Quarterly Journal of Economics*, *84*(3), 488–500. doi:10.2307/1879431

Aquinas, T. (1964). *Commentary on the Nicomachean ethics* (C. I. Litzinger, Trans.). Henry Regnery Company.

Bhandari, H., & Yasunobu, K. (2009). What is social capital? A comprehensive review of the concept. *Asian Journal of Social Science, 37*(3), 480–510. doi:10.1163/156853109X436847

Borchert, D. (2005). *Encyclopedia of philosophy* (2nd ed.). Macmillan Inc.

Casey, T., & Christ, K. (2002). Social capital and economic performance in the American states. *The American Political Science Association Conference.*

Coleman, J. S. (1990). *Foundations of social theory*. Harvard University Press.

Ekman, P. (1985). *Telling lies: Clues to deceit in the marketplace, politics, and marriage*. Norton & Company.

Fukuyama, F. (1995). *Trust: The social virtues and the creation of prosperity*. Free Press.

Glahe, F., & Vorhies, F. (1989). Religion, liberty and economic development: An empirical investigation. *Public Choice, 62*(3), 201–215. doi:10.1007/BF02337742

Grier, K. B., & Tullock, G. (1989). An empirical analysis of cross- -national economic growth. *Journal of Monetary Economics, 24*(2), 259–276. doi:10.1016/0304-3932(89)90006-8

Hitler, A. (1925). *Mein Kampf*. Germany: Franz Eher Nachfolger GmbH: Jankauskas, V., & Šeputienė, J. (2007). The relation between social capital governance and economic performance in Europe. *TeorijaIrPraktika Business: Theory and Practice, VIII*(3), 131–138.

KhanH.BasharO. K. M. R. (2008). *Religion and development: Are they complementary?* U21Global Working Paper Series, No. 006/2008. https://ssrn.com/abstract=1601048 doi:10.2139/ssrn.1601048

Knack, S. (2002). Social capital and the quality of government: Evidence from the State. *American Journal of Political Science, 46*(4), 772–785. doi:10.2307/3088433

Knack, S., & Keefer, P. (1997). Does social capital have an economic payoff? A cross-country investigation. *The Quarterly Journal of Economics, 112*(4), 1251–1288. doi:10.1162/003355300555475

Kormendi, R. C., & Meguire, P. G. (1985). Macroeconomic determinants of growth. *Journal of Monetary Economics, 16*(1), 141–163. doi:10.1016/0304-3932(85)90027-3

Lin, N. (2001). *Social capital: A theory of social structure and action*. Cambridge University Press. doi:10.1017/CBO9780511815447

McCleary, R. M., & Barros, R. J. (2006). Religion and economy. *The Journal of Economic Perspectives*, *20*(2), 49–72. doi:10.1257/jep.20.2.49

Paldam, M. (1999). *Corruption and religion adding to the economic model?* Center for Dynamic Modeling in Economics, Working Paper no. 21.

Paxton, P. (1999). Is social capital declining in the United States? A multiple indicator assessment. *American Journal of Sociology*, *105*(1), 88–127. doi:10.1086/210268

Putnam, R. (1993). *Making democracy work: Civic traditions in modern Italy*. Princeton University Press.

Robison, L. J., Schmid, A. A., & Siles, M. E. (2002). Is social capital really capital? *Review of Social Economy*, *601*(1), 1–21. doi:10.1080/00346760110127074

Savignon, A. B. (2010). *Linking social capital and government performance: A public management perspective*. Working Paper, University of Rome.

Stolle, D., & Rochon, T. R. (1998). Are all associations alike? member diversity, associational type, and the creation of social capital. *The American Behavioral Scientist*, *42*(1), 47–65. doi:10.1177/0002764298042001005

Vrij, A. (2000). *Detecting lies and deceit: The psychology of lying and the implications for professional practice*. John Wiley & Sons.

Wikipedia Contributors. (n.d.). Big Lie. In *Wikipedia*. Retrieved from http://en.wikipedia.org/w/index. php?title=Big_Lie&oldid=77579324

Zak, P. G., & Knack, S. (2001). Trust and growth. *Economic Journal (London)*, *111*(470), 295–321. doi:10.1111/1468-0297.00609

Chapter 9
The Detection of Profit Manipulation:
Assessing the Ability of the Accrual and Revenue Models

Maryam Ebrahimi
https://orcid.org/0000-0001-5837-8864
University of Bayreuth, Germany

ABSTRACT

Profit manipulation refers to bringing reported profits closer to the intended level, which is classified into categories of earnings management, falsification, and creative accounting practices. It is extremely difficult to detect manipulated financial statements using standard business audit procedures because there is a lack of knowledge about extensions and features of management fraud. Auditors have a shortage of the experience to detect falsified financial statements, and managers deliberately attempt to deceive auditors using new methods. The goal of this study is to review mathematical techniques to detect profit management practices and to compare the average profit management and ability to predict earnings management of the accrual and revenue models. The motivation behind this chapter is to provide a basis to compare techniques on detecting financial manipulation.

INTRODUCTION

In recent decades, studies of financial information manipulation have been the focus of analysts and researchers. The recent requirements of the US Securities

DOI: 10.4018/978-1-7998-8235-0.ch009

and Exchange Commission to scrutinize the discovery of fraudulent profits have prompted an investigation. However, the scientific and professional literature on profit manipulation detection is very limited. In the accounting literature, the difference between earnings management and earnings manipulation is not clearly defined, and the distinction between them must be explained (Impink, 2010).

Accounting profit is an important performance indicator used in many economic decisions such as stock valuation, performance appraisal, manager remuneration and profit sharing. This decision can be effective in transferring resources among people, so it causes to pay special attention to the capital market. In a conflict of interest environment, such as a conflict of interest between shareholders and managers, it is always possible for managers to try to manipulate profits. Earnings management is an activity that can be related to various outcomes from a full disclosure perspective in financial reporting. The uncertain nature of this threat and the many consequences of earnings management have forced researchers to measure and identify signs of earnings management and therefore provide models, which are often designed based on accounting variables due to the accounting variables used in earnings management (Taleb Nia and Safari Sarchah, 2014).

Copeland (1968) introduced profit manipulation as the relative ability of managers to reduce or increase reported earnings. The intentional actions of company managers to bring reported profits closer to the intended level, which is classified into three categories in terms of compliance with accounting rules and standards: earnings management, falsification (Merchant, 1990),and Creative Accounting Practices (CAP). Earnings management involves postponing the period affected by an operation by changing measurement methods, accelerating sales, or delaying purchases. Here, we can limit background earnings management to manipulation of accounting figures, not to profit manipulation that includes performance in real business situations. Falsification refers to exposing incorrect data. In this case, such acts may be considered criminal. However, the thin line between the two manipulations remains unclear. The creative accounting is often used to describe the process by which accounting professionals use their knowledge to manipulate the figures in annual accounts (Shah and Butt, 2011).

The purpose of this study is to review mathematical methods using for the detection of profit manipulation and compare the average profit management and ability of accruals and revenue models to predict earnings management in companies.

ACCRUALS MODELS

In the literature on earnings management, manipulations that are explications of standards are mainly discussed, for example, accrual decision making and most research has shown that discretionary accrual models can be an effective tool for identifying earnings manipulation because they can show unusual figures associated with reports and predicted values. Some previous studies on earnings management emphasized on how accounts are manipulated through accruals (DeAngelo, 1986; Healy, 1985). Management of accruals refers to changes in estimates such as useful lives, the possibility of repaying debtors, and other accruals at the end of the year in an effort to change reported earnings to achieve a target. DeAngelo (1986) used the total accruals of the past period, which are scaled by lagged total assets, as a measure of nondiscretionary accruals. Haley (1985) applied the average of total accruals that have been scaled by lagged total assets over the estimated period as a measure of nondiscretionary accruals.

In models that use accruals, researchers compute the extent of earnings management by considering the difference between the total accruals reported in corporate finance reports and accruals estimated as a function of different types of metrics. Total accruals are derived in two ways: cash flow approach and balance sheet approach. In the cash flow approach, total accruals are calculated as the difference between earnings before extraordinary items and operating cash flows. In the balance sheet approach, total accruals are computed using current assets and liabilities. It is stated that the cash flow method gives more accurate results than the balance sheet method (Acar and Coskun, 2020).

Cash Flow Method

$$\frac{ACCR-CF_{i,t}}{TA_{i,t-1}}=\frac{EBXI_{i,t}}{TA_{i,t-1}}-\frac{OCF_{i,t}}{TA_{i,t-1}} \tag{1}$$

ACCR – CF$_{i,t}$**:** Total accruals with the method of cash flow,
TA**:** Total assets,
EBCI**:** Earnings before extraordinary items,
OCF**:** Operating cash flows,
i**:** Company identifier,
t**:** Time identifier in years.

Balance Sheet Method

$$\frac{ACCR-BS_{i,t}}{TA_{i,t-1}}=\frac{\Delta CA_{i,t}}{TA_{i,t-1}}-\frac{\Delta Cash_{i,t}}{TA_{i,t-1}}-\frac{\Delta CL_{i,t}}{TA_{i,t-1}}+\frac{\Delta STD_{i,t}}{TA_{i,t-1}}-\frac{Dep_{i,t}}{TA_{i,t-1}} \quad (2)$$

$\boldsymbol{ACCR-BS_{i,t}}$: Total accruals with the method of balance sheet,
$\boldsymbol{\Delta CA}$: Change in current assets,
$\boldsymbol{\Delta Cash}$: Change in cash and equivalents,
$\boldsymbol{\Delta CL}$: Change in current liabilities,
$\boldsymbol{\Delta STD}$: Change in short-term debt and current portion of long-term debt,
Dep: Depreciation expense.

In the detection of earnings management based on accounting accruals, if the accruals are abnormal, it can be said that earnings management is assumed.

Abnormal accruals = Accounting accruals - Expected accruals (3)

Healy (1985) used the aggregate accruals model while Beneish (1999) used the specific accruals model. However, the accrual model has been used in several types of research and many researchers have questioned the accuracy and usefulness of the accrual model.

Aggregate accrual method approach: "Accruals" are probably the result of the exercise of managerial "discretions'' or may be the result of "changes in economic conditions." Using the regression model, the researcher took total accrual as depended variable and independent variables are sales, assets, equipment, and plant. Here sales are called changes in sales and changes in the level of property plant and equipment (Jones, 1991).

The specific approach of the accrual method: Beneish (1997, 1998) presented this model for measuring the distortions or preconditions of financial statements. The result of this model defined a systematic relationship between the likelihood of manipulation and specific accruals. Moyer (1990) explained that banking and insurance firms often use special accrual methods to manage earnings, such as the bank uses for loan losses and insurance companies provides a reserve for losses.

Total Accruals = Non-discretionary accruals + Discretionary Accruals (4)

Discretionary accrual and nondiscretionary accrual are two types of Accrual and the combination of these two accruals is called total accrual.

The Jones Model

To control the effects of changes in the firm's economic conditions on nondiscretionary accruals Jones (1991) proposed a model. For nondiscretionary accruals in the event year, it is as the following:

$$NDA_t = \alpha 1\left(\frac{1}{A_{t-1}}\right) + \alpha 2\left(\Delta REV_t / A_{t-1}\right) + \alpha 3\left(PPE_t / A_{t-1}\right) \quad (5)$$

Noting that:

***NDA*$_t$:** Nondiscretionary accruals in year t that is scaled based on total assets,
Δ*REV*$_t$: Revenues in year t less revenues in year t - 1;
***PPE*$_t$:** Gross property plant and equipment at the end of year t.
A_{t-1}: Total assets at the end of the year is t – 1,
α1, α2, α3: Company specific parameters.

Estimation of company-specific parameters, α1, α2, and α3, is obtained using the following model in the period of the estimation:

$$\frac{TA_t}{A_{t-1}} = \alpha 1\left(\frac{1}{A_{t-1}}\right) + \alpha 2\left(\frac{\Delta REV_t}{A_{t-1}}\right) + \alpha 3\left(\frac{PPE_t}{A_{t-1}}\right) + \varepsilon t \quad (6)$$

Noting that:

TA_t is the sum of the accruals of year t.

εt refers to the residual, which denotes the portion of the company-specific discretionary for all accruals.

Other variables are like equation (5).

The Modified Jones Model

According to Dechow et al. (1995) and Geiszler (2014):

$$TA_{it}/A_{it-1} = \alpha 1\left(1/A_{it-1}\right) + \alpha 2\left[\left(\Delta REV_{it} - \Delta REC_{it}\right)/A_{it-1}\right] + \alpha 3\left(PPE_{it}/A_{it-1}\right) + \varepsilon_{it} \quad (7)$$

Noting that:

TA_{it}: Total accruals in year t for company i. It is calculated as the change in current assets minus the change in current liabilities minus the change in cash and cash equivalents plus the change in liabilities including current liabilities minus depreciation and the cost of depreciation.

ΔREV_{it}: Revenues in year t less revenues in year t – 1 for company i,

ΔREC_{it}: Net receivables in year t less net receivables in year t – 1 for company i,

PPE_{it}: Gross property, plant, and equipment in year t for company i,

A_{it-1}: Total assets in year t – 1 for company i,

ε_{it}: Error term in year t for company i.

Other Models

Model presented by Kasznik (1999):

$$TA_{it}/A_{it-1} = \alpha_{0i}\left(1/A_{it-1}\right) + \alpha_{1i}\left[\left(\Delta REV_{it} - \Delta REC_{it}\right)/A_{it-1}\right] + \alpha_{2i}\left(PPE_{it}/A_{it-1}\right) + \alpha_{3i}\left(\Delta CFO_{it}/A_{it-1}\right) + \varepsilon_{it} \quad (8)$$

Noting that:

ΔCFO_{it}: Net cash flows from operations from the time t-1 to t.

Other variables are the same as the modified Jones model.

Model presented by Kothari et al. (2005):

$$TA_{it}/A_{it-1} = \alpha_0 + \alpha_i\left(1/A_{it-1}\right) + \alpha_{1i}\left(\Delta REV_{it}/A_{it-1}\right) + \alpha_{2i}\left(PPE_{it}/A_{it-1}\right) + \alpha_{3i} ROA_{i,t-1} + \varepsilon_{it} \quad (9)$$

The modified model of Kothari-Jones:

$$TA_{it}/A_{it-1} = \alpha_0 + \alpha_i\left(1/A_{it-1}\right) + \alpha_{1i}\left[\left(\Delta REV_{it} - \Delta REC_{it}\right)/A_{it-1}\right] + \alpha_{2i}\left(PPE_{it}/A_{it-1}\right) + \alpha_{3i} ROA_{i,t-1} + \varepsilon_{it} \quad (10)$$

Dechow and Dichev Model

This method measures whether current accruals are related to the cash flows of the previous, current or next period. Any accruals that are not related to cash flows reduce the quality of accounting information. The following model is estimated in order to measure accrual quality (Geiszler, 2014):

$$\Delta WC_{it} = \alpha_0 + \alpha_1 CFO_{it-1} + \alpha_2 CFO_{it} + \alpha_3 CFO_{it+1} + \varepsilon_{it} \tag{11}$$

Nothing that:

Change in working capital for company i from year t-1 to year t. It is computed as the change in receivable accounts plus the change in inventory minus the change in payable accounts minus the change in payable taxes plus the change in other assets,

CFO_{it-1}: Company i's cash flow in period t-1,
CFO_{it}: Company i's cash flow in period t,
CFO_{it+1}: Company i's cash flow in period t+1,
$\varepsilon i_{t:}$ Residual for company i in period t.

REVENUE MODEL

The change in receivable accounts can be expressed by the revenue model as a function of discretionary and non-discretionary revenues. The intuition in the model developed by Stubben (2010) is that there is no cash set of discretionary earnings. So, receivable accounts are the sum of discretionary income and uncollected non-discretionary revenues. The error in the revenue model includes the discretionary revenue portion (Geiszler, 2014).

$$\Delta AR_{it} = \alpha + \beta_1 \Delta R1\_3_{it} + \beta_2 \Delta R4_{it} + \varepsilon_{it} \tag{12}$$

Noting that:

ΔAR_{it}: Annual change in receivable accounts for company i in year t,
$\Delta R1_{3it}$: Change in revenues in the first three quarters for company i in year t,
$\Delta R4_{it}$: Change in the fourth quarter revenue for company i in year t,
$\varepsilon i_{t:}$ Discretionary revenues for company i in year t.

As an extension of the revenue model, the conditional revenue model (Stubben 2010) considers different company specific features including credit and inventory polices for different companies. These changes result in the following model (Geiszler, 2014):

$$\Delta AR_{it} = \alpha + \beta_1 \Delta R_{it} + (\beta_2 \Delta R_{it} \times SIZE_{it}) + (\beta_3 \Delta R_{it} \times AGE_{it}) + (\beta_4 \Delta R_{it} \times AGE\_SQ_{it})$$
$$+ (\beta_5 \Delta R_{it} \times GRR\_P_{it}) + (\beta_6 \Delta R_{it} \times GRR\_N_{it}) + (\beta_7 \Delta R_{it} \times GRM_{it}) + (\beta_8 \Delta R_{it} \times GRM\_SQ_{it}) + \varepsilon_{it} \quad (13)$$

Noting that:

ΔAR_{it}: Annual change in receivable accounts for company i in year t,

ΔR_{it}: Annual change in revenue for company i in year t,

$SIZE_{it}$: Natural log of total assets at end of fiscal year for company i in year t,

AGE_{it}: Natural log of the age of the company i per years at year t,

AGE_SQ_{it}: The square root of the natural log of the age of the company i per years at year t,

GRR_P_{it}: The growth of industry-median-adjusted revenue (supposing negative, it will be equal to 0),

GRR_N_{it}: The growth of industry-median-adjusted revenue (supposing positive, it will be equal to 0),

GRM_SQ_{it}: The square root of the industry-median-adjusted gross margin at end of fiscal year for company i in year t,

$\varepsilon i_{t:}$ Discretionary revenues for company i in year t.

STATISTICAL TECHNIQUES

Bell and Carcelo (2000) presented and tested a logistic regression model in order to estimate the probability of fraudulent financial reporting for the audit client, provided there are several risk factors for fraud. Significant risk factors in the final model include weak internal control environment, rapid corporate growth, inadequate or inconsistent relative profitability, management that overemphasizes revenue forecasting, management that lies to the auditor, the level of ownership (public versus private), and the interaction between a weak control environment and an aggressive attitude of management attitude regarding financial reporting.

Lack of specific professional guidance and experience in management fraud has led researchers to create models or decision-making tools to predict management fraud (Hansen et al., 1996). They used a strong generalized qualitative response model to model and predict managerial fraud based on data sets prepared by an international public accounting firm. Beneish (1997, 1999) used a weighted exogenous sample maximum likelihood (WESML) to detect manipulation. Model variables are designed to capture distortions of financial statements that may result from manipulation or preconditions that may compel companies to perform such activities.

Spathis (2002) developed a model for identifying fake financial statements. He used logistic regression statistical method. Two alternative input vectors were applied which include financial ratios. The accuracy reported has exceeded 84%. The results show that it is possible to identify fake financial statements by analyzing the published financial statements. Spathis et al. (2002) used the UTADIS method to prepare a detection model of fake financial statements. This method was based on a non-parametric regression-based framework. They used discriminant analysis and logit regression methods as well. Their results show that UTADIS method is better than other statistical methods in terms of training and validation. The results revealed that the ratio of "total debt / total assets" and "inventory / sales" are explanatory factors related to fake financial statements.

NEURAL NETWORK

Artificial neural network model is a knowledge-inducing technique that creates a classification model by finding existing patterns of input data. Neural networks consist of a set of interconnected processing nodes arranged in input, hidden, and output layers. Data flows from the input layer to the output layer, through this network. The data at first enters the network through the nodes in the input layer. While input nodes transfer data to nodes in the hidden layer (s) so that the network can model complex functions. Nodes in the output layer receive and process all inputs. A number of studies by Green and Choi (1997), Fanning and Cogger (1998), Lin et al. (2003) demonstrated the power of neural network applications in identifying fraudulent financial statements. Green and Choi (1997) proposed the development of a neural network fraud classification model using endogenous financial data and found that their model performed well in this classification. Fanning and Cogger (1998) used an artificial neural network to create a model for detecting management fraud. Using predictors of fake financial statements, they find a model consisting of eight variables with a high probability of detection. Lin et al. (2003) developed a fuzzy neural network to examine the application of information technologies such as the integrated neural network system and fuzzy logic to detect fraud.

DECISION TREE

It is a tree structure, in which each node represents a test on an attribute and each branch represents the test result. The tree tries to divide the observations into separate subgroups. Good division is on the basis of the selecting the attribute that best distinguishes the sample. The sample is divided into subsets sequentially, until either the next division cannot make a statistically significant difference or the subgroups are too small to perform a similar meaningful division.

In automatic interaction detection (AID), the most important t-test is used based on analysis of variance. The chi-square-AID uses chi-square and classification and regression trees (CART) statistics use the diversity index (Koh and Low, 2004). Sequential division of the sample might create a large tree. Some tree branches may reflect anomalies in the training set, such as false values. That is why tree pruning is necessary. Tree pruning involves removing splitting nodes that does not affect the accuracy of the model. In order to classify an object that has not been seen before, the object attribute values are tested against the splitting nodes of the decision tree. On the basis of this test, a path is traced that results in predicting the object class. The main advantages of decision trees are that they provide a meaningful way to display acquired knowledge and facilitate the extraction of IF-THEN classification rules.

METHODOLOGY

Current research is practical in nature and based on correlation method. In this research, the average profit management in all models is examined to test the differences between models in measuring earnings management. Data obtained from the financial statements of selected companies based on convenient sampling between 2008 and 2012 are analyzed. These data is collected through information center of stock exchange organization. Descriptive statistics including average and standard deviation are used for the analysis (Table 1). Additionally, an F-test as a type of statistical test that is very flexible is used to compare the ability of accrual models with revenue model in predicting earnings management (Table 2). Thus, hypotheses (H0 and H1) are as the followings:

H0: The accrual models don't have a higher ability than the revenue model in predicting earnings management.

H1: The accrual models have a higher ability than the revenue model in predicting earnings management.

RESULTS

Table 1 shows the results of this comparison.

Table 1. Descriptive statistics of earnings management index based on different models

Models	No. of observations	Average	Standard deviation
Jones (1991)	1000	0	0.11
The Modified Jones Model	1000	0	0.11
Kasznik (1999)	1000	0	0.09
Kothari et al. (2005)	1000	0	0.10
Kothari-Jones	1000	0	0.10
Revenue Model	1000	0	0.17

Table 2. Comparison of the ability of the models in predicting earnings management

Models	F statistic	Sig.	Adjusted R squared
Jones (1991)	21.58	0	5.8
The Modified Jones Model	9.83	0	2.6
Kasznik (1999)	119.36	0	32.6
Kothari et al. (2005)	44.12	0	14.7
Kothari-Jones	42.40	0	14.2
Revenue Model	14.66	0	3.9

As it is clear from Table 2, the accrual models have higher F-statistic and adjusted R squared than the revenue model at the confidence level of 95%; therefore, their ability in predicting earning management is greater.

DISCUSSION

Since information is important for economic decision making, and without a doubt, its quality can be beneficial for decision making, financial statement can be an important element of information for shareholders to determine stock prices and evaluate management performance (Imeni et al., 2021). The empirical studies on the impact of accounting on earnings management are rare, however its comparability is markedly usefull (Liem and Ntim, 2021).

The results of descriptive statistics in the study show that the average profit management in all models is zero; that is, the different models do not differ much in measuring profit management. But accrual models are better in predicting earnings management than revenue models. Also, the Kasznik's model among accruals models has more power to predict earnings management. This finding is consistent with the results of studies conducted by Aghayi and Chalaki (2009) and Bahar Moghadam and Koohi (2010) and Sajjadi et al. (2012). It should be noted that studies usually referred to accruals models.

Rahmani and Bashiri Manesh (2013) showed that modified Jones model is not efficient in detecting earnings management. However, Bozorg Asl and Ghafar Por (2012) showed that modified Jones model (1995) in accepted companies in Stock Exchange for the detection of profit management has more power.

CONCLUSION

Several researchers in the field of profit management consider accruals the key to earnings manipulation. It is easier to manipulate accruals than cash, therefore, researchers focus on accruals. This research after reviewing mathematical techniques to detect profit management practices compared accrual models with revenue models regarding their average profit management and ability to predict earnings management. Researchers use several models in accounting research to predict corporate earnings management. In this study, six models, including Jones accrual models, modified Jones model, Kasznik model, Kothari et al. (2005) model, Kothari-Jones model, and the revenue model are reviewed and compared. The data used is related to companies listed on Stock Exchange. Using descriptive and F statistics, it was shown that the ability of the Kasznik model compared to other models has been studied is the greatest.

REFERENCES

Acar, G., & Koscun, A. (2020). A comparison of models for predicting discretionary accruals: A cross-country analysis. *Journal of Asian Finance, Economics and Business*, *7*(9), 315–328.

Aghayi, M. A., & Chalaki, P. (2009). Analysis of the relationship between characteristics of corporate governance and earnings management in companies listed on the Tehran Stock Exchange. *Accountability in Research*, *1*(4), 54–77.

Bahar Moghdam, M., & Koohi, A. (2010). Analysis of the earnings management types in in companies listed on the Tehran Stock Exchange. *Accounting Knowledge Journal*, *1*(2), 75–93.

Bell, T., & Carcello, J. (2000). A decision aid for assessing the likelihood of fraudulent financial reporting. *Auditing*, *9*(1), 169–178. doi:10.2308/aud.2000.19.1.169

Beneish, M. D. (1997). Detecting GAAP violation: Implications for assessing earnings management among firms with extreme financial performance. *Journal of Accounting and Public Policy*, *16*(3), 271–309. doi:10.1016/S0278-4254(97)00023-9

Beneish, M. D. (1998). Discussion of 'are accruals during initial public offerings opportunistic?' *Review of Accounting Studies*, *3*(1/2), 209–221. doi:10.1023/A:1009692703952

Beneish, M. D. (1999). The detection of earnings manipulation. *Financial Analysts Journal*, *55*(5), 24–36. doi:10.2469/faj.v55.n5.2296

Bozorg, A. M., & Ghafar Por, F. (2012). Comparison of prediction models for detecting earnings management. *Journal of Applied Research, Financial Reporting, Corporate Audit*, *1*, 27-50.

Copeland, R. M. (1968). Income smoothing. *Journal of Accounting Research, Empirical Research in Accounting, Selected Studies*, *6*(Supplement), 101–116.

DeAngelo, L. E. (1986). Accounting numbers as market valuation substitutes: A study of management buyouts of public stockholders. *The Accounting Review*, *61*(3), 400–420.

Dechow, P., Sloan, R., & Sweeney, A. P. (1995). Detecting earnings management. *The Accounting Review*, *70*(2), 193–225.

Fanning, K., & Cogger, K. O. (1998). Neural network detection of management fraud using published financial data. *Intelligent Systems in Accounting, Finance & Management*, *7*(1), 21–41. doi:10.1002/(SICI)1099-1174(199803)7:1<21::AID-ISAF138>3.0.CO;2-K

Geiszler, M. (2014). *The effect of accrual quality, real activities earnings management and corporate governance on credit ratings* (PhD dissertation). The Graduate School of Management, The Kent State University.

Green, B. P., & Choi, J. H. (1997). Assessing the risk of management fraud through neural network technology. *Auditing*, *16*(1), 14–28.

Hansen, J. V., McDonald, J. B., Messier, W. F. Jr, & Bell, T. B. (1996). A generalized qualitative-response model and the analysis of management fraud. *Management Science*, *42*(7), 1022–1032. doi:10.1287/mnsc.42.7.1022

Healy, P. M. (1985). The Effect of Bonus Schemes on Accounting Decisions. *Journal of Accounting and Economics*, *7*(1-3), 85–107. doi:10.1016/0165-4101(85)90029-1

Imeni, M., Fallah, M., & Edalatpanah, S. A. (2021). *The effect of managerial ability on earnings classification shifting and agency cost of Iranian listed companies*. Retrieved from https://www.hindawi.com/journals/ddns/2021/5565605/

Impink, J. (2010). *Earnings manipulation and bankruptcy: WorldCom, Bachelor paper*. University of Amsterdam.

Jones, J. (1991). Earnings Management during import relief investigations. *Journal of Accounting Research*, *29*(2), 193–228. doi:10.2307/2491047

Kasznik, R. (1999). On the association between voluntary disclosure and earnings management. *Journal of Accounting Research*, *37*(1), 57–81. doi:10.2307/2491396

Koh, H. C., & Low, C. K. (2004). Going Concern Prediction using data mining techniques. *Managerial Auditing Journal*, *19*(3), 462–476. doi:10.1108/02686900410524436

Kothari, S. P., Leone, A. L., & Wasley, C. E. (2005). Performance matched discretionary accrual measures. *Journal of Accounting and Economics*, *39*(1), 163–197. doi:10.1016/j.jacceco.2004.11.002

Liem, N. T., & Ntim, C. G. (2021). Accounting comparability and accruals-based earnings management: Evidence on listed firms in an emerging market. *Cognet Business and Management*, *8*(1). Retrieved from https://www.tandfonline.com/doi/full/10.1080/23311975.2021.1923356

Lin, J.W., Hwang, M., & Becker, J.D. (2003, Spring). A fuzzy neural network for assessing the risk of fraudulent financial reporting. *Managerial Auditing Journal*.

Merchant, K. A. (1990). The effects of financial controls on data manipulation and management myopia. *Accounting, Organizations and Society*, *15*(4), 297–313. doi:10.1016/0361-3682(90)90021-L

Moyer, S. E. (1990). Capital adequacy ratio regulations and accounting choices in commercial banks. *Journal of Accounting and Economics*, *13*(2), 123–154. doi:10.1016/0165-4101(90)90027-2

Rahmani, A., & Bashiri Manesh, N. (2013). Evaluation of detection model of earnings management. *Journal of Accounting and Auditing*, *19*, 1–20.

Sajjadi, S. H., Dastgir, M., Hossinzadeh, A. H., & Akhgar, M. O. (2012). Analysis of methods using management authorities in earnings management reporting and the impact of firms' characteristics on methods using management authorities. *Accounting Knowledge*, *3*(8), 7–30.

Shah, S. Z. A., & Butt, S. (2011). Creative accounting: A tool to help companies in a crisis or a practice to land them into crises. In *International Conference on Business and Economics Research-[IPEDR]*. IACSIT Press.

Spathis, C. (2002). Detecting false financial statements using published data: Some evidence from Greece. *Managerial Auditing Journal*, *17*(4), 179–191. doi:10.1108/02686900210424321

Spathis, C., Doumpos, M., & Zopounidis, C. (2002). Detecting falsified financial statements: A comparative study using multicriteria analysis and multivariate statistical techniques. *European Accounting Review*, *11*(3), 509–535. doi:10.1080/0963818022000000966

Taleb Nia, G., & Safari Sarchah, F. (2014). Comparison of linear accruals models to assess their ability to predict earnings management. *Journal of Applied Environmental and Biological Sciences*, *4*(10), 200–210.

Chapter 10 Misinformation on Social Media Platforms in the Global Crisis of Coronavirus

Elina Ahmadi
Independent Researcher, Australia

ABSTRACT

With COVID-19 turning into a public health crisis, several theories about the origin of the virus on the internet have sparked controversy. Challenges of distinguishing legal content from fake increases the importance of deleting such information through social media networks. Misinformation was created from social media and websites without credible evidence. The COVID-19 epidemic has spread alongside what the World Health Organization calls "infodemic" misinformation. Each social media company responds differently to misinformation and therefore this lack of consistency can lead to confusion among social media users. As the dissemination of such information endangers public health, this chapter focuses on studies to track misinformation on the popular social media. Additionally, one of the consequences of the coronavirus outbreak is the creation of social panic and rapid changes in people's lifestyles caused by social networks. This study investigates the role of social networks in the formation of social phobia and lifestyle changes on account of the corona virus.

INTRODUCTION

Nowadays, the coronavirus outbreak has become a major global crisis affecting many countries. Over the centuries, epidemics such as the black plague (destructive

DOI: 10.4018/978-1-7998-8235-0.ch010

worldwide epidemic of bubonic plague that affected Europe and Asia in the mid-1300s), great Plague of London (from 1665 to 1666), Leprosy (Hansen's disease) in Europe between the 12th and 14th centuries, syphilis (great pox) as an epidemic disease invaded Naples in the first of the Italian Wars, and affected Europe, malaria, and now the corona virus in 2020 indicate the number of victims and the density of corpses in cities, villages and the chaos of public space in different parts of the world.

Examples of these disturbances are mass graves without the names and logos of victims of the corona virus in countries. One of the most important consequences of the coronavirus outbreak is the creation of social anxiety and panic around the world as well as rapid and unbelievable changes in lifestyle. Fear of being exposed to this virus has led to irrational and dramatic behavior in societies (Beck, 1998). Beck defines it as a regular way to deal with the dangers and insecurities of self-renewal. He attributes this to a wide-ranging change he calls the reflexive modernization.

Thus, the reflectivity of people and society binds them to a complex structure of known unknowns. Reflexive modernization is a form of social change driven by seemingly scientific or logical judgments and actions. But in practice consists of reflexes (involved or contaminated with knowledge, image, technology, wealth, power, desire, etc.), so it is intended to create a risky situation (Chang, 2017). Coronavirus outbreaks indicate that endangered communities lead to vulnerable communities. However, pregnant women, families with children, older people, people with disabilities, and low-income people suffer from disproportionate damage in epidemics and natural disasters (Marshall et al., 2020).

An interesting feature of this crisis or epidemic storm is the coronavirus (Chang et al., 2020). There is a synchronicity of gaining knowledge about the virus and the spread of the virus. Not only did the virus itself spread rapidly, but misinformation about the spread of the disease was widely shared. Thus, panic broke out among the public as social media panic moved faster than the spread of the Corona virus (Depoux et al., 2020). In the process of the outbreak of the corona phenomenon, people under the influence of the immediate dangers of becoming infected with the virus, directly and indirectly through virtual social networks, sometimes engaged in uncoordinated and irrational actions. For example, irrational behaviors such as some people rushing to pharmacies and stores for masks and hygiene items can be mentioned; therefore, it can be said that the negative behavior of social networks leads to the formation of social phobia that has common consequences such as confusion and numbness, severe anxiety, excitement and aggression, and perhaps persistent fear.

This chapter is about misinformation on the popular social media. In addition, it examines the role of social networks in the formation of social panic and lifestyle changes by reason of the corona virus.

LITERATURE REVIEW

Another issue that has arisen as a result of the increasing use of virtual social networks in the corona world is rapid lifestyle changes in the shortest possible time. In the process of changing the lifestyle of people who have contact and social relations with each other at the same time, they show intense fear of themselves and try to stay away from each other or show a kind of disorganization that leads to rejection and distance from each other.

How to send key information to the public during a coronavirus outbreak is critical (Lancet, 2020). One of the factors of increasing online informing during the process of coronavirus infection in different countries of the world was social networks, so that the spread of the virus led to a tsunami of social media (Morad et al., 2020). Recently, social networks have become one of the most powerful agents of change and are built on various topics for different populations of society (Ikpi, and Undelikwo, 2019). These networks are an important source of information and news and effective tools for raising awareness of medical knowledge around the world (McGowan et al., 2012).

Social networks also accelerate social change by informing and connecting like-minded groups. Social networks, on the one hand, are the cornerstone of social capital (Lee, 2015). But on the other hand, the edge of these media can lead to the formation of dramatic collective behaviors and major changes in lifestyle in society. These social networks have made it possible to access the latest global information about the corona virus through communication and information sharing in social groups. Whereas the nature of social phobia and the changes that have taken place in the way of life are manifested in a methodical way in the form of mass media these days. On the other hand, these lifestyle changes in traditional societies are harder and more resistant than in large cities.

Ikpi and Undelikwo (2019) in a study sought to determine the extent to which students use social media (Facebook, Twitter and WhatsApp) to change lifestyles related to their health included eating habits, sexual behaviors, smoking and alcohol use, drug use, and engaging in bodybuilding activities. The results showed that the use of social media by students at the University of Calabar had a significant impact on their lifestyle modification. Chukwuere and Chukwuere (2017) in a study showed that social media has changed the way people think, interact, communicate, love and their social lifestyle. Chen and Chiang (2014) showed that presence in virtual social networks has often been for leisure, entertainment, and informing friends.

Baqaei et al. (2011) state that family-based social networks change the attitude of family members towards a healthy lifestyle. Jany et al. (2016) showed that cognitive-behavioral therapy through the Internet has reduced coronary anxiety in health care workers. Rouhani et al. (2017) in a study presented that social networks with components of stress tolerance (tolerance, absorption, evaluation, and regulation) and social fear (fear and avoidance) had significant relationships and students with more use of social networks, tolerated less anxiety and more social fear.

Forghani and Mohajeri (2015) in a study showed that there is a relationship between the components of life style (change in taste in type of clothing, diet, makeup, choice of decoration and home furniture, shopping style, leisure, and changes in interactions and communication) with the use of mobile social networks, so that with increasing hours of use of these networks, changes in each of the components of lifestyle become more.

Pourmoudat and Kajbaf (2017) in a study showed that those who use mobile social networks more, are more likely to be addicted to the Internet and have social anxiety. Sadeghi and Ameri (2016) in a study of the social harms of virtual social networks showed that the formation of virtual social networks, along with positive and constructive opportunities, have caused extensive changes in the behavior of citizens. Kalateh Sadati et al. (2020) concluded that one of the consequences of the coronavirus outbreak is social anxiety and panic around the world which has raised serious concerns for citizens in all countries, even in communities without outbreaks.

Castells (2009) describes the characteristics of social networks as (1) flexibility, meaning the ability to reconstruct for adaptation to environmental changes and pay attention to goals, while changing components and finding new connections; (2) scalability, the ability to expand or contract the size of a network that reduces the likelihood of network disruption; (3) sustainability, which is a sign of the ability of networks, because they do not have a single centrality, but operate on a large scale. The functions of social networks affect social change and transformation, especially among young people. According to Castells, in new communication media, there are new and democratic possibilities for communication and participation. With these facilities, people will be able to create their own virtual worlds, which is the basis for the democratization of ideas and beliefs.

Interaction between information technology, the economic crises of capitalism, and their subsequent restructuring and the flourishing of socio-cultural movements such as libertarianism, human rights, feminism and environmentalism created a new dominant social structure called a society network, a new economy called the global information economy, and a new culture, which is the virtual culture.

It is mentioned that if Corona stays on the planet for up to a year, it will change the culture of social interaction and make friendly gatherings smaller. In this process, the presence and physics of people give way to digital and virtual images. The dominance of phones and the world of the Internet will fill the vacancies of our people and loved ones. In the post-Corona world, there may be many empty tables and chairs that are empty of attendance. Perhaps the post-Corona man owes more to technology than anything else. The human education system will change.

Video conferencing and Internet training is a new chapter in the future of science and education. All schools will inevitably be equipped with the latest means of transmitting knowledge, and the definitions of many educational sciences will change dramatically. This could indirectly and sometimes directly protect the destruction of many forests for the printing of textbooks across the planet.

Misinformation on Social Media

Social networks such as YouTube and Twitter provide a chance of direct access to extraordinary amounts of information and may reinforce rumors and suspicious information. The study of the impact of social media on the understanding of polar issues is also considered in the case of COVID-19. Topics associated with current infodemics are actually explored by the scientific literature from a variety of perspectives, including the dynamics of conspiracy theories, the impact of robots and automated accounts, and the threat of misinformation with regard to dissemination and feedback. Cinelli et al. (2020) published COVID-19 information by extensive data analysis on Twitter, Instagram, YouTube, Reddit and Gab.

Table 1. Posts related to COVID-19 containing misinformation based on various studies

Social media	Total no. of tweets or posts	Tweets or posts including misinformation or jokes or both, no. (%)	No. of retweets or repostings of the tweet or post including misinformation
Twitter	212846	413 (0.2)	NR
Facebook	1 350	97 (7.2)	NR
Twitter	1 923	168 (8.7)	2 338
Twitter	942	100 (10.6)	59955
Weibo	1 923	206 (10.7)	232
Twitter	673	194a (28.8)	NR
Twitter	351	50 (14.2)	NR

COVID-19: coronavirus disease 2019; NR: not reported.
(Gabarron et al., 2021).

In Table 1, misinformation of COVID-19 is tracked in various social media.

Figure 1. Top panel: activity (likes, comments, postings, etc.) distribution for each social media. Middle panel: The most discussed topics about COVID-19 on any social media. Bottom panel: Cumulative number of content (posts, tweets, videos, etc.) generated from January 1st to February 14th. Due to Twitter API restrictions on past data collection, the first data point for Twitter is January 27th
Source: Cinelli et al., 2020

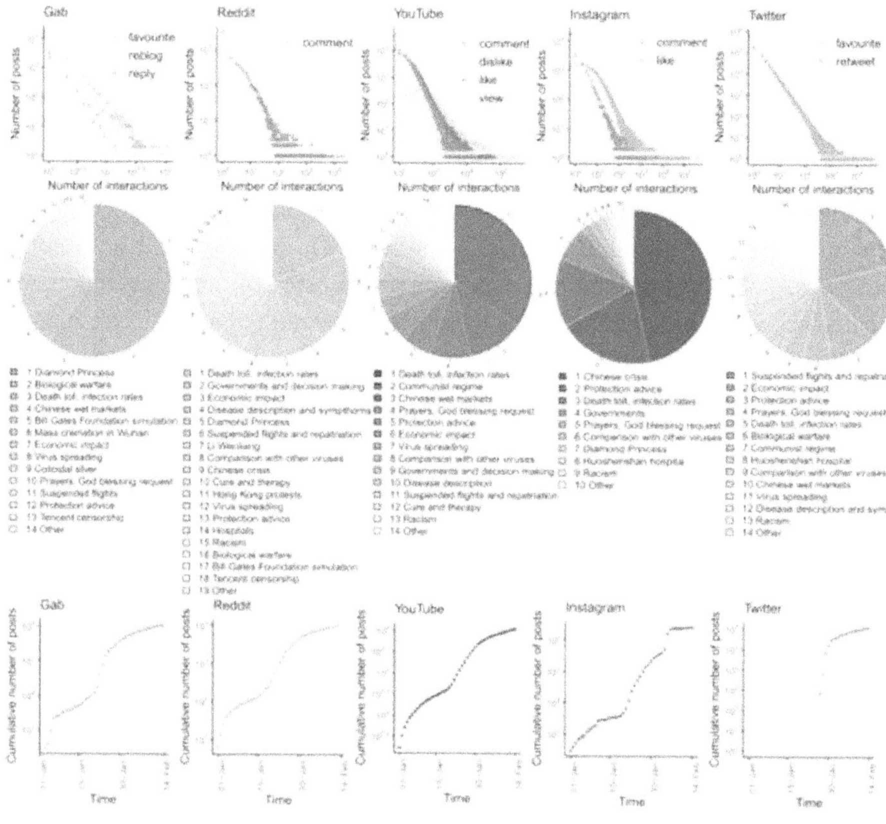

METHODOLOGY

After literature review, the conceptual model, shown in Figure 2 is analyzed through the research methodology.

The present study in terms of approach is quantitative and with regard to strategy and data collection is correlation and descriptive survey type. The statistical population of the study is citizens over 20 years old in a city that is about seven hundred thousand people. The sample size was 320 people who were selected by multi-stage cluster random sampling. Data collection tools were a standard questionnaire for social phobia and a researcher-made questionnaire for lifestyle change. For the validity of the research tool, face and structural validity were used. For face validity, after designing the items, they were provided to university professors and experts. The comments of these people in order to measure the items, eventually led to the selection of appropriate items. The factor analysis using the Kaiser–Meyer–Olkin (KMO) test was more than0.85, which shows that there is no need to remove any items. Bartlett's test showed this significance at a level of at least 95% confidence. The results of Cronbach's alpha showed that the reliability of social fear was 0.807, social avoidance was 0.843, physiological distress was 0.860, social panic was 0.842, and change in life style was 0.920. Pearson correlation test and SPSS software were used for data analysis.

Figure 2. Conceptual model

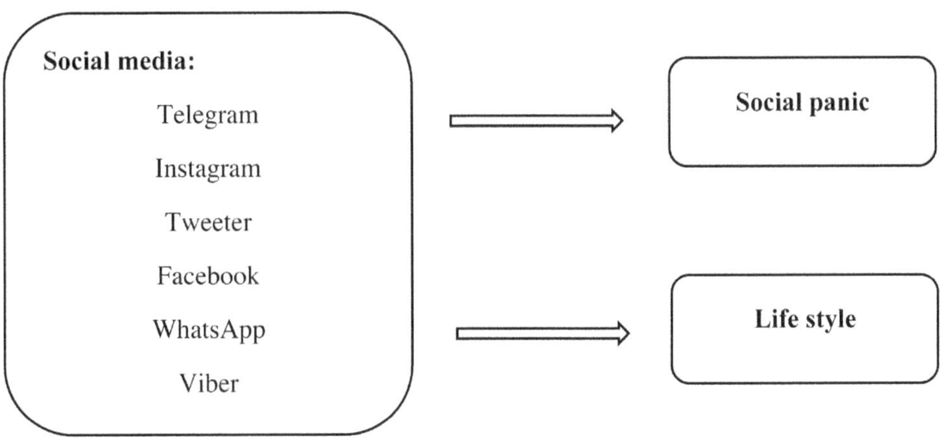

RESULT

The results of the correlation between the use of social networks with the level of fear and the change in lifestyle caused by corona show that the value of Pearson correlation between the use of Viber network with social panic is 0.306, which is the highest of all. Additionally, there is a significant relationship between the use of social networks and the level of social panic and lifestyle changes.

DISCUSSION

Fear of the spread of the coronavirus has affected people around the world. On the other hand, some social networks try to incite social fear. Because of the excessive dominance of these networks over culture and society, they can play a vital role in managing or inciting fear. On the other hand, the social media in connection with the crisis can play the role of dampers to neutralize the effects of fear to some extent, in this situation, fear is controlled and eliminated through numerous discussions. The results show that the average level of social fear in society is lower than expected. But the difference is higher for lifestyle changes. It is inferred that social networks have performed relatively well in managing the crisis of coronary heart disease. To change the lifestyle, these many changes in lifestyle are not unrelated to media and social networks.

Table 2. Correlation between the use of social networks with the level of social panic and lifestyle changes caused by corona

Social networks	Statistic	Social panic				life style
		Social fear	Social Avoidance	Physiological discomfort	Total	
Telegram	Correlation	0.079	0.017	0.189	0.121	0.066
	Significance	0.16	0.76	0.001	0.013	0.23
Instagram	Correlation	0.187	0.201	0.205	0.227	0.07
	Significance	0.001	0.000	0.000	0.000	0.21
Tweeter	Correlation	0.109	0.023	0.157	0.126	0.065
	Significance	0.05	0.68	0.005	0.024	0.24
Facebook	Correlation	0.271	0.101	0.023	0.192	0.023
	Significance	0.000	0.07	0.67	0.001	0.67
WhatsApp	Correlation	0.044	0.043	0.173	0.112	0.039
	Significance	0.43	0.43	0.002	0.045	0.48
Viber	Correlation	0.159	0.184	0.337	0.306	0.096
	Significance	0.004	0.001	0.000	0.000	0.08

CONCLUSION

This chapter was about misinformation on the popular social media. In this regard, after reviewing studies, it presented a conceptual model, which addressed the relationship between social media such as Telegram, Instagram, WhatsApp, Viber, Facebook, and Tweeter with social panic and life style as well. It is concluded that there is a significant relationship between the utilization of social media and the level of social panic and lifestyle changes.

Given the relationship between social networks and social phobia, it is suggested that the relevant authorities manage to counter the Corona rumors by informing the public through the media. In this regard, the growth of collective rationality through raising public awareness is effective in reducing fear. People, while observing health protocols such as physical distance, using masks and personal hygiene, should be aware of the dangerous consequences of this virus, and change their lifestyle in accordance with the most effective ways to deal with this virus.

REFERENCES

Baghaei, N., Kimani, S., Freyne, J., Brindal, E., Berkovsky, S., & Smith, G. (2011). Engaging families in lifestyle changes through social networking. *International Journal of Human-Computer Interaction*, *27*(10), 971–990. doi:10.1080/10447318.2011.555315

Bech, U. (1998). *World risk society*. Wiley.

Castells, M. (2009). *Communication Power*. Oxford University Press.

Chang, D., Lin, M., Wei, L., Xie, L., Zhu, G., Cruz, C. S. D., & Sharma, L. (2020). Epidemiologic and clinical characteristics of novel coronavirus infections involving 13 patients outside Wuhan, China. China [published online ahead of print. *Journal of the American Medical Association*, *323*(11), 1092–1093. doi:10.1001/jama.2020.1623 PMID:32031568

Chang, K. S. (2017). Reflexive modernization. In B. S. Turner (Ed.), *Encyclopedia of social theory*. JohnWiley & Sons, Ltd.

Chen, K. C., Chiang, M., & Poor, H. V. (2014). From technological networks to social networks. *IEEE Journal on Selected Areas in Communications*, *31*(9), 548–572. doi:10.1109/JSAC.2013.SUP.0513049

Cinelli, M., Quattrociocchi, W., Galeazzi, A., Valensise, C. M., Brugnoli, E., Schmidt, A. L., Zola, P., Zollo, F., & Scala, A. (2020). The COVID-19 social media infodemic. *Scientific Reports*, *10*(16598). https://www.nature.com/articles/s41598-020-73510-5 PMID:33024152

Forghani, M. M., & Mohajeri, R. (2015). The relationship between the use of virtual social networks. and changes in the lifestyle of young people. *New Media Studies*, *4*, 259–292.

Gabarron, E., Oyeyemi, S. O., & Wynn, R. (2021). COVID-19-related misinformation on social media: A systematic review. *Bulletin of the World Health Organization*, *99*(6), 455–463A. doi:10.2471/BLT.20.276782 PMID:34108756

Ikpi, N. E., & Undelikwo, V. A. (2019). Social media use and students' health-lifestyle modification in University of Calabar, Nigeria. *European Journal of Interdisciplinary Studies*, *5*(1), 47–54. doi:10.26417/ejis.v5i1.p47-54

Jany, N., Jany, S., & Rahimi, P. (2020). The effect of cognitive-behavioral therapy through the Internet on reducing coronary anxiety. *Information and Communication Technology in Educational Sciences*, *40*, 129–145.

Kalateh Sadati A K, B Lankarani M H, Bagheri Lankarani K. (2020). Risk society, global vulnerability and fragile resilience, sociological view on the coronavirus outbreak, *Shiraz E-Med Journal Online* ahead of Print ; 21(4):e102263. . doi:10.5812/semj.102263

Lancet, T.The Lancet. (2020). COVID-19: Fighting panic with information. *Lancet*, *395*(10224), 537. doi:10.1016/S0140-6736(20)30379-2 PMID:32087777

Lee, S., Seo, K., & Sharma, A. (2015). Corporate social responsibility and firm performance in the airline industry: The moderating role of oil prices. *Tourism Management*, *38*, 20–30. doi:10.1016/j.tourman.2013.02.002

McGowan, B., Wasko, M., Vartabedian, B., Miller, R. S., Freiherr, D. D., & Abdolrasulnia, M. (2012). Understanding the factors that influence the adoption and meaningful use of social media by physicians to share medical information. *Journal of Medical Internet Research*, *14*(5), 1–11. doi:10.2196/jmir.2138 PMID:23006336

Marshall, J., Wiltshire, J., Delva, J., Bello, T., & Masys, A. J. (2020). Natural and manmade disasters: vulnerable populations. In A. Masys, R. Izurieta, & M. Reina Ortiz (Eds.), *Global health security. Advanced sciences and technologies for security applications*. Springer. doi:10.1007/978-3-030-23491-1_7

Mourad, A., Srour, A., Harmanani, H., Jenainatiy, C., & Arafeh, M. (2020). Critical impact of social networks Infodemic on defeating coronavirus COVID-19 pandemic: Twitter-based study and research directions. Retrieved from: https://arxiv.org/abs/2005.08820

Pourmoudat, K., & Kajbaf, M. B. (2017). Study of social anxiety in students using the Internet and virtual social networks. *Social Psychological Review*, *6*(23), 93–105.

Rouhani, N. S., Seyed Mousavi, M., Gorji, M., & Samimi, Z. (2017). Comparison of the effect of tolerance of anxiety and social fear on the use of students' social networks. *Information and Communication Technology in Educational Sciences*, *35*, 33–53.

Sadeghi, A., & Ameri, Z. (2015). Virtual social networks and social harms, case study: Public security. *Journal of Survey in Teaching Humanities*, *2*(5), 51–65.

Compilation of References

Ableev, S. R., & Kuzminskaya, S. I. (2015). Manipulation of Mass Consciousness: Political Mythology and Demonization Strategy. *Bulletin of the Moscow University of the Ministry of Internal Affairs of Russia*, (5), 172–176.

Acar, G., & Koscun, A. (2020). A comparison of models for predicting discretionary accruals: A cross-country analysis. *Journal of Asian Finance, Economics and Business*, *7*(9), 315–328.

Adjei, J. K., Adams, S., Mensah, I. K., Tobbin, P. E., & Odei-Appiah, S. (2020). Digital Identity Management on Social Media: Exploring the Factors That Influence Personal Information Disclosure on Social Media. *Sustainability*, *12*(23), 9994. doi:10.3390u12239994

Agapova, E. A. (2017). On the role of the media in manipulating public consciousness. *Humanities and Social Sciences*, (5), 2–8.

Aghayi, M. A., & Chalaki, P. (2009). Analysis of the relationship between characteristics of corporate governance and earnings management in companies listed on the Tehran Stock Exchange. *Accountability in Research*, *1*(4), 54–77.

Ahmad, A. R., & Murad, H. R. (2020). The impact of social media on panic during the COVID-19 pandemic in Iraqi Kurdistan: Online questionnaire study. *Journal of Medical Internet Research*, *22*(5), e19556. doi:10.2196/19556 PMID:32369026

Ahmed, M. E., Rabin, M. R. I., & Chowdhury, F. N. (2020). *COVID-19: Social media sentiment analysis on reopening.* arXiv preprint arXiv:2006.00804.

Akerlof, G. A. (1970). The market for "Lemons": Quality uncertainty and the market mechanism. *The Quarterly Journal of Economics*, *84*(3), 488–500. doi:10.2307/1879431

Ali, S. (2020). *Combatting against Covid-19 & misinformation: A systematic review.* Human Arenas., doi:10.100742087-020-00139-1

Ambrose, S. (2020). *M'sia Health Minister Drew Flak for Suggesting That Drinking Hot Water Would Prevent COVID-19.* Retrieved from https://goodyfeed.com/msia-health-minister-covid19/

Amineva, E. S. (2018). Techniques and techniques for manipulating public consciousness in the weekly "Arguments and Facts". *Philological sciences. Questions of theory and practice*, *1-2*(79).

Anderson, J., & Rainie, L. (2017). The future of truth and misinformation online. Pew Research Center.

Apuke, O. D., & Omar, B. (2021). Fake news and COVID-19: Modelling the predictors of fake news sharing among social media users. *Telematics and Informatics*, *56*, 101475. doi:10.1016/j.tele.2020.101475

Aquinas, T. (1964). *Commentary on the Nicomachean ethics* (C. I. Litzinger, Trans.). Henry Regnery Company.

Baek, K., Holton, A., Harp, D., & Yaschur, C. (2011). The links that bind: Uncovering novel motivations for linking on Facebook. *Computers in Human Behavior*, *27*(6), 2243–2248. doi:10.1016/j.chb.2011.07.003

Bagchi, K., & Udo, G. (2003). An Analysis of the Growth of Computer and Internet Security Breaches. *Communications of the AIS*, *12*(46), 684–700. doi:10.17705/1CAIS.01246

Baghaei, N., Kimani, S., Freyne, J., Brindal, E., Berkovsky, S., & Smith, G. (2011). Engaging families in lifestyle changes through social networking. *International Journal of Human-Computer Interaction*, *27*(10), 971–990. doi:10.1080/10447318.2011.555315

Bahar Moghdam, M., & Koohi, A. (2010). Analysis of the earnings management types in in companies listed on the Tehran Stock Exchange. *Accounting Knowledge Journal*, *1*(2), 75–93.

Bandura, A. (1986). *Social foundations of thought and action: A social cognitive theory*. Prentice-Hall.

Banerjee, D., & Rai, M. (2020). *Social isolation in COVID-19: The impact of loneliness*. Academic Press.

Baumeister, R. F., DeWall, C. N., Ciarocco, N. J., & Twenge, J. M. (2005). Social exclusion impairs self-regulation. *Journal of Personality and Social Psychology*, *88*(4), 589–604. doi:10.1037/0022-3514.88.4.589 PMID:15796662

Bautista, J. R., Zhang, Y., & Gwizdka, J. (2021). Healthcare professionals' acts of correcting health misinformation on social media. *International Journal of Medical Informatics*, *148*(104375). Advance online publication. doi:10.1016/j.ijmedinf.2021.104375 PMID:33461008

Bech, U. (1998). *World risk society*. Wiley.

Bell, T., & Carcello, J. (2000). A decision aid for assessing the likelihood of fraudulent financial reporting. *Auditing*, *9*(1), 169–178. doi:10.2308/aud.2000.19.1.169

Belousov, A. B. (2012). Edward Bernays: From Public Opinion Manipulation to Consent Engineering. *Policy. Political Studies*, (4), 143–148.

Beneish, M. D. (1997). Detecting GAAP violation: Implications for assessing earnings management among firms with extreme financial performance. *Journal of Accounting and Public Policy*, *16*(3), 271–309. doi:10.1016/S0278-4254(97)00023-9

Beneish, M. D. (1998). Discussion of 'are accruals during initial public offerings opportunistic?' *Review of Accounting Studies*, *3*(1/2), 209–221. doi:10.1023/A:1009692703952

Beneish, M. D. (1999). The detection of earnings manipulation. *Financial Analysts Journal*, *55*(5), 24–36. doi:10.2469/faj.v55.n5.2296

Bento, A., & Bento, R. (2004). Empirical test of a hacking model: An exploratory study. *Communications of the AIS*, *14*(32), 678–690. doi:10.17705/1CAIS.01432

Bernays, E. (2012). Manipulation of Public Opinion: How and Why. Policy. *Political Studies*, (4), 149–159.

Beyens, I., Frison, E., & Eggermont, S. (2016). "I don't want to miss a thing": Adolescents' fear of missing out and its relationship to adolescents' social needs, Facebook use, and Facebook related stress. *Computers in Human Behavior*, *64*, 1–8. doi:10.1016/j.chb.2016.05.083

Bhandari, H., & Yasunobu, K. (2009). What is social capital? A comprehensive review of the concept. *Asian Journal of Social Science*, *37*(3), 480–510. doi:10.1163/156853109X436847

Bhatt, G. (2001). Knowledge management in organization. *Journal of Knowledge Management*, *5*(1), 68–75. doi:10.1108/13673270110384419

Blackwell, D., Leaman, C., Tramposch, R., Osborne, C., & Liss, M. (2017). Extraversion, neuroticism, attachment style and fear of missing out as predictors of social media use and addiction. *Personality and Individual Differences*, *116*, 69–72. doi:10.1016/j.paid.2017.04.039

Bock, G. W., Mahmood, M., Sharma, S., & Kang, Y. J. (2010). The impact of information overload and contribution overload on continued usage of electronic knowledge repositories. *Journal of Organizational Computing and Electronic Commerce*, *20*(3), 257–278. doi:10.1080/10919392.2010.494530

Bode, L., & Vraga, E. K. (2017). See something, say something: Correction of global health misinformation on social media. *Health Communication*, 1–10. doi:10.1080/10410236.2017.1331312 PMID:28622038

Borchert, D. (2005). *Encyclopedia of philosophy* (2nd ed.). Macmillan Inc.

Boyarkin, V. V., & Boyarkina, L. A. (2012). Manipulation of Public Consciousness: Present and Future. In *Proceedings of conferences SIC Sociosphere* (No. 1, pp. 51-53). Vedecko vydavatelske centrum Sociosfera-CZ sro.

Boyd, D. M., & Ellison, N. B. (2007, October). Social network sites: Definition, history, and scholarship. *Journal of Computer-Mediated Communication*, *13*(1), 210–230. doi:10.1111/j.1083-6101.2007.00393.x

Bozorg, A. M., & Ghafar Por, F. (2012). Comparison of prediction models for detecting earnings management. *Journal of Applied Research, Financial Reporting, Corporate Audit*, *1*, 27-50.

Brady, J. T., Kelly, M. E., & Stein, S. L. (2017). The trump effect: With no peer review, how do we know what to really believe on social media? *Clinics in Colon and Rectal Surgery, 30*(04), 270–276. doi:10.1055-0037-1604256 PMID:28924401

Brock, F. J., & Dhillon, G. S. (2001). Managerial information: The basics. *Journal of International Information Management, 10*(2), 45–59.

Brooks, G., Heffner, A., & Henderson, D. (2014). A SWOT analysis of competitive knowledge from social media for a small start-up business. *Review of Business Information Systems, 18*(1), 23–34. doi:10.19030/rbis.v18i1.8540

Carley, K. M. (2000). *Information security: The human perspective.* Department of Social and Decision Sciences, Carnegie Mellon University.

Casey, T., & Christ, K. (2002). Social capital and economic performance in the American states. *The American Political Science Association Conference.*

Castells, M. (2009). *Communication Power.* Oxford University Press.

Chamberlain, P. R. (2010). Twitter as a vector for disinformation. *Journal of Information Warfare, 9*(1), 11-17.

Chan, A. K., Nickson, C. P., Rudolph, J. W., Lee, A., & Joynt, G. M. (2020). *Social media for rapid knowledge dissemination: early experience from the COVID-19 pandemic.* Academic Press.

Chang, D., Lin, M., Wei, L., Xie, L., Zhu, G., Cruz, C. S. D., & Sharma, L. (2020). Epidemiologic and clinical characteristics of novel coronavirus infections involving 13 patients outside Wuhan, China. China [published online ahead of print. *Journal of the American Medical Association, 323*(11), 1092–1093. doi:10.1001/jama.2020.1623 PMID:32031568

Chang, K. S. (2017). Reflexive modernization. In B. S. Turner (Ed.), *Encyclopedia of social theory.* JohnWiley & Sons, Ltd.

Chen, K. C., Chiang, M., & Poor, H. V. (2014). From technological networks to social networks. *IEEE Journal on Selected Areas in Communications, 31*(9), 548–572. doi:10.1109/JSAC.2013.SUP.0513049

Chen, K. C., & Jang, S. J. (2010). Motivation in online learning: Testing a model of self-determination theory. *Computers in Human Behavior, 26*(4), 741–752. doi:10.1016/j.chb.2010.01.011

Chen, X., Sin, S. C. J., Theng, Y. L., & Lee, C. S. (2015). Why students share misinformation on social media: Motivation, gender, and study-level differences. *Journal of Academic Librarianship, 41*(5), 583–592. doi:10.1016/j.acalib.2015.07.003

Chernikova, V.E. (2015). Manipulation of mass consciousness as a phenomenon of the information society. *Philosophical Sciences. Theory and practice of social development, 3,* 141-144. Doi:10.22363/231291822017211203220

Cheung, E. (2015). An outbreak of fear, rumours and stigma: Psychosocial support for the Ebola virus disease outbreak in West Africa. *Intervention (Amstelveen, Netherlands), 13*(1), 70–76. doi:10.1097/WTF.0000000000000079

Chiorando, M. (2020). *Snopes Debunks Meme Claiming No One Is Buying Vegan Food During Coronavirus Stockpiling*. Retrieved from https://plantbasednews.org/news/snopes-debunks-meme-no-one-buying-vegan-food-coronavirus/

Chowdhury, G. G., & Chowdhury, S. C. (2003). *Introduction to digital libraries*. Facet Publishing.

Christofides, E., Muise, A., & Desmarais, S. (2009). Information disclosure and control on Facebook: Are they two sides of the same coin or two different processes? *Cyberpsychology & Behavior, 12*(3), 341–345. doi:10.1089/cpb.2008.0226 PMID:19250020

Cinelli, M., Quattrociocchi, W., Galeazzi, A., Valensise, C. M., Brugnoli, E., Schmidt, A. L., Zola, P., Zollo, F., & Scala, A. (2020). The COVID-19 social media infodemic. *Scientific Reports, 10*(1), 1–10. doi:10.103841598-020-73510-5 PMID:33024152

Coleman, J. S. (1990). *Foundations of social theory*. Harvard University Press.

Colwill, C. (2009). Human factors in information security: The insider threat- Who can you trust these days? *Information Security Technical Report, 14*(4), 186–196. doi:10.1016/j.istr.2010.04.004

Computer Emergency Response Team (CERT). (2004). *CERT Statistics*. Retrieved from https://whatis.techtarget.com/definition/CERT-Computer-Emergency-Readiness-Team

Copeland, R. M. (1968). Income smoothing. *Journal of Accounting Research, Empirical Research in Accounting, Selected Studies, 6*(Supplement), 101–116.

Cuadrado-Garcia, M., Ruiz-Mol, M., & Montoro-Pons, J. D. (2012). Academic contest and social networking to promote technology and information literacy among university students. *Procedia: Social and Behavioral Sciences, 46*(10), 222–226. doi:10.1016/j.sbspro.2012.05.097

Custers, E. J. F. M. (2019). Theories of truth and teaching clinical reasoning and problem solving. *Advances in Health Sciences Education: Theory and Practice, 24*(4), 839–848. doi:10.100710459-018-09871-4 PMID:30671703

Dabbous, A., Barakat, K. A., & Navarro, B. Q. (2021). *Fake news detection and social media trust: a cross-cultural perspective*. Behavior and Information Technology. Retrieved from https://www.tandfonline.com/doi/full/10.1080/0144929X.2021.1963475

Davenport, T. H., & Prusak, L. (1998). *Working knowledge: How organizations manage what they know*. Harvard Business School Press.

De George, R. T. (2003). *The ethics of information technology and business*. Blackwell. doi:10.1002/9780470774144

DeAngelo, L. E. (1986). Accounting numbers as market valuation substitutes: A study of management buyouts of public stockholders. *The Accounting Review, 61*(3), 400–420.

Dechow, P., Sloan, R., & Sweeney, A. P. (1995). Detecting earnings management. *The Accounting Review, 70*(2), 193–225.

Deci, E. L., Eghrari, H., Patrick, B. C., & Leone, D. R. (1994). Facilitating internalization: The self-determination theory perspective. *Journal of Personality, 62*(1), 119–142. doi:10.1111/j.1467-6494.1994.tb00797.x PMID:8169757

Deci, E. L., & Ryan, R. M. (1985). The general causality orientations scale: Self-determination in personality. *Journal of Research in Personality, 19*(2), 109–134. doi:10.1016/0092-6566(85)90023-6

Diddi, A., & LaRose, R. (2006). Getting hooked on news: Uses and gratifications and the formation of news habits among college students in an Internet environment. *Journal of Broadcasting & Electronic Media, 50*(2), 193–210. doi:10.120715506878jobem5002_2

Diviani, N., van den Putte, B., Giani, S., & van Weert, J. C. (2015). Low health literacy and evaluation of online health information: A systematic review of the literature. *Journal of Medical Internet Research, 17*(5), e112. doi:10.2196/jmir.4018 PMID:25953147

Dordevic, M., Safieddine, F., Masri, W., & Pourghomi, P. (2016). Combating misinformation online: Identification of variables and proof-of-concept study. *15th Conference on e-Business, e-Services and e-Society (I3E).*

Dzieza, J. (2014). *Fake news sites are using Facebook to spread Ebola panic.* Retrieved from https://www.theverge.com/2014/10/22/7028983/fake-news-sites-are-using-facebook-to-spread-ebola-panic

Ebrahimi, M. (2021). Analysis of the impact of customer relationship management on innovation acquisition using agent-based modeling. In A. Amini, S. Bushell, & A. Mahmood (Eds.), *Driving innovation and productivity through sustainable automation* (pp. 1–28). IGI Global. doi:10.4018/978-1-7998-5879-9.ch001

Ekman, P. (1985). *Telling lies: Clues to deceit in the marketplace, politics, and marriage.* Norton & Company.

Ermakov, Yu. A. (1995). *Manipulation of a Person: Meaning, Techniques, Consequences.* Yekaterinburg: Publishing house Ural, University.

Fallis, D. (2009). *A conceptual analysis of disinformation.* Paper presented at the iConference.

Fang, J., Wang, X., Wen, Z., & Zhou, J. (2020). Fear of missing out and problematic social media use as mediators between emotional support from social media and phubbing behavior. *Addictive Behaviors, 107*, 106430. doi:10.1016/j.addbeh.2020.106430 PMID:32289745

Fanning, K., & Cogger, K. O. (1998). Neural network detection of management fraud using published financial data. *Intelligent Systems in Accounting, Finance & Management, 7*(1), 21–41. doi:10.1002/(SICI)1099-1174(199803)7:1<21::AID-ISAF138>3.0.CO;2-K

Ferguson, R., Gutberg, J., Schattke, K., Paulin, M., & Jost, N. (2015). Self-determination theory, social media and charitable causes: An in-depth analysis of autonomous motivation. *European Journal of Social Psychology*, *45*(3), 298–307. doi:10.1002/ejsp.2038

Fisher, K. E., Erdelez, S., & McKechnie, L. E. F. (2005). *Theories of information behavior*. Information Today, Inc.

Floridi, L. (2011). *The philosophy of information*. Oxford University Press. doi:10.1093/acprof:oso/9780199232383.001.0001

Forghani, M. M., & Mohajeri, R. (2015). The relationship between the use of virtual social networks. and changes in the lifestyle of young people. *New Media Studies*, *4*, 259–292.

Fox, C. J. (1983). *Information and misinformation: An investigation of the notions of information, misinformation, informing, and misinforming*. Greenwood.

Fukuyama, F. (1995). *Trust: The social virtues and the creation of prosperity*. Free Press.

Gabarron, E., Oyeyemi, S. O., & Wynn, R. (2021). COVID-19-related misinformation on social media: A systematic review. *Bulletin of the World Health Organization*, *99*(6), 455–463A. doi:10.2471/BLT.20.276782 PMID:34108756

Gagné, M., & Deci, E. L. (2005). Self-determination theory and work motivation. *Journal of Organizational Behavior*, *26*(4), 331–362. doi:10.1002/job.322

Garcia. (in press). *Un juez investiga el acoso de neonazis ucranios a un activista oculto en España*. https://elpais.com/espana/catalunya/2021-05-20/un-juez-investiga-el-acoso-de-neonazis-ucranios-a-un-activista-oculto-en-espana.html

Geiszler, M. (2014). *The effect of accrual quality, real activities earnings management and corporate governance on credit ratings* (PhD dissertation). The Graduate School of Management, The Kent State University.

Ghenai, A. (2017). Health Misinformation in Search and Social Media. In *Proceedings of the 2017 International Conference on Digital Health* (2-10), New York, NY: ACM.

Gibbs, J. L., Ellison, N. B., & Heino, R. D. (2006). Self-Presentation in Online Personals: The Role of Anticipated Future Interaction, Self-Disclosure, and Perceived Sucess in Internet Dating. *Communication Research*, *33*(2), 152–177. doi:10.1177/0093650205285368

Glahe, F., & Vorhies, F. (1989). Religion, liberty and economic development: An empirical investigation. *Public Choice*, *62*(3), 201–215. doi:10.1007/BF02337742

Goharian, H. (2015). *Designing an intelligent system for detecting and controlling security risks in the web environment 2* (Master Thesis). Tarbiat Modares University.

Gonzalez, J., & Sawicka, A. (2002). *A framework for human factors in information security*. Retrieved from http://www.wseas.us/e-library/conferences/brazil2002/papers/448-187.pdf

Gordon. (2019). *Posol Vengrii ob ukrainskom yazyke v shkolah Zakarpat'ya: Rebenok dolzhen izuchat' predmety na rodnom yazyke* [Ambassador of Hungary on the Ukrainian language in schools in Transcarpathia: A child should study subjects in their native language]. https://gordonua.com/news/politics/posol-vengrii-ob-ukrainskom-yazyke-v-shkolah-zakarpatya-rebenok-dolzhen-izuchat-predmety-na-rodnom-yazyke-1468964.html

Gordon, L. A., Loeb, M. P., Lucyshyn, W., & Richardson, R. (2004). *The 9th annual CSI/FBI computer crime and security survey*. Computer Security Institute.

Gorina, E. V. (2016). Kommunikativnye tekhnologii manipulyacii v SMI i voprosy informacionnoj bezopasnosti [Communication technologies of media manipulation and information security issues]. Ekaterinburg: Izd-vo Ural. un-ta, Russia.

Gorshkova, L. A. (2019). Functioning of euphemisms in newspaper and journalistic discourse in the process of manipulating public opinion. Media in the modern world. 58th Petersburg Readings, 173-175.

Grech, V., & Masukume, G. (2017). Fake news of baby booms 9 months after major sporting events distorts the public's understanding of early human development science. *Early Human Development, 115*, 16–17. doi:10.1016/j.earlhumdev.2017.08.007

Green, B. P., & Choi, J. H. (1997). Assessing the risk of management fraud through neural network technology. *Auditing, 16*(1), 14–28.

Grier, K. B., & Tullock, G. (1989). An empirical analysis of cross- -national economic growth. *Journal of Monetary Economics, 24*(2), 259–276. doi:10.1016/0304-3932(89)90006-8

Guess, A. M., Lerner, M., Lyons, B., Montgomery, J. M., Nyhan, B., Reifler, J., & Sircar, N. (2020). A digital media literacy intervention increases discernment between mainstream and false news in the United States and India. *Proceedings of the National Academy of Sciences of the United States of America, 117*(27), 15536–15545. doi:10.1073/pnas.1920498117 PMID:32571950

Gureeva, M. A. (2019). Manipulirovanie soznaniem i povedeniem lyudej v sisteme massovoj kul'tury [Manipulation of consciousness and behavior of people in the system of mass culture]. Sociology in the modern world: Science, education, creativity. Izd-vo Alt. un-ta.

Ha, L., Yoon, K., & Zhang, X. (2013). Consumption and dependency of social network sites as a news medium: A comparison between college students and general population. *Journal of Communication and Media Research, 5*(1), 1.

Hair, J. F., Hult, G. T. M., Ringle, C., & Sarstedt, M. (2014). *A primer on partial least squares structural equation modeling*. Sage.

Hansen, J. V., McDonald, J. B., Messier, W. F. Jr, & Bell, T. B. (1996). A generalized qualitative-response model and the analysis of management fraud. *Management Science, 42*(7), 1022–1032. doi:10.1287/mnsc.42.7.1022

Hazari, S., Hargrave, W., & Clenney, B. (2008). An empirical investigation of factors influencing information security behavior. *Journal of Information Privacy & Security*, *4*(4), 3–20. doi:10.1080/2333696X.2008.10855849

Healy, P. M. (1985). The Effect of Bonus Schemes on Accounting Decisions. *Journal of Accounting and Economics*, *7*(1-3), 85–107. doi:10.1016/0165-4101(85)90029-1

Henseler, J., Ringle, C. M., & Sarstedt, M. (2015). A new criterion for assessing discriminant validity in variance-based structural equation modeling. *Journal of the Academy of Marketing Science*, *43*(1), 115–135. doi:10.100711747-014-0403-8

Hinson, G. (2003). *Human factors in information security, Innovative information security awareness programs*. Notice Bored.

Hitler, A. (1925). *Mein Kampf.* Germany: Franz Eher Nachfolger GmbH: Jankauskas, V., & Šeputienė, J. (2007). The relation between social capital governance and economic performance in Europe. *TeorijaIrPraktika Business: Theory and Practice*, *VIII*(3), 131–138.

Hoetjes, M. (2013). *(Compulsive) Mobile Phone Checking Behavior Out of a Fear of Missing Out: Development, Psychometric Properties and Test-Retest Reliability of a C-FoMO-Scale Beata Hato ANR: 610304*. Academic Press.

Hu, C., & Racherla, P. (2008). Visual representation of knowledge networks: A social network analysis of hospitality research domain. *International Journal of Hospitality Management*, *27*(2), 302–312. doi:10.1016/j.ijhm.2007.01.002

Ibragimov, L. K. (2015). Internet manipulation technologies in the network space of politics. *The Contours of Global Transformations: Politics, Economics, Law*, *8*(2).

Ikpi, N. E., & Undelikwo, V. A. (2019). Social media use and students' health-lifestyle modification in University of Calabar, Nigeria. *European Journal of Interdisciplinary Studies*, *5*(1), 47–54. doi:10.26417/ejis.v5i1.p47-54

Imeni, M., Fallah, M., & Edalatpanah, S. A. (2021). *The effect of managerial ability on earnings classification shifting and agency cost of Iranian listed companies*. Retrieved from https://www.hindawi.com/journals/ddns/2021/5565605/

Impink, J. (2010). *Earnings manipulation and bankruptcy: WorldCom, Bachelor paper*. University of Amsterdam.

Islam, A. N., Laato, S., Talukder, S., & Sutinen, E. (2020). Misinformation sharing and social media fatigue during COVID-19: An affordance and cognitive load perspective. *Technological Forecasting and Social Change*, *159*, 120201. doi:10.1016/j.techfore.2020.120201 PMID:32834137

Jackson, T. W., & Farzaneh, P. (2012). Theory-based model of factors affecting information overload. *International Journal of Information Management*, *32*(6), 523–532. doi:10.1016/j.ijinfomgt.2012.04.006

Jany, N., Jany, S., & Rahimi, P. (2020). The effect of cognitive-behavioral therapy through the Internet on reducing coronary anxiety. *Information and Communication Technology in Educational Sciences*, *40*, 129–145.

Jia-lin, W., & Zeng-yi, Z. (2018). The Generation, Dissemination, Identification and Control of Misinformation—A Review of Existing Studies. *Science and Society*, *8*(3), 108–122.

Jones, J. (1991). Earnings Management during import relief investigations. *Journal of Accounting Research*, *29*(2), 193–228. doi:10.2307/2491047

Jouini, M., Rabai, L. B. A., & Aissa, A. B. (2014). Classification of security threats in information systems. *Procedia Computer Science*, *32*, 489–496. doi:10.1016/j.procs.2014.05.452

Jourard, S. M., & Friedman, R. (1970). Experimenter-subject" distance" and self-disclosure. *Journal of Personality and Social Psychology*, *15*(3), 278–282. doi:10.1037/h0029388 PMID:5485418

Kaigo, M. (2003). Initial Findings in the Perceptions and Behavioural Change by News on SARS in Japan. *Media Asia*, *30*(4), 216–219. doi:10.1080/01296612.2003.11726728

Kalateh Sadati A K, B Lankarani M H, Bagheri Lankarani K. (2020). Risk society, global vulnerability and fragile resilience, sociological view on the coronavirus outbreak, *Shiraz E-Med Journal Online* ahead of Print ; 21(4):e102263. . doi:10.5812/semj.102263

Kanekar, A. S., & Thombre, A. (2019). Fake medical news: Avoiding pitfalls and perils. *Family Medicine and Community Health*, *7*(4), e000142. doi:10.1136/fmch-2019-000142 PMID:32148726

Kaplan, A., & Haenlein, M. (2010). Users of the world, unite! The challenges and opportunities of social media. *Business Horizons*, *53*(1), 59–68. doi:10.1016/j.bushor.2009.09.003

Kara Murza, S. (2017). *Consciousness manipulation. XXI century*. Lites.

Karahanna, E., Xu, S. X., Xu, Y., & Zhang, N. A. (2018). The needs–affordances–features perspective for the use of social media. *Management Information Systems Quarterly*, *42*(3), 737–756. doi:10.25300/MISQ/2018/11492

Karlova, N. A., & Fisher, K. E. (2013). *A social diffusion model of misinformation and disinformation for understanding human information behaviour*. Retrieved from http://www.informationr.net/ir/18-1/paper573.html

Kasznik, R. (1999). On the association between voluntary disclosure and earnings management. *Journal of Accounting Research*, *37*(1), 57–81. doi:10.2307/2491396

Katz, E. J., & Aspden, P. (1997). A nation of strangers? *Communications of the ACM, 40*(12), 81-86. doi:10.1145/265563.265575

Kearns, G. S. (2006). The effect of top management support of SISP on strategic IS management: Insights from the US electric power industry. *Omega*, *34*(3), 236–253. doi:10.1016/j.omega.2004.10.008

Keshavarz, H. (2014). How credible is information on the web: Reflections on misinformation and disinformation. *Infopreneurship Journal*, *1*(2), 1–17.

KhanH.BasharO. K. M. R. (2008). *Religion and development: Are they complementary?* U21Global Working Paper Series, No. 006/2008. https://ssrn.com/abstract=1601048 doi:10.2139/ssrn.1601048

Khan, M. L., & Idris, I. K. (2019). Recognise misinformation and verify before sharing: A reasoned action and information literacy perspective. *Behaviour & Information Technology*, *38*(12), 1194–1212. doi:10.1080/0144929X.2019.1578828

Khan, S. A. (2017). A STRIDE model based threat modelling using unified and-or fuzzy operator for computer network security. *International Journal of Computing and Network Technology*, *5*(1), 13–20. doi:10.12785/ijcnt/050103

Khlopkov, K.A. (2009). The importance of mass media in the manipulation of mass consciousness. *Bulletin of the Krasnoyarsk State Pedagogical University by V.P. Astafieva*, (2).

Khrienko, A. P., & Khrienko, Al. P. (2008). Electoral ratings as a tool for manipulating public opinion. *RGGU Bulletin. Series "Philosophy. Sociology. Art Criticism,"* (2), 99–106.

Khvatov, K. Y., Timofeev, A. I., & Gulenko, P. I. (2014). Development and Application of Technologies for Manipulating Public Opinion: A Historical Review. Topical issues of development of the Russian economy, 45-52.

Kim, S. H., Yang, K. H., & Park, S. (2014). An integrative behavioral model of information security policy compliance. *TheScientificWorldJournal*, *3*, 1–12. doi:10.1155/2014/463870 PMID:24971373

Kirchherr, J., & Charles, K. (2018). Enhancing the sample diversity of snowball samples: Recommendations from a research project on anti-dam movements in Southeast Asia. *PLoS One*, *13*(8), e0201710. doi:10.1371/journal.pone.0201710 PMID:30133457

Knack, S. (2002). Social capital and the quality of government: Evidence from the State. *American Journal of Political Science*, *46*(4), 772–785. doi:10.2307/3088433

Knack, S., & Keefer, P. (1997). Does social capital have an economic payoff? A cross- country investigation. *The Quarterly Journal of Economics*, *112*(4), 1251–1288. doi:10.1162/003355300555475

Knapp, K. J., Marshall, T. E., Rainer, R. K., & Ford, N. (2005). *Managerial dimensions in information security: A theoretical model of organizational effectiveness*. Management Information Systems Department College of Business, Auburn University.

Knapp, K. J., Marshall, T. E., Rainer, R. K. Jr, & Morrow, D. W. (2004). *Top ranked information security issues: The 2004 International Information Systems Security Certification Consortium (ISC) 2 Survey Results*. Auburn University.

Koh, H. C., & Low, C. K. (2004). Going Concern Prediction using data mining techniques. *Managerial Auditing Journal, 19*(3), 462–476. doi:10.1108/02686900410524436

Kolosheina, M. G. (2020). Ugrozy ekonomicheskoj bezopasnosti i ih minimizacia [Threats to economic security and their minimization]. *Sovremennye tekhnologii v nauke i obrazovanii-STNO-2020.*

Koohang, A., & Weiss, E. (2003). Misinformation: Toward Creating a Prevention Framework. *Information Science.* Retrieved from https://proceedings.informingscience.org/IS2003Proceedings/docs/025Kooha.pdf

Kormendi, R. C., & Meguire, P. G. (1985). Macroeconomic determinants of growth. *Journal of Monetary Economics, 16*(1), 141–163. doi:10.1016/0304-3932(85)90027-3

Kothari, S. P., Leone, A. L., & Wasley, C. E. (2005). Performance matched discretionary accrual measures. *Journal of Accounting and Economics, 39*(1), 163–197. doi:10.1016/j.jacceco.2004.11.002

Kotulic, A. G., & Clark, J. G. (2004). Why there aren't more information security research studies. *Information & Management, 41*(5), 597–607. doi:10.1016/j.im.2003.08.001

Kovalik, E. V., & Gubin, A. I. (2019). Aktual'nost' razvitia mediakommunikacii [Relevance of media communication development]. Penzenskij gosudarstvennyj universitet, g. Penza.

Kozan, H., Baloğlu, M., Kesici, Ş., & Arpaci, İ. (2019). *The role of personality and psychological needs on the problematic internet use and problematic social media use.* Academic Press.

Kozlov, K. N. (2019). Mechanisms of manipulation of public opinion in modern politics. In Society and Power: History and Modernity (pp. 475-479). Academic Press.

Kozlova, O. N. (2010). Manipulyaciya soznaniem i sub"ektnost' v XXI veke [Manipulation of consciousness and subjectivity in the XXI century]. *Vestnik RGGU. Seriya. Filosofiya. Sociologiya. Iskusstvovedenie*, (3 (46)), 113–130.

Krainova, K. A. (2013). The Internet as a means of political manipulation in modern political governance. *PolitBook*, (2), 60–67.

Krasnova, H., Kolesnikova, E., & Guenther, O. (2009). *"It won't happen to me!" Self-disclosure in online social networks.* Academic Press.

Kraut, R., Kiesler, S., Boneva, B., Cummings, J., Helgeson, V., & Crawford, A. (2002). Internet paradox revisited. *Journal of Social Issues, 58*(1), 49-74.

Laato, S., Islam, A. N., Islam, M. N., & Whelan, E. (2020). What drives unverified information sharing and cyberchondria during the COVID-19 pandemic? *European Journal of Information Systems, 29*(3), 288–305. doi:10.1080/0960085X.2020.1770632

Lancet, T.The Lancet. (2020). COVID-19: Fighting panic with information. *Lancet, 395*(10224), 537. doi:10.1016/S0140-6736(20)30379-2 PMID:32087777

Larionova, D. P. (2015). Information as a social weapon. *Electronic Bulletin of the Rostov Social and Economic Institute*, (3-4), 1082–1086.

Lee, S., Seo, K., & Sharma, A. (2015). Corporate social responsibility and firm performance in the airline industry: The moderating role of oil prices. *Tourism Management*, *38*, 20–30. doi:10.1016/j.tourman.2013.02.002

Levashov, V. I. (2011). Manipulation of public opinion in the election campaign. *Metropolitan Management*, (3), 98–106.

Lewandowsky, S. U., Ecker, K. H., Seifert, C. M., Schwarz, N., & Cook, J. (2012). Misinformation and its correction. *Psychological Science in the Public Interest*, *13*(3), 106–131. doi:10.1177/1529100612451018 PMID:26173286

Lewis, A., Lord, A. S., Czeisler, B. M., & Caplan, A. (2016). Public education and misinformation on brain death in mainstream media. *Clinical Transplantation*, *9*(30), 1082–1089. doi:10.1111/ctr.12791 PMID:27314625

Liem, N. T., & Ntim, C. G. (2021). Accounting comparability and accruals-based earnings management: Evidence on listed firms in an emerging market. *Cognet Business and Management*, *8*(1). Retrieved from https://www.tandfonline.com/doi/full/10.1080/23311975.2021.1923356

Lin, J.W., Hwang, M., & Becker, J.D. (2003, Spring). A fuzzy neural network for assessing the risk of fraudulent financial reporting. *Managerial Auditing Journal*.

Lin, N. (2001). *Social capital: A theory of social structure and action*. Cambridge University Press. doi:10.1017/CBO9780511815447

Lozovsky, B. N. (2011). Kto i kak manipuliruet zhurnalistami. Manipulyativnye tekhnologii vliyaniya na sredstva massovoj informacii [Who and how manipulates journalists. Manipulative technologies of influence on the media]. Izdatel'stvo Ural'skogo Universiteta.

Magklaras, G. B., & Furnell, S. M. (2005). A preliminary model of end user sophistication for insider threat prediction in IT systems. *Computers & Security*, *24*(5), 371–38. doi:10.1016/j.cose.2004.10.003

Mahmoudi, H., & Taheri, A. (2015). Relation between information literacy and health literacy of students in Ferdowsi University of Mashhad. *Human Information Interaction*, *2*(2), 31–41.

Maier, J., & Richter, T. (2014). Fostering multiple text comprehension: How metacognitive strategies and motivation moderate the text-belief consistency effect. Ryan. *Metacognition and Learning*, *9*(1), 51–74. doi:10.100711409-013-9111-x

Makarychev, V.N. (2019). Marketing and manipulation of public opinion. *Advertising: Theory and Practice*, (4), 302-308.

Ma, L., Lee, C. S., & Goh, D. H. L. (2011, June). That's news to me: The influence of perceived gratifications and personal experience on news sharing in social media. In *Proceedings of the 11th annual international ACM/IEEE joint conference on Digital libraries* (pp. 141-144). 10.1145/1998076.1998103

Malinova, O. (2004). Public opinion and public policy models. *Public policy: collection of articles*. Norma. https://www.civisbook.ru/files/File/Malinova_obsh_mn.pdf

Marshall, J., Wiltshire, J., Delva, J., Bello, T., & Masys, A. J. (2020). Natural and manmade disasters: vulnerable populations. In A. Masys, R. Izurieta, & M. Reina Ortiz (Eds.), *Global health security. Advanced sciences and technologies for security applications*. Springer. doi:10.1007/978-3-030-23491-1_7

McCleary, R. M., & Barros, R. J. (2006). Religion and economy. *The Journal of Economic Perspectives*, *20*(2), 49–72. doi:10.1257/jep.20.2.49

McGowan, B., Wasko, M., Vartabedian, B., Miller, R. S., Freiherr, D. D., & Abdolrasulnia, M. (2012). Understanding the factors that influence the adoption and meaningful use of social media by physicians to share medical information. *Journal of Medical Internet Research*, *14*(5), 1–11. doi:10.2196/jmir.2138 PMID:23006336

Meier, J., Mackman, A., Dunner, M., Vasireddy, S., Escamilla, R., & Murukan, A. (2003). *Improving web application security: threats and counter measures*. Microsoft Redmond.

Merchant, K. A. (1990). The effects of financial controls on data manipulation and management myopia. *Accounting, Organizations and Society*, *15*(4), 297–313. doi:10.1016/0361-3682(90)90021-L

Merchant, R. M., & Asch, D. A. (2018). Protecting the value of medical science in the age of social media and "Fake News". *Journal of the American Medical Association*, *320*(23), 2415–2416. doi:10.1001/jama.2018.18416 PMID:30453315

Metalidou, E., Marinagi, C., Trivellas, P., Eberhagen, N., Skourlas, C., & Giannakopoulos, G. (2014). The human factor of information security: Unintentional damage perspective. *Procedia: Social and Behavioral Sciences*, *147*, 424–428. doi:10.1016/j.sbspro.2014.07.133

Mittal, Y. K., Roy, S., & Saxena, M. (2010). Role of knowledge management in enhancing information security. *IJCSI International Journal of Computer Science Issues*, *7*(6), 320–324.

Moradi, R., Aliabadi, K., Khazayi, A., & Rasuli, B. (2014). The relationship between critical thinking and information literacy in medical students. *Teaching Strategies in Medical Sciences*, *3*(7), 141–147.

Morozova, J., & Magamedli, N. (2019). Media as a subject of public opinion manipulation. *Topical issues of education and science development in modern society*, 247-251.

Mourad, A., Srour, A., Harmanani, H., Jenainatiy, C., & Arafeh, M. (2020). Critical impact of social networks Infodemic on defeating coronavirus COVID-19 pandemic: Twitter-based study and research directions. Retrieved from: https://arxiv.org/abs/2005.08820

Moyer, S. E. (1990). Capital adequacy ratio regulations and accounting choices in commercial banks. *Journal of Accounting and Economics, 13*(2), 123–154. doi:10.1016/0165-4101(90)90027-2

Nafieva, N. R. (2019). Manipulation of public counsciousness as a news media. *Electronic Scientific Journal,* 35-36. https://sibac.info/archive/journal/student/5%2849_1%29.pdf#page=36

Nambisan, P. (2011). Information seeking and social support in online health communities: Impact on patients' perceived empathy. *Journal of the American Medical Informatics Association: JAMIA, 18*(3), 298–304. doi:10.1136/amiajnl-2010-000058 PMID:21486888

Napoleoncat. (2020). *Social media users in Malaysia.* Retrieved from https://napoleoncat.com/stats/social-media-users-in-malaysia/2020/03

Nasr Mohammadi, M. (2013). *Detection of anomalies in the network using the illustration of security warnings* (Master's thesis). Tarbiat Modares University.

Nasyrova, O.A., & Zamyatina, E. V. (2013). Mass consciousness manipulation is one of the ways to manage people in the field of information technology. *Actual Problems of Aviation and Cosmonautics, 2*(9), 258-259.

Nikkar, M. (2008). Information literacy training plan in distance learning environment. *Peyke Nour, 6*(3), 43-51.

Nimmo, B. (2016). *Identifying disinformation: An ABC approach.* Institute for European Studies. Policy Brief. Retrieved from http://www.ies. be/node/3612

Nottingham Trent University. (2016). *FOMO, a vicious circle for social media users.* Retrieved from: https://www.ntu.ac.uk/about-us/news/news-articles/2016/10/fomo-a-vicious-circle-for-social-media-users

Ozyumenko, V. (2017). Media Discourse in an Atmosphere of Information Warfare. *Manipulation to Aggression. Russian Journal of Linguistics, 21*(1), 203–220. doi:10.22363/2312-9182-2017-21-1-203-220

Paige, S. R., Krieger, J. L., & Stellefson, M. L. (2017). The influence of e-health literacy on perceived trust in online health communication channels and sources. *Journal of Health Communication, 22*(1), 53–65. doi:10.1080/10810730.2016.1250846 PMID:28001489

Pakdaman, R. (2009). *Designing the structure and process of certification and accreditation of information and information security* (Master Thesis). Tarbiat Modares University.

Paldam, M. (1999). *Corruption and religion adding to the economic model?* Center for Dynamic Modeling in Economics, Working Paper no. 21.

Parirokh, M., Moghadaszadeh, H. (1999). Information Literacy: A research on how to acquire information literacy. *Journal of the Faculty of Literature and Humanities*, (1-2), 318-334.

Park, J., Cha, M., Kim, H., & Jeong, J. (2012). Managing bad news in social media: A case study on Domino's pizza crisis. *Proceedings of the Sixth International AAAI Conference on Weblogs and Social Media*, 282-289.

Paxton, P. (1999). Is social capital declining in the United States? A multiple indicator assessment. *American Journal of Sociology, 105*(1), 88–127. doi:10.1086/210268

Pennycook, G., McPhetres, J., Zhang, Y., Lu, J. G., & Rand, D. G. (2020). Fighting COVID-19 misinformation on social media: Experimental evidence for a scalable accuracy-nudge intervention. *Psychological Science, 31*(7), 770–780. doi:10.1177/0956797620939054 PMID:32603243

Pennycook, G., & Rand, D. G. (2019). Fighting misinformation on social media using crowdsourced judgments of news source quality. *Proceedings of the National Academy of Sciences of the United States of America, 116*(7), 2521–2526. doi:10.1073/pnas.1806781116 PMID:30692252

Phelps, D. (2005). *Information system security: self-efficacy and security effectiveness in Florida Libraries*. PhD dissertation

Popovich, Z. (2017). *Law on education: where will language passions lead in Zacarpathia?* https://www.bbc.com/ukrainian/features-russian-41265262

Pourmoudat, K., & Kajbaf, M. B. (2017). Study of social anxiety in students using the Internet and virtual social networks. *Social Psychological Review*, *6*(23), 93–105.

Prokopenko, I. S. (2012). *Storm of consciousness. The truth about manipulating human consciousness*. Eksmo.

Prudon, P. (2015). Confirmatory factor analysis as a tool in research using questionnaires: A critique. *Comprehensive Psychology*, *4*(10), 1–19. doi:10.2466/03.CP.4.10

Przybylski, A. K., Murayama, K., DeHaan, C. R., & Gladwell, V. (2013). Motivational, emotional, and behavioral correlates of fear of missing out. *Computers in Human Behavior*, *29*(4), 1841–1848. doi:10.1016/j.chb.2013.02.014

Putnam, R. (1993). *Making democracy work: Civic traditions in modern Italy*. Princeton University Press.

Qiu, L., Rui, H., & Whinston, A. (2013). Information Exchange in Prediction Markets: Do Social Net-works Promote Forecast Efficiency? *System Sciences (HICSS), 46th Hawaii International Conference on System Sciences*, 3982-3991. 10.1109/HICSS.2013.269

Quinn, K. (2018). Cognitive effects of social media use: A case of older adults. *Social Media + Society*, *4*(3), 2056305118787203. doi:10.1177/2056305118787203

Rahmani, A., & Bashiri Manesh, N. (2013). Evaluation of detection model of earnings management. *Journal of Accounting and Auditing*, *19*, 1–20.

Ransbotham, S., & Sabyasachi, M. (2009). Choice and chance: A conceptual model of paths to information security compromise. *Information Systems Research*, *20*(1), 121–139. doi:10.1287/isre.1080.0174

Rapid7. (2011). Retrieved form https://www.rapid7.com/blog/post/2011/07/19/the-attackers-triad/

Richard, F. M., & Hübl, T. (2021). *Harvard Health Blog. Numb from the news? Understanding why and what to do may help.* Retrieved from https://www.health.harvard.edu/blog/numb-from-the-news-understanding-why-and-what-to-do-may-help-2021031822176

Robison, L. J., Schmid, A. A., & Siles, M. E. (2002). Is social capital really capital? *Review of Social Economy*, *601*(1), 1–21. doi:10.1080/00346760110127074

Rouhani, N. S., Seyed Mousavi, M., Gorji, M., & Samimi, Z. (2017). Comparison of the effect of tolerance of anxiety and social fear on the use of students' social networks. *Information and Communication Technology in Educational Sciences*, *35*, 33–53.

Rovetta, A., & Bhagavathula, A. S. (2020). COVID-19-related web search behaviors and infodemic attitudes in Italy: Infodemiological study. *JMIR Public Health and Surveillance*, *6*(2), e19374. doi:10.2196/19374 PMID:32338613

Ryan, R. M., & Deci, E. L. (2000). Self-determination theory and the facilitation of intrinsic motivation, social development, and well-being. *The American Psychologist*, *55*(1), 68–78. doi:10.1037/0003-066X.55.1.68 PMID:11392867

Ryan, R. M., & Deci, E. L. (2017). *Self-determination theory: Basic psychological needs in motivation, development, and wellness.* Guilford Publications. doi:10.1521/978.14625/28806

Sadeghi, A., & Ameri, Z. (2015). Virtual social networks and social harms, case study: Public security. *Journal of Survey in Teaching Humanities*, *2*(5), 51–65.

Sahoo, H., and Krotov, V. (2018). The value map for social networking. *JCS, 26*(3, 4), 248-267.

Sajjadi, S. H., Dastgir, M., Hossinzadeh, A. H., & Akhgar, M. O. (2012). Analysis of methods using management authorities in earnings management reporting and the impact of firms' characteristics on methods using management authorities. *Accounting Knowledge*, *3*(8), 7–30.

Salanova, M., Grau, R. M., Cifre, E., & Llorens, S. (2000). Computer training, frequency of usage and burnout: The moderating role of computer self-efficacy. *Computers in Human Behavior*, *16*(6), 575–590. doi:10.1016/S0747-5632(00)00028-5

Savignon, A. B. (2010). *Linking social capital and government performance: A public management perspective.* Working Paper, University of Rome.

Sazhin, N. O. (2013). Manipulation of public opinion on the Internet. In *Materials of the International Congress of FSBEI HPE "SibADI" Architecture. Building. Transport. Technologies. Innovation* (pp. 279-285). Academic Press.

Schlienger, T., & Teufel, S. (2003). Analyzing information security culture: Increasing trust by an appropriate information security culture. *The 14th International Conference on Database and Expert Systems Applications (DEXA 2003).*

Schou, C. D., & Trimmer, K. J. (2004). Information assurance and security. *Journal of Organizational and End User Computing, 16*(3), i–vii.

Seymour, B., Getman, R., Saraf, A., Zhang, L. H., & Kalenderian, E. (2015). When advocacy obscures accuracy online: Digital pandemics of public health misinformation through an antifluoride case study. *American Journal of Public Health, 105*(3), 517–523. doi:10.2105/AJPH.2014.302437 PMID:25602893

Shah, S. Z. A., & Butt, S. (2011). Creative accounting: A tool to help companies in a crisis or a practice to land them into crises. In *International Conference on Business and Economics Research-[IPEDR].* IACSIT Press.

Sharkova, I. V. (2020). *Methods of manipulating public opinion in modern mass media and social networks*. Modern Media and the Media Market.

Shayan, A. (2008). *Designing a comprehensive model of information security management in electronic banking* (Master Thesis). Tarbiat Modares University.

Shcheglov, A. V., & Makarychev, V. N. (2020). Manipulation of public opinion. *Economic Security Bulletin*, (1), 285–288.

Shostack, A. (2014). *Threat modeling: Designing for security*. John Wiley & Sons.

Shustina, I. V. (2016). *Speech means of manipulating public opinion in modern political advertising*. Man in the Information Space.

Singaevskaya, M. V. (2020). Public Opinion Management Technologies. *Sociology*, (2), 71–80.

Sladkova, O. B. (2006). Manipulation of public consciousness in the information society. *Observatory of Culture*, (6), 4–12.

Smith, J. (2004). Social cognitive theory of organizational management. *Academy of Management Journal.*

Soleimanipoor, R. (2010). Social networks, opportunities and threats. *Rahavarde Nour Journal, 31*, 14–19.

Solmsa, B., & Solms, R. (2005). From information security to business security? *Computers & Security, 24*(4), 271–273. doi:10.1016/j.cose.2005.04.004

Solms, B. (2006). Information ssecurity – the fourth wave. *Computers & Security, 25*(3), 165–168. doi:10.1016/j.cose.2006.03.004

Sommariva, S., Vamos, Ch., Mantzarlis, A., Đào, L. U. L., & Martinez Tyson, D. (2018). Spreading the (fake) news: Exploring health messages on social media and the implications for health professionals using a case study. *American Journal of Health Education, 49*(4), 246–255. doi:10.1080/19325037.2018.1473178

Sotnykov, A. V. (2018). Manipulation in mass media: Components and resistance. *Research Journal of Drohobych Ivan Franco State Pedagogical University. Series. Philology (Linguistics), 9*, 208–210.

Spathis, C. (2002). Detecting false financial statements using published data: Some evidence from Greece. *Managerial Auditing Journal, 17*(4), 179–191. doi:10.1108/02686900210424321

Spathis, C., Doumpos, M., & Zopounidis, C. (2002). Detecting falsified financial statements: A comparative study using multicriteria analysis and multivariate statistical techniques. *European Accounting Review, 11*(3), 509–535. doi:10.1080/09638180220000966

Stahl, B. (2006). On the difference or equality of information, misinformation, and disinformation: A critical research perspective. *Informing Science Journal, 9*, 83–96. doi:10.28945/473

Stair, R., & Reynolds, G. (2017). *Principles of information systems*. Course Technology.

Staroverov, V. I., & Levashov, V. I. (2009). Manipulating Public Opinion: Sociological Aspects of Analysis. *Sociology of Power*, (4).

Stec, E., & Varlejs, J. (2014). *Factors affecting students' information literacy as they transition from high school to college*. School Library Media Research. Retreived 2016, May 31 from https://www.ala.org/aasl/sites/ala.org.aasl/files/content/aaslpubsandjournals/slr/vol17/SLR_FactorsAffecting_V17.pdf

Stolle, D., & Rochon, T. R. (1998). Are all associations alike? member diversity, associational type, and the creation of social capital. *The American Behavioral Scientist, 42*(1), 47–65. doi:10.1177/0002764298042001005

Sultana, A. (2016). Information seeking behaviour of academics of Maulana Azad national Urdu University in the digital environment. In S. Dhanavandan (Ed.), Transition in librarianship (pp. 245-252). Dominant Publishers annd Distributions Pvt ltd.

Sur, E.I. (2012). Manipulation: concept, main features and structure. *Actual problems of the humanities and natural sciences, 3,* 143-146.

Swar, B., Hameed, T., & Reychav, I. (2017). Information overload, psychological ill-being, and behavioral intention to continue online healthcare information search. *Computers in Human Behavior, 70*, 416–425. doi:10.1016/j.chb.2016.12.068

Sweller, J. (2011). Cognitive load theory. *Psychology of Learning and Motivation, 55*, 37–76. doi:10.1016/B978-0-12-387691-1.00002-8

Tabatabai, M. H. (1990). *The principles of philosophy and the method of realism*. Sadra Publishing.

Taleb Nia, G., & Safari Sarchah, F. (2014). Comparison of linear accruals models to assess their ability to predict earnings management. *Journal of Applied Environmental and Biological Sciences*, *4*(10), 200–210.

Talwar, S., Dhir, A., Kaur, P., Zafar, N., & Alrasheedy, M. (2019). Why do people share fake news? Associations between the dark side of social media use and fake news sharing behavior. *Journal of Retailing and Consumer Services*, *51*, 72–82. doi:10.1016/j.jretconser.2019.05.026

Talwar, S., Dhir, A., Singh, D., Virk, G. S., & Salo, J. (2020). Sharing of fake news on social media: Application of the honeycomb framework and the third-person effect hypothesis. *Journal of Retailing and Consumer Services*, *57*, 102197. doi:10.1016/j.jretconser.2020.102197

Terry, A. (2021). *Jurist. Legal News and Commentary. Malaysia government uses emergency powers to enforce anti fake-news law*. Retrieved from https://www.jurist.org/news/2021/03/malaysia-government-uses-emergency-powers-to-enforce-anti-fake-news-law/

Theoharidou, M., Kokolakis, S., Karyda, M., & Kiountouzis, E. (2005). The insider threat to information systems and the effectiveness of ISO17799. *Computers & Security*, *24*(6), 472–484. doi:10.1016/j.cose.2005.05.002

Thompson, N., Wang, X., & Daya, P. (2020). Determinants of news sharing behavior on social media. *Journal of Computer Information Systems*, *60*(6), 593–601. doi:10.1080/08874417.2019.1566803

Tibinko, N. D. (2011). Manipulation in political discourse. *Bulletin of the Chelyabinsk State University*, *3*(218), 134-137.

Toffler, A. (1980). *The third wave*. William Morrow.

Topaloglu, M., & Tekkanat, E. (2015). Identifying the usage of information technologies and literacy levels. *Procedia-Social and Behavioral Sciences*, *182*(3), 574–583. doi:10.1016/j.sbspro.2015.04.784

Torgovanova, O. N., & Shabanova, A. E. (2016). Manipulation of public opinion in political discourse (on the example of Barack Obama's speech). *Bulletin of Tver State University. Series. Philosophy*, (4), 93–98.

Trethewey, S. P. (2020). Strategies to combat medical misinformation on social media. *Postgraduate Medical Journal*, *96*(1131), 4–6. doi:10.1136/postgradmedj-2019-137201 PMID:31732511

Tudjman, M., & Mikelic, N. (2003). Information science: Science about information, misinformation and disinformation. *Informing Science*, *4*, 1513–1527.

Turkman, F., & Shahabi, Z. (2016). Rumors and social factors affecting its acceptance. *Socio-Cultural Strategy*, *5*(19), 191-216.

Tustin, N. (2010). The role of patient satisfaction in online health information seeking. *Journal of Health Communication*, *15*(1), 3–17. doi:10.1080/10810730903465491 PMID:20390974

Tutarashvili, R. Y., & Gushchina, L. V. (2015). Manipulation of public consciousness within the framework of political discourse: the role of the media in manipulating public consciousness, the main types of manipulative technologies. *International Research Journal*, *3-2*(34), 85-87.

Twitter. (2020). *World Health Organization (WHO) Live with @DrTedros on health security from the @MunSecConf. #MSC2020*. https://twitter.com/WHO/status/1228680399733194756

Ulrich, W. (2001). A philosophical staircase for information systems definition, design, and development. *Journal of Information Technology Theory and Application*, *3*(3), 55–84.

Valero, P.P., Oliveira, L. (2018). Fake news: una revision sistemática de la literatura. *Observatorio*, 54-78.

Vasiliev, A. A. (2016). Manipulation of public opinion through virtual communities. *Christian Reading*, (5), 207–222. doi:10.24411/1814-5574-2016-00074

Vermeclen, C., & von Solms, R. (1999). Information security policy. Department of Computer Science.

Volgutova, A. V. (2014). Mass media and power: Specificity of public opinion manipulation. *Ogarev-Online*, (5 (19)), 6.

Vraga, E. K., & Bode, L. (2020). Correction as a solution for health misinformation on social media. *American Journal of Public Health, 110*(53). https://ajph.aphapublications.org/doi/abs/10.2105/AJPH.2020.305916 PMID:33001724

Vraga, E. K., & Bode, L. (2020). Using expert sources to correct health misinformation in social media. *Science Communication*, *39*(5), 621–645. doi:10.1177/1075547017731776

Vrij, A. (2000). *Detecting lies and deceit: The psychology of lying and the implications for professional practice*. John Wiley & Sons.

Vroom, C., & Solms, R. (2004). Towards information security behavioral compliance. *Computers & Security*, *23*(3), 191–198. doi:10.1016/j.cose.2004.01.012

Vuuren, I. E. V. (2016). IT Security Trust Model—Securing the Human Perimeter. *International Journal of Social Science and Humanity*, *6*(11), 852–858. doi:10.18178/ijssh.2016.V6.761

Walsham, G. (2001). *Making a world of difference - IT in a global context*. Wiley.

Waszak, P.M., Kasprzycka-Waszak, W., & Kubanek, A. (n.d.). The spread of medical fake news in social media – The pilot quantitative study. *Health Policy and Technology, 7*(2), 115-8. doi:10.1016/j.hlpt.2018.03.002

Watson, B. W. (1990). *United States intelligence: An encyclopedia*. Garland Publishing, Inc.

Whelan, E., Islam, A. N., & Brooks, S. (2020). Applying the SOBC paradigm to explain how social media overload affects academic performance. *Computers & Education*, *143*, 103692. doi:10.1016/j.compedu.2019.103692

Whelan, E., Islam, A. N., & Brooks, S. (2020). Is boredom proneness related to social media overload and fatigue? A stress–strain–outcome approach. *Internet Research*, *30*(3), 869–887. doi:10.1108/INTR-03-2019-0112

Wikipedia Contributors. (n.d.). Big Lie. In *Wikipedia*. Retrieved from http://en.wikipedia.org/w/index. php?title=Big_Lie&oldid=77579324

Winter, S., Neubaum, G., Eimler, S. C., Gordon, V., Theil, J., Herrmann, J., Meinert, J., & Krämer, N. C. (2014). Another brick in the Facebook wall–How personality traits relate to the content of status updates. *Computers in Human Behavior*, *34*, 194–202. doi:10.1016/j.chb.2014.01.048

won Kim, J. (2014). Scan and click: The uses and gratifications of social recommendation systems. *Computers in Human Behavior, 33*, 184-191.

Wood, C. (2000). An unappreciated reason why security policies fail. *Computer Fraud & Security*, *10*(10), 13–14. doi:10.1016/S1361-3723(00)10029-6

Xiang, D., & Lehmann, L. S. (2021). Confronting the misinformation pandemic. *Health Policy and Technology*, *10*(3), 100520. doi:10.1016/j.hlpt.2021.100520 PMID:34002131

Yakovleva, E. L. Lyulkin S. N. (2015). Manipulation of information as a violation of human rights. *Балтийский гуманитарный журнал, 3(12)*, 85-88.

Yang, Y., & Lim, H. (2011). A cognitive ability measuring system with cognitive loading task. In *Future Information Technology* (pp. 325–328). Springer.

Yen, C. H., Chen, I. C., Lai, S. C., & Chuang, Y. R. (2015). An analytics-based approach to managing cognitive load by using log data of learning management systems and footprints of social media. *Journal of Educational Technology & Society*, *18*(4), 141–158.

Yu, S. C., Chen, H. R., Liu, A. C., & Lee, H. Y. (2020, December). Toward COVID-19 Information: Infodemic or Fear of Missing Out? []). Multidisciplinary Digital Publishing Institute.]. *Health Care*, *8*(4), 550.

Zak, P. G., & Knack, S. (2001). Trust and growth. *Economic Journal (London)*, *111*(470), 295–321. doi:10.1111/1468-0297.00609

Zarocostas, J. (2020). How to fight an infodemic. *Lancet*, *395*(10225), 676.

Zerehsaz, M. (2015). *Analysis of the relationship between psychological and skill capabilities of users with their guiding behavior based on the modified model of Marchionni information* (PhD thesis). Shahid Ferdowsi University of Mashhad, Faculty of Educational Sciences and Psychology.

Zhao, Y., & Zhang, J. (2017). Consumer health information seeking in social media: A literature review. *Health Information and Libraries Journal*, *34*(4), 268–283. doi:10.1111/hir.12192 PMID:29045011

Zhukovets, O. Yu. (2013). Methods and techniques for manipulating public opinion used by sectarian-type organizations. *Humanities and Social Sciences*, (5).

Zhuravleva, O. (2021). *Law on state language: in the service sector now only Ukrainian*. https://www.dw.com/ru/zakon-o-gosjazyke-v-sfere-uslug-teper-tolko-ukrainskij/a-56225227

Ziaee Parvar, H., & Aghili, S. V. (2009). Investigating the influence of social networks among Iranian users. *Rashaneh*, *20*(4), 23–42.

Znamenskaya, T. A. (2015). The use of metaphors as a means of manipulating public opinion in English-language publications about Ukraine. *CETERIS PARIBUS*, (1), 67–69.

Related References

To continue our tradition of advancing information science and technology research, we have compiled a list of recommended IGI Global readings. These references will provide additional information and guidance to further enrich your knowledge and assist you with your own research and future publications.

Adesina, K., Ganiu, O., & R., O. S. (2018). Television as Vehicle for Community Development: A Study of Lotunlotun Programme on (B.C.O.S.) Television, Nigeria. In A. Salawu, & T. Owolabi (Eds.), *Exploring Journalism Practice and Perception in Developing Countries* (pp. 60-84). Hershey, PA: IGI Global. doi:10.4018/978-1-5225-3376-4.ch004

Adigun, G. O., Odunola, O. A., & Sobalaje, A. J. (2016). Role of Social Networking for Information Seeking in a Digital Library Environment. In A. Tella (Ed.), *Information Seeking Behavior and Challenges in Digital Libraries* (pp. 272–290). Hershey, PA: IGI Global. doi:10.4018/978-1-5225-0296-8.ch013

Ahmad, M. B., Pride, C., & Corsy, A. K. (2016). Free Speech, Press Freedom, and Democracy in Ghana: A Conceptual and Historical Overview. In L. Mukhongo & J. Macharia (Eds.), *Political Influence of the Media in Developing Countries* (pp. 59–73). Hershey, PA: IGI Global. doi:10.4018/978-1-4666-9613-6.ch005

Ahmad, R. H., & Pathan, A. K. (2017). A Study on M2M (Machine to Machine) System and Communication: Its Security, Threats, and Intrusion Detection System. In M. Ferrag & A. Ahmim (Eds.), *Security Solutions and Applied Cryptography in Smart Grid Communications* (pp. 179–214). Hershey, PA: IGI Global. doi:10.4018/978-1-5225-1829-7.ch010

Akanni, T. M. (2018). In Search of Women-Supportive Media for Sustainable Development in Nigeria. In A. Salawu & T. Owolabi (Eds.), *Exploring Journalism Practice and Perception in Developing Countries* (pp. 126–149). Hershey, PA: IGI Global. doi:10.4018/978-1-5225-3376-4.ch007

Akçay, D. (2017). The Role of Social Media in Shaping Marketing Strategies in the Airline Industry. In V. Benson, R. Tuninga, & G. Saridakis (Eds.), *Analyzing the Strategic Role of Social Networking in Firm Growth and Productivity* (pp. 214–233). Hershey, PA: IGI Global. doi:10.4018/978-1-5225-0559-4.ch012

Al-Rabayah, W. A. (2017). Social Media as Social Customer Relationship Management Tool: Case of Jordan Medical Directory. In W. Al-Rabayah, R. Khasawneh, R. Abu-shamaa, & I. Alsmadi (Eds.), *Strategic Uses of Social Media for Improved Customer Retention* (pp. 108–123). Hershey, PA: IGI Global. doi:10.4018/978-1-5225-1686-6.ch006

Almjeld, J. (2017). Getting “Girly” Online: The Case for Gendering Online Spaces. In E. Monske & K. Blair (Eds.), *Handbook of Research on Writing and Composing in the Age of MOOCs* (pp. 87–105). Hershey, PA: IGI Global. doi:10.4018/978-1-5225-1718-4.ch006

Altaş, A. (2017). Space as a Character in Narrative Advertising: A Qualitative Research on Country Promotion Works. In R. Yılmaz (Ed.), *Narrative Advertising Models and Conceptualization in the Digital Age* (pp. 303–319). Hershey, PA: IGI Global. doi:10.4018/978-1-5225-2373-4.ch017

Altıparmak, B. (2017). The Structural Transformation of Space in Turkish Television Commercials as a Narrative Component. In R. Yılmaz (Ed.), *Narrative Advertising Models and Conceptualization in the Digital Age* (pp. 153–166). Hershey, PA: IGI Global. doi:10.4018/978-1-5225-2373-4.ch009

An, Y., & Harvey, K. E. (2016). Public Relations and Mobile: Becoming Dialogic. In X. Xu (Ed.), *Handbook of Research on Human Social Interaction in the Age of Mobile Devices* (pp. 284–311). Hershey, PA: IGI Global. doi:10.4018/978-1-5225-0469-6.ch013

Assay, B. E. (2018). Regulatory Compliance, Ethical Behaviour, and Sustainable Growth in Nigeria’s Telecommunications Industry. In I. Oncioiu (Ed.), *Ethics and Decision-Making for Sustainable Business Practices* (pp. 90–108). Hershey, PA: IGI Global. doi:10.4018/978-1-5225-3773-1.ch006

Averweg, U. R., & Leaning, M. (2018). The Qualities and Potential of Social Media. In M. Khosrow-Pour, D.B.A. (Ed.), Encyclopedia of Information Science and Technology, Fourth Edition (pp. 7106-7115). Hershey, PA: IGI Global. doi:10.4018/978-1-5225-2255-3.ch617

Azemi, Y., & Ozuem, W. (2016). Online Service Failure and Recovery Strategy: The Mediating Role of Social Media. In W. Ozuem & G. Bowen (Eds.), *Competitive Social Media Marketing Strategies* (pp. 112–135). Hershey, PA: IGI Global. doi:10.4018/978-1-4666-9776-8.ch006

Baarda, R. (2017). Digital Democracy in Authoritarian Russia: Opportunity for Participation, or Site of Kremlin Control? In R. Luppicini & R. Baarda (Eds.), *Digital Media Integration for Participatory Democracy* (pp. 87–100). Hershey, PA: IGI Global. doi:10.4018/978-1-5225-2463-2.ch005

Bacallao-Pino, L. M. (2016). Radical Political Communication and Social Media: The Case of the Mexican #YoSoy132. In T. Deželan & I. Vobič (Eds.), *R)evolutionizing Political Communication through Social Media* (pp. 56–74). Hershey, PA: IGI Global. doi:10.4018/978-1-4666-9879-6.ch004

Baggio, B. G. (2016). Why We Would Rather Text than Talk: Personality, Identity, and Anonymity in Modern Virtual Environments. In B. Baggio (Ed.), *Analyzing Digital Discourse and Human Behavior in Modern Virtual Environments* (pp. 110–125). Hershey, PA: IGI Global. doi:10.4018/978-1-4666-9899-4.ch006

Başal, B. (2017). Actor Effect: A Study on Historical Figures Who Have Shaped the Advertising Narration. In R. Yılmaz (Ed.), *Narrative Advertising Models and Conceptualization in the Digital Age* (pp. 34–60). Hershey, PA: IGI Global. doi:10.4018/978-1-5225-2373-4.ch003

Behjati, M., & Cosmas, J. (2017). Self-Organizing Network Solutions: A Principal Step Towards Real 4G and Beyond. In D. Singh (Ed.), *Routing Protocols and Architectural Solutions for Optimal Wireless Networks and Security* (pp. 241–253). Hershey, PA: IGI Global. doi:10.4018/978-1-5225-2342-0.ch011

Bekafigo, M., & Pingley, A. C. (2017). Do Campaigns "Go Negative" on Twitter? In Y. Ibrahim (Ed.), *Politics, Protest, and Empowerment in Digital Spaces* (pp. 178–191). Hershey, PA: IGI Global. doi:10.4018/978-1-5225-1862-4.ch011

Bender, S., & Dickenson, P. (2016). Utilizing Social Media to Engage Students in Online Learning: Building Relationships Outside of the Learning Management System. In P. Dickenson & J. Jaurez (Eds.), *Increasing Productivity and Efficiency in Online Teaching* (pp. 84–105). Hershey, PA: IGI Global. doi:10.4018/978-1-5225-0347-7.ch005

Bermingham, N., & Prendergast, M. (2016). Bespoke Mobile Application Development: Facilitating Transition of Foundation Students to Higher Education. In L. Briz-Ponce, J. Juanes-Méndez, & F. García-Peñalvo (Eds.), *Handbook of Research on Mobile Devices and Applications in Higher Education Settings* (pp. 222–249). Hershey, PA: IGI Global. doi:10.4018/978-1-5225-0256-2.ch010

Bishop, J. (2017). Developing and Validating the "This Is Why We Can't Have Nice Things Scale": Optimising Political Online Communities for Internet Trolling. In Y. Ibrahim (Ed.), *Politics, Protest, and Empowerment in Digital Spaces* (pp. 153–177). Hershey, PA: IGI Global. doi:10.4018/978-1-5225-1862-4.ch010

Bolat, N. (2017). The Functions of the Narrator in Digital Advertising. In R. Yılmaz (Ed.), *Narrative Advertising Models and Conceptualization in the Digital Age* (pp. 184–201). Hershey, PA: IGI Global. doi:10.4018/978-1-5225-2373-4.ch011

Bowen, G., & Bowen, D. (2016). Social Media: Strategic Decision Making Tool. In W. Ozuem & G. Bowen (Eds.), *Competitive Social Media Marketing Strategies* (pp. 94–111). Hershey, PA: IGI Global. doi:10.4018/978-1-4666-9776-8.ch005

Brown, M. A. Sr. (2017). SNIP: High Touch Approach to Communication. In *Solutions for High-Touch Communications in a High-Tech World* (pp. 71–88). Hershey, PA: IGI Global. doi:10.4018/978-1-5225-1897-6.ch004

Brown, M. A. Sr. (2017). Comparing FTF and Online Communication Knowledge. In *Solutions for High-Touch Communications in a High-Tech World* (pp. 103–113). Hershey, PA: IGI Global. doi:10.4018/978-1-5225-1897-6.ch006

Brown, M. A. Sr. (2017). Where Do We Go from Here? In *Solutions for High-Touch Communications in a High-Tech World* (pp. 137–159). Hershey, PA: IGI Global. doi:10.4018/978-1-5225-1897-6.ch008

Brown, M. A. Sr. (2017). Bridging the Communication Gap. In *Solutions for High-Touch Communications in a High-Tech World* (pp. 1–22). Hershey, PA: IGI Global. doi:10.4018/978-1-5225-1897-6.ch001

Brown, M. A. Sr. (2017). Key Strategies for Communication. In *Solutions for High-Touch Communications in a High-Tech World* (pp. 179–202). Hershey, PA: IGI Global. doi:10.4018/978-1-5225-1897-6.ch010

Bryant, K. N. (2017). WordUp!: Student Responses to Social Media in the Technical Writing Classroom. In K. Bryant (Ed.), *Engaging 21st Century Writers with Social Media* (pp. 231–245). Hershey, PA: IGI Global. doi:10.4018/978-1-5225-0562-4.ch014

Buck, E. H. (2017). Slacktivism, Supervision, and #Selfies: Illuminating Social Media Composition through Reception Theory. In K. Bryant (Ed.), *Engaging 21st Century Writers with Social Media* (pp. 163–178). Hershey, PA: IGI Global. doi:10.4018/978-1-5225-0562-4.ch010

Bucur, B. (2016). Sociological School of Bucharest's Publications and the Romanian Political Propaganda in the Interwar Period. In A. Fox (Ed.), *Global Perspectives on Media Events in Contemporary Society* (pp. 106–120). Hershey, PA: IGI Global. doi:10.4018/978-1-4666-9967-0.ch008

Bull, R., & Pianosi, M. (2017). Social Media, Participation, and Citizenship: New Strategic Directions. In V. Benson, R. Tuninga, & G. Saridakis (Eds.), *Analyzing the Strategic Role of Social Networking in Firm Growth and Productivity* (pp. 76–94). Hershey, PA: IGI Global. doi:10.4018/978-1-5225-0559-4.ch005

Camillo, A. A., & Camillo, I. C. (2016). The Ethics of Strategic Managerial Communication in the Global Context. In A. Normore, L. Long, & M. Javidi (Eds.), *Handbook of Research on Effective Communication, Leadership, and Conflict Resolution* (pp. 566–590). Hershey, PA: IGI Global. doi:10.4018/978-1-4666-9970-0.ch030

Cassard, A., & Sloboda, B. W. (2016). Faculty Perception of Virtual 3-D Learning Environment to Assess Student Learning. In D. Choi, A. Dailey-Hebert, & J. Simmons Estes (Eds.), *Emerging Tools and Applications of Virtual Reality in Education* (pp. 48–74). Hershey, PA: IGI Global. doi:10.4018/978-1-4666-9837-6.ch003

Castellano, S., & Khelladi, I. (2017). Play It Like Beckham!: The Influence of Social Networks on E-Reputation – The Case of Sportspeople and Their Online Fan Base. In A. Mesquita (Ed.), *Research Paradigms and Contemporary Perspectives on Human-Technology Interaction* (pp. 43–61). Hershey, PA: IGI Global. doi:10.4018/978-1-5225-1868-6.ch003

Castellet, A. (2016). What If Devices Take Command: Content Innovation Perspectives for Smart Wearables in the Mobile Ecosystem. *International Journal of Handheld Computing Research, 7*(2), 16–33. doi:10.4018/IJHCR.2016040102

Chugh, R., & Joshi, M. (2017). Challenges of Knowledge Management amidst Rapidly Evolving Tools of Social Media. In R. Chugh (Ed.), *Harnessing Social Media as a Knowledge Management Tool* (pp. 299–314). Hershey, PA: IGI Global. doi:10.4018/978-1-5225-0495-5.ch014

Cockburn, T., & Smith, P. A. (2016). Leadership in the Digital Age: Rhythms and the Beat of Change. In A. Normore, L. Long, & M. Javidi (Eds.), *Handbook of Research on Effective Communication, Leadership, and Conflict Resolution* (pp. 1–20). Hershey, PA: IGI Global. doi:10.4018/978-1-4666-9970-0.ch001

Cole, A. W., & Salek, T. A. (2017). Adopting a Parasocial Connection to Overcome Professional Kakoethos in Online Health Information. In M. Folk & S. Apostel (Eds.), *Establishing and Evaluating Digital Ethos and Online Credibility* (pp. 104–120). Hershey, PA: IGI Global. doi:10.4018/978-1-5225-1072-7.ch006

Cossiavelou, V. (2017). ACTA as Media Gatekeeping Factor: The EU Role as Global Negotiator. *International Journal of Interdisciplinary Telecommunications and Networking*, *9*(1), 26–37. doi:10.4018/IJITN.2017010103

Costanza, F. (2017). Social Media Marketing and Value Co-Creation: A System Dynamics Approach. In S. Rozenes & Y. Cohen (Eds.), *Handbook of Research on Strategic Alliances and Value Co-Creation in the Service Industry* (pp. 205–230). Hershey, PA: IGI Global. doi:10.4018/978-1-5225-2084-9.ch011

Cross, D. E. (2016). Globalization and Media's Impact on Cross Cultural Communication: Managing Organizational Change. In A. Normore, L. Long, & M. Javidi (Eds.), *Handbook of Research on Effective Communication, Leadership, and Conflict Resolution* (pp. 21–41). Hershey, PA: IGI Global. doi:10.4018/978-1-4666-9970-0.ch002

Damásio, M. J., Henriques, S., Teixeira-Botelho, I., & Dias, P. (2016). Mobile Media and Social Interaction: Mobile Services and Content as Drivers of Social Interaction. In J. Aguado, C. Feijóo, & I. Martínez (Eds.), *Emerging Perspectives on the Mobile Content Evolution* (pp. 357–379). Hershey, PA: IGI Global. doi:10.4018/978-1-4666-8838-4.ch018

Davis, A., & Foley, L. (2016). Digital Storytelling. In B. Guzzetti & M. Lesley (Eds.), *Handbook of Research on the Societal Impact of Digital Media* (pp. 317–342). Hershey, PA: IGI Global. doi:10.4018/978-1-4666-8310-5.ch013

Davis, S., Palmer, L., & Etienne, J. (2016). The Geography of Digital Literacy: Mapping Communications Technology Training Programs in Austin, Texas. In B. Passarelli, J. Straubhaar, & A. Cuevas-Cerveró (Eds.), *Handbook of Research on Comparative Approaches to the Digital Age Revolution in Europe and the Americas* (pp. 371–384). Hershey, PA: IGI Global. doi:10.4018/978-1-4666-8740-0.ch022

Delello, J. A., & McWhorter, R. R. (2016). New Visual Literacies and Competencies for Education and the Workplace. In B. Guzzetti & M. Lesley (Eds.), *Handbook of Research on the Societal Impact of Digital Media* (pp. 127–162). Hershey, PA: IGI Global. doi:10.4018/978-1-4666-8310-5.ch006

Di Virgilio, F., & Antonelli, G. (2018). Consumer Behavior, Trust, and Electronic Word-of-Mouth Communication: Developing an Online Purchase Intention Model. In F. Di Virgilio (Ed.), *Social Media for Knowledge Management Applications in Modern Organizations* (pp. 58–80). Hershey, PA: IGI Global. doi:10.4018/978-1-5225-2897-5.ch003

Dixit, S. K. (2016). eWOM Marketing in Hospitality Industry. In A. Singh, & P. Duhan (Eds.), Managing Public Relations and Brand Image through Social Media (pp. 266-280). Hershey, PA: IGI Global. doi:10.4018/978-1-5225-0332-3.ch014

Duhan, P., & Singh, A. (2016). Facebook Experience Is Different: An Empirical Study in Indian Context. In S. Rathore & A. Panwar (Eds.), *Capturing, Analyzing, and Managing Word-of-Mouth in the Digital Marketplace* (pp. 188–212). Hershey, PA: IGI Global. doi:10.4018/978-1-4666-9449-1.ch011

Dunne, D. J. (2016). The Scholar's Ludo-Narrative Game and Multimodal Graphic Novel: A Comparison of Fringe Scholarship. In A. Connor & S. Marks (Eds.), *Creative Technologies for Multidisciplinary Applications* (pp. 182–207). Hershey, PA: IGI Global. doi:10.4018/978-1-5225-0016-2.ch008

DuQuette, J. L. (2017). Lessons from Cypris Chat: Revisiting Virtual Communities as Communities. In G. Panconesi & M. Guida (Eds.), *Handbook of Research on Collaborative Teaching Practice in Virtual Learning Environments* (pp. 299–316). Hershey, PA: IGI Global. doi:10.4018/978-1-5225-2426-7.ch016

Ekhlassi, A., Niknejhad Moghadam, M., & Adibi, A. (2018). The Concept of Social Media: The Functional Building Blocks. In *Building Brand Identity in the Age of Social Media: Emerging Research and Opportunities* (pp. 29–60). Hershey, PA: IGI Global. doi:10.4018/978-1-5225-5143-0.ch002

Ekhlassi, A., Niknejhad Moghadam, M., & Adibi, A. (2018). Social Media Branding Strategy: Social Media Marketing Approach. In *Building Brand Identity in the Age of Social Media: Emerging Research and Opportunities* (pp. 94–117). Hershey, PA: IGI Global. doi:10.4018/978-1-5225-5143-0.ch004

Ekhlassi, A., Niknejhad Moghadam, M., & Adibi, A. (2018). The Impact of Social Media on Brand Loyalty: Achieving "E-Trust" Through Engagement. In *Building Brand Identity in the Age of Social Media: Emerging Research and Opportunities* (pp. 155–168). Hershey, PA: IGI Global. doi:10.4018/978-1-5225-5143-0.ch007

Elegbe, O. (2017). An Assessment of Media Contribution to Behaviour Change and HIV Prevention in Nigeria. In O. Nelson, B. Ojebuyi, & A. Salawu (Eds.), *Impacts of the Media on African Socio-Economic Development* (pp. 261–280). Hershey, PA: IGI Global. doi:10.4018/978-1-5225-1859-4.ch017

Endong, F. P. (2018). Hashtag Activism and the Transnationalization of Nigerian-Born Movements Against Terrorism: A Critical Appraisal of the #BringBackOurGirls Campaign. In F. Endong (Ed.), *Exploring the Role of Social Media in Transnational Advocacy* (pp. 36–54). Hershey, PA: IGI Global. doi:10.4018/978-1-5225-2854-8.ch003

Erragcha, N. (2017). Using Social Media Tools in Marketing: Opportunities and Challenges. In M. Brown Sr., (Ed.), *Social Media Performance Evaluation and Success Measurements* (pp. 106–129). Hershey, PA: IGI Global. doi:10.4018/978-1-5225-1963-8.ch006

Ezeh, N. C. (2018). Media Campaign on Exclusive Breastfeeding: Awareness, Perception, and Acceptability Among Mothers in Anambra State, Nigeria. In A. Salawu & T. Owolabi (Eds.), *Exploring Journalism Practice and Perception in Developing Countries* (pp. 172–193). Hershey, PA: IGI Global. doi:10.4018/978-1-5225-3376-4.ch009

Fawole, O. A., & Osho, O. A. (2017). Influence of Social Media on Dating Relationships of Emerging Adults in Nigerian Universities: Social Media and Dating in Nigeria. In M. Wright (Ed.), *Identity, Sexuality, and Relationships among Emerging Adults in the Digital Age* (pp. 168–177). Hershey, PA: IGI Global. doi:10.4018/978-1-5225-1856-3.ch011

Fayoyin, A. (2017). Electoral Polling and Reporting in Africa: Professional and Policy Implications for Media Practice and Political Communication in a Digital Age. In N. Mhiripiri & T. Chari (Eds.), *Media Law, Ethics, and Policy in the Digital Age* (pp. 164–181). Hershey, PA: IGI Global. doi:10.4018/978-1-5225-2095-5.ch009

Fayoyin, A. (2018). Rethinking Media Engagement Strategies for Social Change in Africa: Context, Approaches, and Implications for Development Communication. In A. Salawu & T. Owolabi (Eds.), *Exploring Journalism Practice and Perception in Developing Countries* (pp. 257–280). Hershey, PA: IGI Global. doi:10.4018/978-1-5225-3376-4.ch013

Fechine, Y., & Rêgo, S. C. (2018). Transmedia Television Journalism in Brazil: Jornal da Record News as Reference. In R. Gambarato & G. Alzamora (Eds.), *Exploring Transmedia Journalism in the Digital Age* (pp. 253–265). Hershey, PA: IGI Global. doi:10.4018/978-1-5225-3781-6.ch015

Feng, J., & Lo, K. (2016). Video Broadcasting Protocol for Streaming Applications with Cooperative Clients. In D. Kanellopoulos (Ed.), *Emerging Research on Networked Multimedia Communication Systems* (pp. 205–229). Hershey, PA: IGI Global. doi:10.4018/978-1-4666-8850-6.ch006

Fiore, C. (2017). The Blogging Method: Improving Traditional Student Writing Practices. In K. Bryant (Ed.), *Engaging 21st Century Writers with Social Media* (pp. 179–198). Hershey, PA: IGI Global. doi:10.4018/978-1-5225-0562-4.ch011

Fleming, J., & Kajimoto, M. (2016). The Freedom of Critical Thinking: Examining Efforts to Teach American News Literacy Principles in Hong Kong, Vietnam, and Malaysia. In M. Yildiz & J. Keengwe (Eds.), *Handbook of Research on Media Literacy in the Digital Age* (pp. 208–235). Hershey, PA: IGI Global. doi:10.4018/978-1-4666-9667-9.ch010

Gambarato, R. R., Alzamora, G. C., & Tárcia, L. P. (2018). 2016 Rio Summer Olympics and the Transmedia Journalism of Planned Events. In R. Gambarato & G. Alzamora (Eds.), *Exploring Transmedia Journalism in the Digital Age* (pp. 126–146). Hershey, PA: IGI Global. doi:10.4018/978-1-5225-3781-6.ch008

Ganguin, S., Gemkow, J., & Haubold, R. (2017). Information Overload as a Challenge and Changing Point for Educational Media Literacies. In R. Marques & J. Batista (Eds.), *Information and Communication Overload in the Digital Age* (pp. 302–328). Hershey, PA: IGI Global. doi:10.4018/978-1-5225-2061-0.ch013

Gao, Y. (2016). Reviewing Gratification Effects in Mobile Gaming. In X. Xu (Ed.), *Handbook of Research on Human Social Interaction in the Age of Mobile Devices* (pp. 406–428). Hershey, PA: IGI Global. doi:10.4018/978-1-5225-0469-6.ch017

Gardner, G. C. (2017). The Lived Experience of Smartphone Use in a Unit of the United States Army. In F. Topor (Ed.), *Handbook of Research on Individualism and Identity in the Globalized Digital Age* (pp. 88–117). Hershey, PA: IGI Global. doi:10.4018/978-1-5225-0522-8.ch005

Giessen, H. W. (2016). The Medium, the Content, and the Performance: An Overview on Media-Based Learning. In B. Khan (Ed.), *Revolutionizing Modern Education through Meaningful E-Learning Implementation* (pp. 42–55). Hershey, PA: IGI Global. doi:10.4018/978-1-5225-0466-5.ch003

Giltenane, J. (2016). Investigating the Intention to Use Social Media Tools Within Virtual Project Teams. In G. Silvius (Ed.), *Strategic Integration of Social Media into Project Management Practice* (pp. 83–105). Hershey, PA: IGI Global. doi:10.4018/978-1-4666-9867-3.ch006

Golightly, D., & Houghton, R. J. (2018). Social Media as a Tool to Understand Behaviour on the Railways. In S. Kohli, A. Kumar, J. Easton, & C. Roberts (Eds.), *Innovative Applications of Big Data in the Railway Industry* (pp. 224–239). Hershey, PA: IGI Global. doi:10.4018/978-1-5225-3176-0.ch010

Goovaerts, M., Nieuwenhuysen, P., & Dhamdhere, S. N. (2016). VLIR-UOS Workshop 'E-Info Discovery and Management for Institutes in the South': Presentations and Conclusions, Antwerp, 8-19 December, 2014. In E. de Smet, & S. Dhamdhere (Eds.), E-Discovery Tools and Applications in Modern Libraries (pp. 1-40). Hershey, PA: IGI Global. doi:10.4018/978-1-5225-0474-0.ch001

Grützmann, A., Carvalho de Castro, C., Meireles, A. A., & Rodrigues, R. C. (2016). Organizational Architecture and Online Social Networks: Insights from Innovative Brazilian Companies. In G. Jamil, J. Poças Rascão, F. Ribeiro, & A. Malheiro da Silva (Eds.), *Handbook of Research on Information Architecture and Management in Modern Organizations* (pp. 508–524). Hershey, PA: IGI Global. doi:10.4018/978-1-4666-8637-3.ch023

Gundogan, M. B. (2017). In Search for a "Good Fit" Between Augmented Reality and Mobile Learning Ecosystem. In G. Kurubacak & H. Altinpulluk (Eds.), *Mobile Technologies and Augmented Reality in Open Education* (pp. 135–153). Hershey, PA: IGI Global. doi:10.4018/978-1-5225-2110-5.ch007

Gupta, H. (2018). Impact of Digital Communication on Consumer Behaviour Processes in Luxury Branding Segment: A Study of Apparel Industry. In S. Dasgupta, S. Biswal, & M. Ramesh (Eds.), *Holistic Approaches to Brand Culture and Communication Across Industries* (pp. 132–157). Hershey, PA: IGI Global. doi:10.4018/978-1-5225-3150-0.ch008

Hai-Jew, S. (2017). Creating "(Social) Network Art" with NodeXL. In S. Hai-Jew (Ed.), *Social Media Data Extraction and Content Analysis* (pp. 342–393). Hershey, PA: IGI Global. doi:10.4018/978-1-5225-0648-5.ch011

Hai-Jew, S. (2017). Employing the Sentiment Analysis Tool in NVivo 11 Plus on Social Media Data: Eight Initial Case Types. In N. Rao (Ed.), *Social Media Listening and Monitoring for Business Applications* (pp. 175–244). Hershey, PA: IGI Global. doi:10.4018/978-1-5225-0846-5.ch010

Hai-Jew, S. (2017). Conducting Sentiment Analysis and Post-Sentiment Data Exploration through Automated Means. In S. Hai-Jew (Ed.), *Social Media Data Extraction and Content Analysis* (pp. 202–240). Hershey, PA: IGI Global. doi:10.4018/978-1-5225-0648-5.ch008

Hai-Jew, S. (2017). Applied Analytical "Distant Reading" using NVivo 11 Plus. In S. Hai-Jew (Ed.), *Social Media Data Extraction and Content Analysis* (pp. 159–201). Hershey, PA: IGI Global. doi:10.4018/978-1-5225-0648-5.ch007

Hai-Jew, S. (2017). Flickering Emotions: Feeling-Based Associations from Related Tags Networks on Flickr. In S. Hai-Jew (Ed.), *Social Media Data Extraction and Content Analysis* (pp. 296–341). Hershey, PA: IGI Global. doi:10.4018/978-1-5225-0648-5.ch010

Hai-Jew, S. (2017). Manually Profiling Egos and Entities across Social Media Platforms: Evaluating Shared Messaging and Contents, User Networks, and Metadata. In V. Benson, R. Tuninga, & G. Saridakis (Eds.), *Analyzing the Strategic Role of Social Networking in Firm Growth and Productivity* (pp. 352–405). Hershey, PA: IGI Global. doi:10.4018/978-1-5225-0559-4.ch019

Hai-Jew, S. (2017). Exploring "User," "Video," and (Pseudo) Multi-Mode Networks on YouTube with NodeXL. In S. Hai-Jew (Ed.), *Social Media Data Extraction and Content Analysis* (pp. 242–295). Hershey, PA: IGI Global. doi:10.4018/978-1-5225-0648-5.ch009

Hai-Jew, S. (2018). Exploring "Mass Surveillance" Through Computational Linguistic Analysis of Five Text Corpora: Academic, Mainstream Journalism, Microblogging Hashtag Conversation, Wikipedia Articles, and Leaked Government Data. In *Techniques for Coding Imagery and Multimedia: Emerging Research and Opportunities* (pp. 212–286). Hershey, PA: IGI Global. doi:10.4018/978-1-5225-2679-7.ch004

Hai-Jew, S. (2018). Exploring Identity-Based Humor in a #Selfies #Humor Image Set From Instagram. In *Techniques for Coding Imagery and Multimedia: Emerging Research and Opportunities* (pp. 1–90). Hershey, PA: IGI Global. doi:10.4018/978-1-5225-2679-7.ch001

Hai-Jew, S. (2018). See Ya!: Exploring American Renunciation of Citizenship Through Targeted and Sparse Social Media Data Sets and a Custom Spatial-Based Linguistic Analysis Dictionary. In *Techniques for Coding Imagery and Multimedia: Emerging Research and Opportunities* (pp. 287–393). Hershey, PA: IGI Global. doi:10.4018/978-1-5225-2679-7.ch005

Han, H. S., Zhang, J., Peikazadi, N., Shi, G., Hung, A., Doan, C. P., & Filippelli, S. (2016). An Entertaining Game-Like Learning Environment in a Virtual World for Education. In S. D'Agustino (Ed.), *Creating Teacher Immediacy in Online Learning Environments* (pp. 290–306). Hershey, PA: IGI Global. doi:10.4018/978-1-4666-9995-3.ch015

Harrin, E. (2016). Barriers to Social Media Adoption on Projects. In G. Silvius (Ed.), *Strategic Integration of Social Media into Project Management Practice* (pp. 106–124). Hershey, PA: IGI Global. doi:10.4018/978-1-4666-9867-3.ch007

Harvey, K. E. (2016). Local News and Mobile: Major Tipping Points. In X. Xu (Ed.), *Handbook of Research on Human Social Interaction in the Age of Mobile Devices* (pp. 171–199). Hershey, PA: IGI Global. doi:10.4018/978-1-5225-0469-6.ch009

Harvey, K. E., & An, Y. (2016). Marketing and Mobile: Increasing Integration. In X. Xu (Ed.), *Handbook of Research on Human Social Interaction in the Age of Mobile Devices* (pp. 220–247). Hershey, PA: IGI Global. doi:10.4018/978-1-5225-0469-6.ch011

Harvey, K. E., Auter, P. J., & Stevens, S. (2016). Educators and Mobile: Challenges and Trends. In X. Xu (Ed.), *Handbook of Research on Human Social Interaction in the Age of Mobile Devices* (pp. 61–95). Hershey, PA: IGI Global. doi:10.4018/978-1-5225-0469-6.ch004

Hasan, H., & Linger, H. (2017). Connected Living for Positive Ageing. In S. Gordon (Ed.), *Online Communities as Agents of Change and Social Movements* (pp. 203–223). Hershey, PA: IGI Global. doi:10.4018/978-1-5225-2495-3.ch008

Hashim, K., Al-Sharqi, L., & Kutbi, I. (2016). Perceptions of Social Media Impact on Social Behavior of Students: A Comparison between Students and Faculty. *International Journal of Virtual Communities and Social Networking*, *8*(2), 1–11. doi:10.4018/IJVCSN.2016040101

Henriques, S., & Damasio, M. J. (2016). The Value of Mobile Communication for Social Belonging: Mobile Apps and the Impact on Social Interaction. *International Journal of Handheld Computing Research*, *7*(2), 44–58. doi:10.4018/IJHCR.2016040104

Hersey, L. N. (2017). CHOICES: Measuring Return on Investment in a Nonprofit Organization. In M. Brown Sr., (Ed.), *Social Media Performance Evaluation and Success Measurements* (pp. 157–179). Hershey, PA: IGI Global. doi:10.4018/978-1-5225-1963-8.ch008

Heuva, W. E. (2017). Deferring Citizens' "Right to Know" in an Information Age: The Information Deficit in Namibia. In N. Mhiripiri & T. Chari (Eds.), *Media Law, Ethics, and Policy in the Digital Age* (pp. 245–267). Hershey, PA: IGI Global. doi:10.4018/978-1-5225-2095-5.ch014

Hopwood, M., & McLean, H. (2017). Social Media in Crisis Communication: The Lance Armstrong Saga. In V. Benson, R. Tuninga, & G. Saridakis (Eds.), *Analyzing the Strategic Role of Social Networking in Firm Growth and Productivity* (pp. 45–58). Hershey, PA: IGI Global. doi:10.4018/978-1-5225-0559-4.ch003

Hotur, S. K. (2018). Indian Approaches to E-Diplomacy: An Overview. In S. Bute (Ed.), *Media Diplomacy and Its Evolving Role in the Current Geopolitical Climate* (pp. 27–35). Hershey, PA: IGI Global. doi:10.4018/978-1-5225-3859-2.ch002

Ibadildin, N., & Harvey, K. E. (2016). Business and Mobile: Rapid Restructure Required. In X. Xu (Ed.), *Handbook of Research on Human Social Interaction in the Age of Mobile Devices* (pp. 312–350). Hershey, PA: IGI Global. doi:10.4018/978-1-5225-0469-6.ch014

Iwasaki, Y. (2017). Youth Engagement in the Era of New Media. In M. Adria & Y. Mao (Eds.), *Handbook of Research on Citizen Engagement and Public Participation in the Era of New Media* (pp. 90–105). Hershey, PA: IGI Global. doi:10.4018/978-1-5225-1081-9.ch006

Jamieson, H. V. (2017). We have a Situation!: Cyberformance and Civic Engagement in Post-Democracy. In R. Shin (Ed.), *Convergence of Contemporary Art, Visual Culture, and Global Civic Engagement* (pp. 297–317). Hershey, PA: IGI Global. doi:10.4018/978-1-5225-1665-1.ch017

Jimoh, J., & Kayode, J. (2018). Imperative of Peace and Conflict-Sensitive Journalism in Development. In A. Salawu & T. Owolabi (Eds.), *Exploring Journalism Practice and Perception in Developing Countries* (pp. 150–171). Hershey, PA: IGI Global. doi:10.4018/978-1-5225-3376-4.ch008

Johns, R. (2016). Increasing Value of a Tangible Product through Intangible Attributes: Value Co-Creation and Brand Building within Online Communities – Virtual Communities and Value. In R. English & R. Johns (Eds.), *Gender Considerations in Online Consumption Behavior and Internet Use* (pp. 112–124). Hershey, PA: IGI Global. doi:10.4018/978-1-5225-0010-0.ch008

Kanellopoulos, D. N. (2018). Group Synchronization for Multimedia Systems. In M. Khosrow-Pour, D.B.A. (Ed.), Encyclopedia of Information Science and Technology, Fourth Edition (pp. 6435-6446). Hershey, PA: IGI Global. doi:10.4018/978-1-5225-2255-3.ch559

Kapepo, M. I., & Mayisela, T. (2017). Integrating Digital Literacies Into an Undergraduate Course: Inclusiveness Through Use of ICTs. In C. Ayo & V. Mbarika (Eds.), *Sustainable ICT Adoption and Integration for Socio-Economic Development* (pp. 152–173). Hershey, PA: IGI Global. doi:10.4018/978-1-5225-2565-3.ch007

Karahoca, A., & Yengin, İ. (2018). Understanding the Potentials of Social Media in Collaborative Learning. In M. Khosrow-Pour, D.B.A. (Ed.), Encyclopedia of Information Science and Technology, Fourth Edition (pp. 7168-7180). Hershey, PA: IGI Global. doi:10.4018/978-1-5225-2255-3.ch623

Karataş, S., Ceran, O., Ülker, Ü., Gün, E. T., Köse, N. Ö., Kılıç, M., ... Tok, Z. A. (2016). A Trend Analysis of Mobile Learning. In D. Parsons (Ed.), *Mobile and Blended Learning Innovations for Improved Learning Outcomes* (pp. 248–276). Hershey, PA: IGI Global. doi:10.4018/978-1-5225-0359-0.ch013

Kasemsap, K. (2016). Role of Social Media in Brand Promotion: An International Marketing Perspective. In A. Singh & P. Duhan (Eds.), *Managing Public Relations and Brand Image through Social Media* (pp. 62–88). Hershey, PA: IGI Global. doi:10.4018/978-1-5225-0332-3.ch005

Kasemsap, K. (2016). The Roles of Social Media Marketing and Brand Management in Global Marketing. In W. Ozuem & G. Bowen (Eds.), *Competitive Social Media Marketing Strategies* (pp. 173–200). Hershey, PA: IGI Global. doi:10.4018/978-1-4666-9776-8.ch009

Kasemsap, K. (2017). Professional and Business Applications of Social Media Platforms. In V. Benson, R. Tuninga, & G. Saridakis (Eds.), *Analyzing the Strategic Role of Social Networking in Firm Growth and Productivity* (pp. 427–450). Hershey, PA: IGI Global. doi:10.4018/978-1-5225-0559-4.ch021

Kasemsap, K. (2017). Mastering Social Media in the Modern Business World. In N. Rao (Ed.), *Social Media Listening and Monitoring for Business Applications* (pp. 18–44). Hershey, PA: IGI Global. doi:10.4018/978-1-5225-0846-5.ch002

Kato, Y., & Kato, S. (2016). Mobile Phone Use during Class at a Japanese Women's College. In M. Yildiz & J. Keengwe (Eds.), *Handbook of Research on Media Literacy in the Digital Age* (pp. 436–455). Hershey, PA: IGI Global. doi:10.4018/978-1-4666-9667-9.ch021

Kaufmann, H. R., & Manarioti, A. (2017). Consumer Engagement in Social Media Platforms. In *Encouraging Participative Consumerism Through Evolutionary Digital Marketing: Emerging Research and Opportunities* (pp. 95–123). Hershey, PA: IGI Global. doi:10.4018/978-1-68318-012-8.ch004

Kavoura, A., & Kefallonitis, E. (2018). The Effect of Social Media Networking in the Travel Industry. In M. Khosrow-Pour, D.B.A. (Ed.), Encyclopedia of Information Science and Technology, Fourth Edition (pp. 4052-4063). Hershey, PA: IGI Global. doi:10.4018/978-1-5225-2255-3.ch351

Kawamura, Y. (2018). Practice and Modeling of Advertising Communication Strategy: Sender-Driven and Receiver-Driven. In T. Ogata & S. Asakawa (Eds.), *Content Generation Through Narrative Communication and Simulation* (pp. 358–379). Hershey, PA: IGI Global. doi:10.4018/978-1-5225-4775-4.ch013

Kell, C., & Czerniewicz, L. (2017). Visibility of Scholarly Research and Changing Research Communication Practices: A Case Study from Namibia. In A. Esposito (Ed.), *Research 2.0 and the Impact of Digital Technologies on Scholarly Inquiry* (pp. 97–116). Hershey, PA: IGI Global. doi:10.4018/978-1-5225-0830-4.ch006

Khalil, G. E. (2016). Change through Experience: How Experiential Play and Emotional Engagement Drive Health Game Success. In D. Novák, B. Tulu, & H. Brendryen (Eds.), *Handbook of Research on Holistic Perspectives in Gamification for Clinical Practice* (pp. 10–34). Hershey, PA: IGI Global. doi:10.4018/978-1-4666-9522-1.ch002

Kılınç, U. (2017). Create It! Extend It!: Evolution of Comics Through Narrative Advertising. In R. Yılmaz (Ed.), *Narrative Advertising Models and Conceptualization in the Digital Age* (pp. 117–132). Hershey, PA: IGI Global. doi:10.4018/978-1-5225-2373-4.ch007

Kim, J. H. (2016). Pedagogical Approaches to Media Literacy Education in the United States. In M. Yildiz & J. Keengwe (Eds.), *Handbook of Research on Media Literacy in the Digital Age* (pp. 53–74). Hershey, PA: IGI Global. doi:10.4018/978-1-4666-9667-9.ch003

Kirigha, J. M., Mukhongo, L. L., & Masinde, R. (2016). Beyond Web 2.0. Social Media and Urban Educated Youths Participation in Kenyan Politics. In L. Mukhongo & J. Macharia (Eds.), *Political Influence of the Media in Developing Countries* (pp. 156–174). Hershey, PA: IGI Global. doi:10.4018/978-1-4666-9613-6.ch010

Krochmal, M. M. (2016). Training for Mobile Journalism. In D. Mentor (Ed.), *Handbook of Research on Mobile Learning in Contemporary Classrooms* (pp. 336–362). Hershey, PA: IGI Global. doi:10.4018/978-1-5225-0251-7.ch017

Kumar, P., & Sinha, A. (2018). Business-Oriented Analytics With Social Network of Things. In H. Bansal, G. Shrivastava, G. Nguyen, & L. Stanciu (Eds.), *Social Network Analytics for Contemporary Business Organizations* (pp. 166–187). Hershey, PA: IGI Global. doi:10.4018/978-1-5225-5097-6.ch009

Kunock, A. I. (2017). Boko Haram Insurgency in Cameroon: Role of Mass Media in Conflict Management. In N. Mhiripiri & T. Chari (Eds.), *Media Law, Ethics, and Policy in the Digital Age* (pp. 226–244). Hershey, PA: IGI Global. doi:10.4018/978-1-5225-2095-5.ch013

Labadie, J. A. (2018). Digitally Mediated Art Inspired by Technology Integration: A Personal Journey. In A. Ursyn (Ed.), *Visual Approaches to Cognitive Education With Technology Integration* (pp. 121–162). Hershey, PA: IGI Global. doi:10.4018/978-1-5225-5332-8.ch008

Lefkowith, S. (2017). Credibility and Crisis in Pseudonymous Communities. In M. Folk & S. Apostel (Eds.), *Establishing and Evaluating Digital Ethos and Online Credibility* (pp. 190–236). Hershey, PA: IGI Global. doi:10.4018/978-1-5225-1072-7.ch010

Lemoine, P. A., Hackett, P. T., & Richardson, M. D. (2016). The Impact of Social Media on Instruction in Higher Education. In L. Briz-Ponce, J. Juanes-Méndez, & F. García-Peñalvo (Eds.), *Handbook of Research on Mobile Devices and Applications in Higher Education Settings* (pp. 373–401). Hershey, PA: IGI Global. doi:10.4018/978-1-5225-0256-2.ch016

Liampotis, N., Papadopoulou, E., Kalatzis, N., Roussaki, I. G., Kosmides, P., Sykas, E. D., ... Taylor, N. K. (2016). Tailoring Privacy-Aware Trustworthy Cooperating Smart Spaces for University Environments. In A. Panagopoulos (Ed.), *Handbook of Research on Next Generation Mobile Communication Systems* (pp. 410–439). Hershey, PA: IGI Global. doi:10.4018/978-1-4666-8732-5.ch016

Luppicini, R. (2017). Technoethics and Digital Democracy for Future Citizens. In R. Luppicini & R. Baarda (Eds.), *Digital Media Integration for Participatory Democracy* (pp. 1–21). Hershey, PA: IGI Global. doi:10.4018/978-1-5225-2463-2.ch001

Mahajan, I. M., Rather, M., Shafiq, H., & Qadri, U. (2016). Media Literacy Organizations. In M. Yildiz & J. Keengwe (Eds.), *Handbook of Research on Media Literacy in the Digital Age* (pp. 236–248). Hershey, PA: IGI Global. doi:10.4018/978-1-4666-9667-9.ch011

Maher, D. (2018). Supporting Pre-Service Teachers' Understanding and Use of Mobile Devices. In J. Keengwe (Ed.), *Handbook of Research on Mobile Technology, Constructivism, and Meaningful Learning* (pp. 160–177). Hershey, PA: IGI Global. doi:10.4018/978-1-5225-3949-0.ch009

Makhwanya, A. (2018). Barriers to Social Media Advocacy: Lessons Learnt From the Project "Tell Them We Are From Here". In F. Endong (Ed.), *Exploring the Role of Social Media in Transnational Advocacy* (pp. 55–72). Hershey, PA: IGI Global. doi:10.4018/978-1-5225-2854-8.ch004

Manli, G., & Rezaei, S. (2017). Value and Risk: Dual Pillars of Apps Usefulness. In S. Rezaei (Ed.), *Apps Management and E-Commerce Transactions in Real-Time* (pp. 274–292). Hershey, PA: IGI Global. doi:10.4018/978-1-5225-2449-6.ch013

Manrique, C. G., & Manrique, G. G. (2017). Social Media's Role in Alleviating Political Corruption and Scandals: The Philippines during and after the Marcos Regime. In K. Demirhan & D. Çakır-Demirhan (Eds.), *Political Scandal, Corruption, and Legitimacy in the Age of Social Media* (pp. 205–222). Hershey, PA: IGI Global. doi:10.4018/978-1-5225-2019-1.ch009

Manzoor, A. (2016). Cultural Barriers to Organizational Social Media Adoption. In A. Goel & P. Singhal (Eds.), *Product Innovation through Knowledge Management and Social Media Strategies* (pp. 31–45). Hershey, PA: IGI Global. doi:10.4018/978-1-4666-9607-5.ch002

Manzoor, A. (2016). Social Media for Project Management. In G. Silvius (Ed.), *Strategic Integration of Social Media into Project Management Practice* (pp. 51–65). Hershey, PA: IGI Global. doi:10.4018/978-1-4666-9867-3.ch004

Marovitz, M. (2017). Social Networking Engagement and Crisis Communication Considerations. In M. Brown Sr., (Ed.), *Social Media Performance Evaluation and Success Measurements* (pp. 130–155). Hershey, PA: IGI Global. doi:10.4018/978-1-5225-1963-8.ch007

Mathur, D., & Mathur, D. (2016). Word of Mouth on Social Media: A Potent Tool for Brand Building. In S. Rathore & A. Panwar (Eds.), *Capturing, Analyzing, and Managing Word-of-Mouth in the Digital Marketplace* (pp. 45–60). Hershey, PA: IGI Global. doi:10.4018/978-1-4666-9449-1.ch003

Maulana, I. (2018). Spontaneous Taking and Posting Selfie: Reclaiming the Lost Trust. In S. Hai-Jew (Ed.), *Selfies as a Mode of Social Media and Work Space Research* (pp. 28–50). Hershey, PA: IGI Global. doi:10.4018/978-1-5225-3373-3.ch002

Mayo, S. (2018). A Collective Consciousness Model in a Post-Media Society. In M. Khosrow-Pour (Ed.), *Enhancing Art, Culture, and Design With Technological Integration* (pp. 25–49). Hershey, PA: IGI Global. doi:10.4018/978-1-5225-5023-5.ch002

Mazur, E., Signorella, M. L., & Hough, M. (2018). The Internet Behavior of Older Adults. In M. Khosrow-Pour, D.B.A. (Ed.), Encyclopedia of Information Science and Technology, Fourth Edition (pp. 7026-7035). Hershey, PA: IGI Global. doi:10.4018/978-1-5225-2255-3.ch609

McGuire, M. (2017). Reblogging as Writing: The Role of Tumblr in the Writing Classroom. In K. Bryant (Ed.), *Engaging 21st Century Writers with Social Media* (pp. 116–131). Hershey, PA: IGI Global. doi:10.4018/978-1-5225-0562-4.ch007

McKee, J. (2018). Architecture as a Tool to Solve Business Planning Problems. In M. Khosrow-Pour, D.B.A. (Ed.), Encyclopedia of Information Science and Technology, Fourth Edition (pp. 573-586). Hershey, PA: IGI Global. doi:10.4018/978-1-5225-2255-3.ch050

McMahon, D. (2017). With a Little Help from My Friends: The Irish Radio Industry's Strategic Appropriation of Facebook for Commercial Growth. In V. Benson, R. Tuninga, & G. Saridakis (Eds.), *Analyzing the Strategic Role of Social Networking in Firm Growth and Productivity* (pp. 157–171). Hershey, PA: IGI Global. doi:10.4018/978-1-5225-0559-4.ch009

McPherson, M. J., & Lemon, N. (2017). The Hook, Woo, and Spin: Academics Creating Relations on Social Media. In A. Esposito (Ed.), *Research 2.0 and the Impact of Digital Technologies on Scholarly Inquiry* (pp. 167–187). Hershey, PA: IGI Global. doi:10.4018/978-1-5225-0830-4.ch009

Melro, A., & Oliveira, L. (2018). Screen Culture. In M. Khosrow-Pour, D.B.A. (Ed.), Encyclopedia of Information Science and Technology, Fourth Edition (pp. 4255-4266). Hershey, PA: IGI Global. doi:10.4018/978-1-5225-2255-3.ch369

Merwin, G. A. Jr, McDonald, J. S., Bennett, J. R. Jr, & Merwin, K. A. (2016). Social Media Applications Promote Constituent Involvement in Government Management. In G. Silvius (Ed.), *Strategic Integration of Social Media into Project Management Practice* (pp. 272–291). Hershey, PA: IGI Global. doi:10.4018/978-1-4666-9867-3.ch016

Mhiripiri, N. A., & Chikakano, J. (2017). Criminal Defamation, the Criminalisation of Expression, Media and Information Dissemination in the Digital Age: A Legal and Ethical Perspective. In N. Mhiripiri & T. Chari (Eds.), *Media Law, Ethics, and Policy in the Digital Age* (pp. 1–24). Hershey, PA: IGI Global. doi:10.4018/978-1-5225-2095-5.ch001

Miliopoulou, G., & Cossiavelou, V. (2016). Brands and Media Gatekeeping in the Social Media: Current Trends and Practices – An Exploratory Research. *International Journal of Interdisciplinary Telecommunications and Networking*, *8*(4), 51–64. doi:10.4018/IJITN.2016100105

Miron, E., Palmor, A., Ravid, G., Sharon, A., Tikotsky, A., & Zirkel, Y. (2017). Principles and Good Practices for Using Wikis within Organizations. In R. Chugh (Ed.), *Harnessing Social Media as a Knowledge Management Tool* (pp. 143–176). Hershey, PA: IGI Global. doi:10.4018/978-1-5225-0495-5.ch008

Mishra, K. E., Mishra, A. K., & Walker, K. (2016). Leadership Communication, Internal Marketing, and Employee Engagement: A Recipe to Create Brand Ambassadors. In A. Normore, L. Long, & M. Javidi (Eds.), *Handbook of Research on Effective Communication, Leadership, and Conflict Resolution* (pp. 311–329). Hershey, PA: IGI Global. doi:10.4018/978-1-4666-9970-0.ch017

Moeller, C. L. (2018). Sharing Your Personal Medical Experience Online: Is It an Irresponsible Act or Patient Empowerment? In S. Sekalala & B. Niezgoda (Eds.), *Global Perspectives on Health Communication in the Age of Social Media* (pp. 185–209). Hershey, PA: IGI Global. doi:10.4018/978-1-5225-3716-8.ch007

Mosanako, S. (2017). Broadcasting Policy in Botswana: The Case of Botswana Television. In O. Nelson, B. Ojebuyi, & A. Salawu (Eds.), *Impacts of the Media on African Socio-Economic Development* (pp. 217–230). Hershey, PA: IGI Global. doi:10.4018/978-1-5225-1859-4.ch014

Nazari, A. (2016). Developing a Social Media Communication Plan. In G. Silvius (Ed.), *Strategic Integration of Social Media into Project Management Practice* (pp. 194–217). Hershey, PA: IGI Global. doi:10.4018/978-1-4666-9867-3.ch012

Neto, B. M. (2016). From Information Society to Community Service: The Birth of E-Citizenship. In B. Passarelli, J. Straubhaar, & A. Cuevas-Cerveró (Eds.), *Handbook of Research on Comparative Approaches to the Digital Age Revolution in Europe and the Americas* (pp. 101–123). Hershey, PA: IGI Global. doi:10.4018/978-1-4666-8740-0.ch007

Noguti, V., Singh, S., & Waller, D. S. (2016). Gender Differences in Motivations to Use Social Networking Sites. In R. English & R. Johns (Eds.), *Gender Considerations in Online Consumption Behavior and Internet Use* (pp. 32–49). Hershey, PA: IGI Global. doi:10.4018/978-1-5225-0010-0.ch003

Noor, R. (2017). Citizen Journalism: News Gathering by Amateurs. In M. Adria & Y. Mao (Eds.), *Handbook of Research on Citizen Engagement and Public Participation in the Era of New Media* (pp. 194–229). Hershey, PA: IGI Global. doi:10.4018/978-1-5225-1081-9.ch012

Nwagbara, U., Oruh, E. S., & Brown, C. (2016). State Fragility and Stakeholder Engagement: New Media and Stakeholders' Voice Amplification in the Nigerian Petroleum Industry. In W. Ozuem & G. Bowen (Eds.), *Competitive Social Media Marketing Strategies* (pp. 136–154). Hershey, PA: IGI Global. doi:10.4018/978-1-4666-9776-8.ch007

Obermayer, N., Csepregi, A., & Kővári, E. (2017). Knowledge Sharing Relation to Competence, Emotional Intelligence, and Social Media Regarding Generations. In A. Bencsik (Ed.), *Knowledge Management Initiatives and Strategies in Small and Medium Enterprises* (pp. 269–290). Hershey, PA: IGI Global. doi:10.4018/978-1-5225-1642-2.ch013

Obermayer, N., Gaál, Z., Szabó, L., & Csepregi, A. (2017). Leveraging Knowledge Sharing over Social Media Tools. In R. Chugh (Ed.), *Harnessing Social Media as a Knowledge Management Tool* (pp. 1–24). Hershey, PA: IGI Global. doi:10.4018/978-1-5225-0495-5.ch001

Ogwezzy-Ndisika, A. O., & Faustino, B. A. (2016). Gender Responsive Election Coverage in Nigeria: A Score Card of 2011 General Elections. In L. Mukhongo & J. Macharia (Eds.), *Political Influence of the Media in Developing Countries* (pp. 234–249). Hershey, PA: IGI Global. doi:10.4018/978-1-4666-9613-6.ch015

Okoroafor, O. E. (2018). New Media Technology and Development Journalism in Nigeria. In A. Salawu & T. Owolabi (Eds.), *Exploring Journalism Practice and Perception in Developing Countries* (pp. 105–125). Hershey, PA: IGI Global. doi:10.4018/978-1-5225-3376-4.ch006

Olaleye, S. A., Sanusi, I. T., & Ukpabi, D. C. (2018). Assessment of Mobile Money Enablers in Nigeria. In F. Mtenzi, G. Oreku, D. Lupiana, & J. Yonazi (Eds.), *Mobile Technologies and Socio-Economic Development in Emerging Nations* (pp. 129–155). Hershey, PA: IGI Global. doi:10.4018/978-1-5225-4029-8.ch007

Ozuem, W., Pinho, C. A., & Azemi, Y. (2016). User-Generated Content and Perceived Customer Value. In W. Ozuem & G. Bowen (Eds.), *Competitive Social Media Marketing Strategies* (pp. 50–63). Hershey, PA: IGI Global. doi:10.4018/978-1-4666-9776-8.ch003

Pacchiega, C. (2017). An Informal Methodology for Teaching Through Virtual Worlds: Using Internet Tools and Virtual Worlds in a Coordinated Pattern to Teach Various Subjects. In G. Panconesi & M. Guida (Eds.), *Handbook of Research on Collaborative Teaching Practice in Virtual Learning Environments* (pp. 163–180). Hershey, PA: IGI Global. doi:10.4018/978-1-5225-2426-7.ch009

Pase, A. F., Goss, B. M., & Tietzmann, R. (2018). A Matter of Time: Transmedia Journalism Challenges. In R. Gambarato & G. Alzamora (Eds.), *Exploring Transmedia Journalism in the Digital Age* (pp. 49–66). Hershey, PA: IGI Global. doi:10.4018/978-1-5225-3781-6.ch004

Passarelli, B., & Paletta, F. C. (2016). Living inside the NET: The Primacy of Interactions and Processes. In B. Passarelli, J. Straubhaar, & A. Cuevas-Cerveró (Eds.), *Handbook of Research on Comparative Approaches to the Digital Age Revolution in Europe and the Americas* (pp. 1–15). Hershey, PA: IGI Global. doi:10.4018/978-1-4666-8740-0.ch001

Patkin, T. T. (2017). Social Media and Knowledge Management in a Crisis Context: Barriers and Opportunities. In R. Chugh (Ed.), *Harnessing Social Media as a Knowledge Management Tool* (pp. 125–142). Hershey, PA: IGI Global. doi:10.4018/978-1-5225-0495-5.ch007

Pavlíček, A. (2017). Social Media and Creativity: How to Engage Users and Tourists. In A. Kiráľová (Ed.), *Driving Tourism through Creative Destinations and Activities* (pp. 181–202). Hershey, PA: IGI Global. doi:10.4018/978-1-5225-2016-0.ch009

Pillay, K., & Maharaj, M. (2017). The Business of Advocacy: A Case Study of Greenpeace. In V. Benson, R. Tuninga, & G. Saridakis (Eds.), *Analyzing the Strategic Role of Social Networking in Firm Growth and Productivity* (pp. 59–75). Hershey, PA: IGI Global. doi:10.4018/978-1-5225-0559-4.ch004

Piven, I. P., & Breazeale, M. (2017). Desperately Seeking Customer Engagement: The Five-Sources Model of Brand Value on Social Media. In V. Benson, R. Tuninga, & G. Saridakis (Eds.), *Analyzing the Strategic Role of Social Networking in Firm Growth and Productivity* (pp. 283–313). Hershey, PA: IGI Global. doi:10.4018/978-1-5225-0559-4.ch016

Pokharel, R. (2017). New Media and Technology: How Do They Change the Notions of the Rhetorical Situations? In B. Gurung & M. Limbu (Eds.), *Integration of Cloud Technologies in Digitally Networked Classrooms and Learning Communities* (pp. 120–148). Hershey, PA: IGI Global. doi:10.4018/978-1-5225-1650-7.ch008

Popoola, I. S. (2016). The Press and the Emergent Political Class in Nigeria: Media, Elections, and Democracy. In L. Mukhongo & J. Macharia (Eds.), *Political Influence of the Media in Developing Countries* (pp. 45–58). Hershey, PA: IGI Global. doi:10.4018/978-1-4666-9613-6.ch004

Porlezza, C., Benecchi, E., & Colapinto, C. (2018). The Transmedia Revitalization of Investigative Journalism: Opportunities and Challenges of the Serial Podcast. In R. Gambarato & G. Alzamora (Eds.), *Exploring Transmedia Journalism in the Digital Age* (pp. 183–201). Hershey, PA: IGI Global. doi:10.4018/978-1-5225-3781-6.ch011

Ramluckan, T., Ally, S. E., & van Niekerk, B. (2017). Twitter Use in Student Protests: The Case of South Africa's #FeesMustFall Campaign. In M. Korstanje (Ed.), *Threat Mitigation and Detection of Cyber Warfare and Terrorism Activities* (pp. 220–253). Hershey, PA: IGI Global. doi:10.4018/978-1-5225-1938-6.ch010

Rao, N. R. (2017). Social Media: An Enabler for Governance. In N. Rao (Ed.), *Social Media Listening and Monitoring for Business Applications* (pp. 151–164). Hershey, PA: IGI Global. doi:10.4018/978-1-5225-0846-5.ch008

Rathore, A. K., Tuli, N., & Ilavarasan, P. V. (2016). Pro-Business or Common Citizen?: An Analysis of an Indian Woman CEO's Tweets. *International Journal of Virtual Communities and Social Networking*, *8*(1), 19–29. doi:10.4018/IJVCSN.2016010102

Redi, F. (2017). Enhancing Coopetition Among Small Tourism Destinations by Creativity. In A. Kiráľová (Ed.), *Driving Tourism through Creative Destinations and Activities* (pp. 223–244). Hershey, PA: IGI Global. doi:10.4018/978-1-5225-2016-0.ch011

Reeves, M. (2016). Social Media: It Can Play a Positive Role in Education. In R. English & R. Johns (Eds.), *Gender Considerations in Online Consumption Behavior and Internet Use* (pp. 82–95). Hershey, PA: IGI Global. doi:10.4018/978-1-5225-0010-0.ch006

Reis, Z. A. (2016). Bring the Media Literacy of Turkish Pre-Service Teachers to the Table. In M. Yildiz & J. Keengwe (Eds.), *Handbook of Research on Media Literacy in the Digital Age* (pp. 405–422). Hershey, PA: IGI Global. doi:10.4018/978-1-4666-9667-9.ch019

Resuloğlu, F., & Yılmaz, R. (2017). A Model for Interactive Advertising Narration. In R. Yılmaz (Ed.), *Narrative Advertising Models and Conceptualization in the Digital Age* (pp. 1–20). Hershey, PA: IGI Global. doi:10.4018/978-1-5225-2373-4.ch001

Ritzhaupt, A. D., Poling, N., Frey, C., Kang, Y., & Johnson, M. (2016). A Phenomenological Study of Games, Simulations, and Virtual Environments Courses: What Are We Teaching and How? *International Journal of Gaming and Computer-Mediated Simulations*, *8*(3), 59–73. doi:10.4018/IJGCMS.2016070104

Ross, D. B., Eleno-Orama, M., & Salah, E. V. (2018). The Aging and Technological Society: Learning Our Way Through the Decades. In V. Bryan, A. Musgrove, & J. Powers (Eds.), *Handbook of Research on Human Development in the Digital Age* (pp. 205–234). Hershey, PA: IGI Global. doi:10.4018/978-1-5225-2838-8.ch010

Rusko, R., & Merenheimo, P. (2017). Co-Creating the Christmas Story: Digitalizing as a Shared Resource for a Shared Brand. In I. Oncioiu (Ed.), *Driving Innovation and Business Success in the Digital Economy* (pp. 137–157). Hershey, PA: IGI Global. doi:10.4018/978-1-5225-1779-5.ch010

Sabao, C., & Chikara, T. O. (2018). Social Media as Alternative Public Sphere for Citizen Participation and Protest in National Politics in Zimbabwe: The Case of #thisflag. In F. Endong (Ed.), *Exploring the Role of Social Media in Transnational Advocacy* (pp. 17–35). Hershey, PA: IGI Global. doi:10.4018/978-1-5225-2854-8.ch002

Samarthya-Howard, A., & Rogers, D. (2018). Scaling Mobile Technologies to Maximize Reach and Impact: Partnering With Mobile Network Operators and Governments. In S. Takavarasha Jr & C. Adams (Eds.), *Affordability Issues Surrounding the Use of ICT for Development and Poverty Reduction* (pp. 193–211). Hershey, PA: IGI Global. doi:10.4018/978-1-5225-3179-1.ch009

Sandoval-Almazan, R. (2017). Political Messaging in Digital Spaces: The Case of Twitter in Mexico's Presidential Campaign. In Y. Ibrahim (Ed.), *Politics, Protest, and Empowerment in Digital Spaces* (pp. 72–90). Hershey, PA: IGI Global. doi:10.4018/978-1-5225-1862-4.ch005

Schultz, C. D., & Dellnitz, A. (2018). Attribution Modeling in Online Advertising. In K. Yang (Ed.), *Multi-Platform Advertising Strategies in the Global Marketplace* (pp. 226–249). Hershey, PA: IGI Global. doi:10.4018/978-1-5225-3114-2.ch009

Schultz, C. D., & Holsing, C. (2018). Differences Across Device Usage in Search Engine Advertising. In K. Yang (Ed.), *Multi-Platform Advertising Strategies in the Global Marketplace* (pp. 250–279). Hershey, PA: IGI Global. doi:10.4018/978-1-5225-3114-2.ch010

Senadheera, V., Warren, M., Leitch, S., & Pye, G. (2017). Facebook Content Analysis: A Study into Australian Banks' Social Media Community Engagement. In S. Hai-Jew (Ed.), *Social Media Data Extraction and Content Analysis* (pp. 412–432). Hershey, PA: IGI Global. doi:10.4018/978-1-5225-0648-5.ch013

Sharma, A. R. (2018). Promoting Global Competencies in India: Media and Information Literacy as Stepping Stone. In M. Yildiz, S. Funk, & B. De Abreu (Eds.), *Promoting Global Competencies Through Media Literacy* (pp. 160–174). Hershey, PA: IGI Global. doi:10.4018/978-1-5225-3082-4.ch010

Sillah, A. (2017). Nonprofit Organizations and Social Media Use: An Analysis of Nonprofit Organizations' Effective Use of Social Media Tools. In M. Brown Sr., (Ed.), *Social Media Performance Evaluation and Success Measurements* (pp. 180–195). Hershey, PA: IGI Global. doi:10.4018/978-1-5225-1963-8.ch009

Škorić, M. (2017). Adaptation of Winlink 2000 Emergency Amateur Radio Email Network to a VHF Packet Radio Infrastructure. In A. El Oualkadi & J. Zbitou (Eds.), *Handbook of Research on Advanced Trends in Microwave and Communication Engineering* (pp. 498–528). Hershey, PA: IGI Global. doi:10.4018/978-1-5225-0773-4.ch016

Skubida, D. (2016). Can Some Computer Games Be a Sport?: Issues with Legitimization of eSport as a Sporting Activity. *International Journal of Gaming and Computer-Mediated Simulations*, *8*(4), 38–52. doi:10.4018/IJGCMS.2016100103

Sonnenberg, C. (2016). Mobile Content Adaptation: An Analysis of Techniques and Frameworks. In J. Aguado, C. Feijóo, & I. Martínez (Eds.), *Emerging Perspectives on the Mobile Content Evolution* (pp. 177–199). Hershey, PA: IGI Global. doi:10.4018/978-1-4666-8838-4.ch010

Sonnevend, J. (2016). More Hope!: Ceremonial Media Events Are Still Powerful in the Twenty-First Century. In A. Fox (Ed.), *Global Perspectives on Media Events in Contemporary Society* (pp. 132–140). Hershey, PA: IGI Global. doi:10.4018/978-1-4666-9967-0.ch010

Sood, T. (2017). Services Marketing: A Sector of the Current Millennium. In T. Sood (Ed.), *Strategic Marketing Management and Tactics in the Service Industry* (pp. 15–42). Hershey, PA: IGI Global. doi:10.4018/978-1-5225-2475-5.ch002

Stairs, G. A. (2016). The Amplification of the Sunni-Shia Divide through Contemporary Communications Technology: Fear and Loathing in the Modern Middle East. In S. Gibson & A. Lando (Eds.), *Impact of Communication and the Media on Ethnic Conflict* (pp. 214–231). Hershey, PA: IGI Global. doi:10.4018/978-1-4666-9728-7.ch013

Stokinger, E., & Ozuem, W. (2016). The Intersection of Social Media and Customer Retention in the Luxury Beauty Industry. In W. Ozuem & G. Bowen (Eds.), *Competitive Social Media Marketing Strategies* (pp. 235–258). Hershey, PA: IGI Global. doi:10.4018/978-1-4666-9776-8.ch012

Sudarsanam, S. K. (2017). Social Media Metrics. In N. Rao (Ed.), *Social Media Listening and Monitoring for Business Applications* (pp. 131–149). Hershey, PA: IGI Global. doi:10.4018/978-1-5225-0846-5.ch007

Swiatek, L. (2017). Accessing the Finest Minds: Insights into Creativity from Esteemed Media Professionals. In N. Silton (Ed.), *Exploring the Benefits of Creativity in Education, Media, and the Arts* (pp. 240–263). Hershey, PA: IGI Global. doi:10.4018/978-1-5225-0504-4.ch012

Switzer, J. S., & Switzer, R. V. (2016). Virtual Teams: Profiles of Successful Leaders. In B. Baggio (Ed.), *Analyzing Digital Discourse and Human Behavior in Modern Virtual Environments* (pp. 1–24). Hershey, PA: IGI Global. doi:10.4018/978-1-4666-9899-4.ch001

Tabbane, R. S., & Debabi, M. (2016). Electronic Word of Mouth: Definitions and Concepts. In S. Rathore & A. Panwar (Eds.), *Capturing, Analyzing, and Managing Word-of-Mouth in the Digital Marketplace* (pp. 1–27). Hershey, PA: IGI Global. doi:10.4018/978-1-4666-9449-1.ch001

Tellería, A. S. (2016). The Role of the Profile and the Digital Identity on the Mobile Content. In J. Aguado, C. Feijóo, & I. Martínez (Eds.), *Emerging Perspectives on the Mobile Content Evolution* (pp. 263–282). Hershey, PA: IGI Global. doi:10.4018/978-1-4666-8838-4.ch014

Teurlings, J. (2017). What Critical Media Studies Should Not Take from Actor-Network Theory. In M. Spöhrer & B. Ochsner (Eds.), *Applying the Actor-Network Theory in Media Studies* (pp. 66–78). Hershey, PA: IGI Global. doi:10.4018/978-1-5225-0616-4.ch005

Tomé, V. (2018). Assessing Media Literacy in Teacher Education. In M. Yildiz, S. Funk, & B. De Abreu (Eds.), *Promoting Global Competencies Through Media Literacy* (pp. 1–19). Hershey, PA: IGI Global. doi:10.4018/978-1-5225-3082-4.ch001

Toscano, J. P. (2017). Social Media and Public Participation: Opportunities, Barriers, and a New Framework. In M. Adria & Y. Mao (Eds.), *Handbook of Research on Citizen Engagement and Public Participation in the Era of New Media* (pp. 73–89). Hershey, PA: IGI Global. doi:10.4018/978-1-5225-1081-9.ch005

Trauth, E. (2017). Creating Meaning for Millennials: Bakhtin, Rosenblatt, and the Use of Social Media in the Composition Classroom. In K. Bryant (Ed.), *Engaging 21st Century Writers with Social Media* (pp. 151–162). Hershey, PA: IGI Global. doi:10.4018/978-1-5225-0562-4.ch009

Ugangu, W. (2016). Kenya's Difficult Political Transitions Ethnicity and the Role of Media. In L. Mukhongo & J. Macharia (Eds.), *Political Influence of the Media in Developing Countries* (pp. 12–24). Hershey, PA: IGI Global. doi:10.4018/978-1-4666-9613-6.ch002

Uprety, S. (2018). Print Media's Role in Securitization: National Security and Diplomacy Discourses in Nepal. In S. Bute (Ed.), *Media Diplomacy and Its Evolving Role in the Current Geopolitical Climate* (pp. 56–82). Hershey, PA: IGI Global. doi:10.4018/978-1-5225-3859-2.ch004

Van der Merwe, L. (2016). Social Media Use within Project Teams: Practical Application of Social Media on Projects. In G. Silvius (Ed.), *Strategic Integration of Social Media into Project Management Practice* (pp. 139–159). Hershey, PA: IGI Global. doi:10.4018/978-1-4666-9867-3.ch009

van der Vyver, A. G. (2018). A Model for Economic Development With Telecentres and the Social Media: Overcoming Affordability Constraints. In S. Takavarasha Jr & C. Adams (Eds.), *Affordability Issues Surrounding the Use of ICT for Development and Poverty Reduction* (pp. 112–140). Hershey, PA: IGI Global. doi:10.4018/978-1-5225-3179-1.ch006

van Dokkum, E., & Ravesteijn, P. (2016). Managing Project Communication: Using Social Media for Communication in Projects. In G. Silvius (Ed.), *Strategic Integration of Social Media into Project Management Practice* (pp. 35–50). Hershey, PA: IGI Global. doi:10.4018/978-1-4666-9867-3.ch003

van Niekerk, B. (2018). Social Media Activism From an Information Warfare and Security Perspective. In F. Endong (Ed.), *Exploring the Role of Social Media in Transnational Advocacy* (pp. 1–16). Hershey, PA: IGI Global. doi:10.4018/978-1-5225-2854-8.ch001

Varnali, K., & Gorgulu, V. (2017). Determinants of Brand Recall in Social Networking Sites. In W. Al-Rabayah, R. Khasawneh, R. Abu-shamaa, & I. Alsmadi (Eds.), *Strategic Uses of Social Media for Improved Customer Retention* (pp. 124–153). Hershey, PA: IGI Global. doi:10.4018/978-1-5225-1686-6.ch007

Varty, C. T., O'Neill, T. A., & Hambley, L. A. (2017). Leading Anywhere Workers: A Scientific and Practical Framework. In Y. Blount & M. Gloet (Eds.), *Anywhere Working and the New Era of Telecommuting* (pp. 47–88). Hershey, PA: IGI Global. doi:10.4018/978-1-5225-2328-4.ch003

Vatikiotis, P. (2016). Social Media Activism: A Contested Field. In T. Deželan & I. Vobič (Eds.), *R)evolutionizing Political Communication through Social Media* (pp. 40–54). Hershey, PA: IGI Global. doi:10.4018/978-1-4666-9879-6.ch003

Velikovsky, J. T. (2018). The Holon/Parton Structure of the Meme, or The Unit of Culture. In M. Khosrow-Pour, D.B.A. (Ed.), Encyclopedia of Information Science and Technology, Fourth Edition (pp. 4666-4678). Hershey, PA: IGI Global. doi:10.4018/978-1-5225-2255-3.ch405

Venkatesh, R., & Jayasingh, S. (2017). Transformation of Business through Social Media. In N. Rao (Ed.), *Social Media Listening and Monitoring for Business Applications* (pp. 1–17). Hershey, PA: IGI Global. doi:10.4018/978-1-5225-0846-5.ch001

Vesnic-Alujevic, L. (2016). European Elections and Facebook: Political Advertising and Deliberation? In T. Deželan & I. Vobič (Eds.), *R)evolutionizing Political Communication through Social Media* (pp. 191–209). Hershey, PA: IGI Global. doi:10.4018/978-1-4666-9879-6.ch010

Virkar, S. (2017). Trolls Just Want to Have Fun: Electronic Aggression within the Context of E-Participation and Other Online Political Behaviour in the United Kingdom. In M. Korstanje (Ed.), *Threat Mitigation and Detection of Cyber Warfare and Terrorism Activities* (pp. 111–162). Hershey, PA: IGI Global. doi:10.4018/978-1-5225-1938-6.ch006

Wakabi, W. (2017). When Citizens in Authoritarian States Use Facebook for Social Ties but Not Political Participation. In Y. Ibrahim (Ed.), *Politics, Protest, and Empowerment in Digital Spaces* (pp. 192–214). Hershey, PA: IGI Global. doi:10.4018/978-1-5225-1862-4.ch012

Weisberg, D. J. (2016). Methods and Strategies in Using Digital Literacy in Media and the Arts. In M. Yildiz & J. Keengwe (Eds.), *Handbook of Research on Media Literacy in the Digital Age* (pp. 456–471). Hershey, PA: IGI Global. doi:10.4018/978-1-4666-9667-9.ch022

Weisgerber, C., & Butler, S. H. (2016). Debranding Digital Identity: Personal Branding and Identity Work in a Networked Age. *International Journal of Interactive Communication Systems and Technologies*, *6*(1), 17–34. doi:10.4018/IJICST.2016010102

Wijngaard, P., Wensveen, I., Basten, A., & de Vries, T. (2016). Projects without Email, Is that Possible? In G. Silvius (Ed.), *Strategic Integration of Social Media into Project Management Practice* (pp. 218–235). Hershey, PA: IGI Global. doi:10.4018/978-1-4666-9867-3.ch013

Wright, K. (2018). "Show Me What You Are Saying": Visual Literacy in the Composition Classroom. In A. August (Ed.), *Visual Imagery, Metadata, and Multimodal Literacies Across the Curriculum* (pp. 24–49). Hershey, PA: IGI Global. doi:10.4018/978-1-5225-2808-1.ch002

Yang, K. C. (2018). Understanding How Mexican and U.S. Consumers Decide to Use Mobile Social Media: A Cross-National Qualitative Study. In K. Yang (Ed.), *Multi-Platform Advertising Strategies in the Global Marketplace* (pp. 168–198). Hershey, PA: IGI Global. doi:10.4018/978-1-5225-3114-2.ch007

Yang, K. C., & Kang, Y. (2016). Exploring Female Hispanic Consumers' Adoption of Mobile Social Media in the U.S. In R. English & R. Johns (Eds.), *Gender Considerations in Online Consumption Behavior and Internet Use* (pp. 185–207). Hershey, PA: IGI Global. doi:10.4018/978-1-5225-0010-0.ch012

Yao, Q., & Wu, M. (2016). Examining the Role of WeChat in Advertising. In X. Xu (Ed.), *Handbook of Research on Human Social Interaction in the Age of Mobile Devices* (pp. 386–405). Hershey, PA: IGI Global. doi:10.4018/978-1-5225-0469-6.ch016

Yarchi, M., Wolfsfeld, G., Samuel-Azran, T., & Segev, E. (2017). Invest, Engage, and Win: Online Campaigns and Their Outcomes in an Israeli Election. In M. Brown Sr., (Ed.), *Social Media Performance Evaluation and Success Measurements* (pp. 225–248). Hershey, PA: IGI Global. doi:10.4018/978-1-5225-1963-8.ch011

Yeboah-Banin, A. A., & Amoakohene, M. I. (2018). The Dark Side of Multi-Platform Advertising in an Emerging Economy Context. In K. Yang (Ed.), *Multi-Platform Advertising Strategies in the Global Marketplace* (pp. 30–53). Hershey, PA: IGI Global. doi:10.4018/978-1-5225-3114-2.ch002

Yılmaz, R., Çakır, A., & Resuloğlu, F. (2017). Historical Transformation of the Advertising Narration in Turkey: From Stereotype to Digital Media. In R. Yılmaz (Ed.), *Narrative Advertising Models and Conceptualization in the Digital Age* (pp. 133–152). Hershey, PA: IGI Global. doi:10.4018/978-1-5225-2373-4.ch008

Yusuf, S., Hassan, M. S., & Ibrahim, A. M. (2018). Cyberbullying Among Malaysian Children Based on Research Evidence. In M. Khosrow-Pour, D.B.A. (Ed.), Encyclopedia of Information Science and Technology, Fourth Edition (pp. 1704-1722). Hershey, PA: IGI Global. doi:10.4018/978-1-5225-2255-3.ch149

Zervas, P., & Alexandraki, C. (2016). Facilitating Open Source Software and Standards to Assembly a Platform for Networked Music Performance. In D. Kanellopoulos (Ed.), *Emerging Research on Networked Multimedia Communication Systems* (pp. 334–365). Hershey, PA: IGI Global. doi:10.4018/978-1-4666-8850-6.ch011

About the Contributors

Maryam Ebrahimi has working experience as an assistant professor at some universities and a senior researcher in several industries. She is currently an independent researcher in Germany. Her post-doctoral research was in the area of Information Systems Management funded by the Alexander von Humboldt Foundation, Germany. She has oriented her studies towards systems science in business management. Her interest is the use of modeling and simulation methodologies for the purpose of policymaking. A few of her publications are 'hybrid simulation approach for technological innovation policymaking in developing countries' and 'modeling and simulation techniques for improved business processes'.

* * *

Elina Ahmadi is independent researcher in Australia and her main interests are cluster development, innovation management, and security studies.

Mahshid Ebrahimi graduated from Tehran University with a master's degree in Public Management - Human Resource Management in 2013. She has had an experience of working in insurance industry. Since 2014 she has worked in the banking industry. Her interest is studying technological changes especially in these industries.

Mohammad Tariqul Islam Khan is a Senior Lecturer at the Faculty of Business, Multimedia University (MMU), Malaysia. He is actively involved in teaching, research, and supervision. He has published numerous articles in indexed journals. Dr. Khan's research interests are mainly in the area of financial technology and behavioral finance.

Nadezhda Lebedeva is a Doctor of Philosophy in the field of Cultural Studies, professor of the International Personnel Academy (Kyiv, Ukraine). She is the author of more than 100 scientific articles. The focus of her research is the cultural and social aspects of regional development.

Tze Wei Liew is a Senior Lecturer at the Faculty of Business, Multimedia University Malaysia. He leads the Human-Centric Technology Interaction SIG, and his research domains include communication sciences, learning sciences, human-computer interaction, and media effects.

John Ryan has a Ph.D. degree in Information Technology Management and for a period of 10 years, he was involved in a number of research activities in various universities and institutes in the area of ICT.

Thong Bing Tai is a research scholar at the Faculty of Business, Multimedia University Malaysia. Her research domains concern information management with social media platforms such as Facebook, Instagram, and Tik Tok.

Su-Mae Tan is a Senior Lecturer at the Faculty of Information Science and Technology, Multimedia University, Malaysia. Her research areas are human-computer interaction, media effects, and learning sciences.

Index

www.ingramcontent.com/pod-product-compliance
Lightning Source LLC
LaVergne TN
LVHW081323300926
849161LV00008B/1865

* 9 7 8 1 7 9 9 8 8 2 3 5 0 *